DISCARD

# A Confederate Nurse

Ada Bacot in old age
(*courtesy of Lillian Earle Clarke James*)

# A Confederate Nurse

The Diary of Ada W. Bacot,
1860–1863

Edited by Jean V. Berlin

University of South Carolina Press

# Women's Diaries and Letters of the Nineteenth-Century South

Carol Bleser, Series Editor

*A Woman Doctor's Civil War: Esther Hill Hawks' Diary*
edited by Gerald Schwartz

*A Rebel Came Home:*
*The Diary and Letters of Floride Clemson, 1863–1866*
edited by Ernest McPherson Lander, Jr., and Charles M. McGee, Jr.

*The Shattered Dream: The Day Book of Margaret Sloan, 1900–1902*
edited by Harold Woodell

*George Washington's Beautiful Nelly: The Letters of Eleanor Parke Custis Lewis*
*to Elizabeth Bordley Gibson, 1794–1851*
edited by Patricia Brady

*A Confederate Lady Comes of Age:*
*The Journal of Pauline DeCaradeuc Heyward, 1863–1888*
edited by Mary D. Robertson

*The Letters of a Victorian Madwoman*
edited by John S. Hughes

*A Plantation Mistress on the Eve of the Civil War:*
*The Diary of Keziah Goodwyn Hopkins Brevard, 1860–1861*
edited by John Hammond Moore

*A Northern Woman in the Plantation South:*
*Letters of Tryphena Blanche Holder Fox, 1856–1876*
edited by Wilma King

*A Confederate Nurse: The Diary of Ada W. Bacot, 1860–1863*
edited by Jean V. Berlin

Copyright © 1994 University of South Carolina

Published in Columbia, South Carolina, by the
University of South Carolina Press

Manufactured in the United States of America

**Library of Congress Cataloging-in-Publication**
Bacot, Ada W. (Ada White)
    A Confederate nurse : the diary of Ada W. Bacot, 1860–1863 /
edited by Jean V. Berlin.
        p.    cm.
    Includes bibliographical references (p.) and index.
    ISBN 0–87249–970–7
    1. Bacot, Ada W. (Ada White)—Diaries.    2. United States—History—
Civil War, 1861–1865—Medical care.    3. United States—History—
Civil War, 1861–1865—Personal narratives, Confederate.    4. Nurses—
Confederate States of America—Diaries.    I. Berlin, Jean V. (Jean
Vance), 1962–    .  II. Title.
E625.B33   1994
973.7'75—dc20

93-30098

For Brooks

# Contents

# Series Editor's Introduction

*A Confederate Nurse: The Diary of Ada W. Bacot, 1860–1863* is the ninth volume in an ongoing series of women's diaries and letters of the nineteenth-century South. This series published by the University of South Carolina Press includes a number of never-before-published diaries, some collections of unpublished correspondence, and a few published diaries that are being reprinted—a potpourri of nineteenth-century women's writings.

The Women's Diaries and Letters of the Nineteenth-Century South Series enables women to speak for themselves, providing readers with a rarely opened window into Southern society before, during, and after the American Civil War. The significance of these letters and journals lies not only in the personal revelations and the writing talents of these women authors but also in the range and versatility of the documents' contents. Taken together these publications will tell us much about the heyday and the fall of the Cotton Kingdom, the mature years of the "peculiar institution," the war years, and the adjustment of the South to a new social order following the defeat of the Confederacy. Through their writings the reader will also be presented with first-hand accounts of everyday life and social events, courtships and marriages, family life and travels, religion and education, and the life-and-death matters which made up the ordinary and extraordinary world of the nineteenth-century South.

Ada Bacot's diary of a Confederate nurse, edited by Jean V. Berlin, is an excellent companion in the series to *A Woman Doctor's Civil War*. The Civil War was the first major American conflict in which women as nurses played a significant role. Many were middle- and upper-class women who had never worked for wages, seen the inside of a hospital, or been responsible for the physical care of others. Most of these women, Northern and Southern, left no written record of their nursing service, but one who did keep a diary was Ada Bacot, a wealthy plantation owner from Darlington County, South Carolina.

A young and childless widow, Bacot was motivated to enter the ranks of Confederate nursing, in part, by her effort to break away from the chains of Southern patriarchy, and in part, by her fierce patriotism for her native state of South Carolina. She offered her services as a nurse "to the gallant men who are to fight for the deliverance of my beloved country," as she wrote in her diary, only two weeks after South Carolina seceded from the Union. It would be almost a year, however, before Ada Bacot arrived in Charlottesville, Virginia, to join other volunteer nurses in caring for Southern soldiers in the Virginia theater of war.

Much of this young Southern widow's compelling wartime diary centers in the social relationships with her coworkers. According to the editor, despite the horror of war, the camaraderie of the medical staff described in Ada Bacot's diary was much like that depicted in the television series "M*A*S*H" and "China Beach." A Confederate Nurse is an invaluable source for anyone who is interested in Southern, women's, or Civil War history.

Carol Bleser

# Preface

Ada White Bacot's diary consists of six brown, gold-stamped leather books measuring approximately 5 by 7½ inches and a slim notebook of the same dimensions carrying a partial patient diet list kept during the time she was a nurse. Volume 1 is dated September 11, 1860–April 29, 1861; volume 2, May 1–September 21, 1861; volume 3, September 21, 1861–January 26, 1862; volume 4, January 27–April 30, 1862; volume 5, May 1–September 6, 1862; and volume 6, September 7, 1862–January 18, 1863. The unpublished diary is in the manuscript collection of the South Caroliniana Library at the University of South Carolina in Columbia and was sold to it in 1964 by Lillian Clarke James, a granddaughter of Ada Bacot. Also in the collection are the papers of Peter Samuel Bacot, Ada's father, donated by another Bacot descendant in 1969. Family recollection holds that there may have been a seventh volume of Ada Bacot's diary, but if there was, it has vanished. The six volumes that do remain total approximately a thousand pages and have been put on microfilm as part of the series *American Women's Diaries, Southern Women* (New Canaan, CT: Readex Micrographics), edited by Jane Begos.

Since the contents of many of Ada Bacot's entries overlap or repeat themselves, it was deemed best to present a selected version of the text covering two years and four months of her life, including her time as a Confederate nurse. Approximately twenty to twenty-five percent of her entries before she went off to be a nurse in Charlottesville, Virginia, are included. About forty percent of her entries after she arrived in Charlottesville are included for they are longer and more varied than those she wrote in South Carolina before December 1861 and it is Bacot's work as a nurse that will be of most interest to scholars and general readers. I have divided the diary into eight chapters and chosen illustrative quotations to head them. The first chapter ends with her removal to her South Carolina plantation at Arnmore to avoid conflict with her brother Peter and his wife. The second ends just before her renewed and successful attempts to go to Charlottesville to become a nurse. The third encompasses her preparations and trip to Charlottesville and her initial role there as housekeeper for the hospital employees. The fourth chapter begins with her becoming an assistant matron at the hospital and ends when she and the other employees of the Monticello Hospital feel themselves such a unit that they stand united against the meddling of a new arrival. The fifth chapter ends just before her extended illness; the sixth picks up with her recuperation and ends with the adjustment period following the Confederate government's assumption of control over the Monticello Hospital. The seventh begins with her bitter confrontation with two of the black servants and ends with her stated desire to go home. The eighth and final chapter takes her home to South Carolina and then chronicles her return to Charlottesville.

Ada Bacot left the text of her diary virtually unchanged over the years; in a very few places, she corrected names, but that is the extent of her own editing. Her style is a loquacious narrative of the events of her life as a Confederate nurse. When her entries are terse or restrained, she usually reveals in the text that she feels exhausted or ill. Her handwriting is usually clear, unless she is upset or rushed. Her spelling, like many diarists of her time, is erratic, and her punctuation leaves a great deal to be desired. Her most common fault is to separate two clearly different sentences with a comma instead of a period. On the other hand, unlike other diarists, she rarely uses the dash. She uses few paragraph divisions and sometimes marks them by a long blank in the text on a line rather than breaking off the text and indenting the next line. If she is unsure of a name or word, she writes as much of it as she knows and follows that with a blank space. This has been replaced with a conjectured reading or several dashes.

Bacot's text has been left much as she wrote it, but missing plural forms have been supplied silently. Abbreviated place names have been written out when their meaning is not absolutely clear. Initials of proper names have been extended where necessary and possible, and periods inserted after those initials that have been retained. The spelling of proper names has been corrected throughout the text because

Bacot spells names phonetically and her renderings are often highly inaccurate. In fact, many men and women in her diary may have had their names misspelled to such a degree as to preclude their identification. Bacot's use of the word "patience" for "patients" and vice versa has been silently corrected to prevent confusion. Periods have been inserted in brackets where two completely independent sentences are separated by commas or spaces; in certain instances, periods and commas have been inserted for the sake of clarity. Duplicated words have been dropped. Words, usually verbs, inserted by the editor to make Bacot's meaning clear are in square brackets. Conjectured readings of the text are enclosed in braces; instances of illegible text are indicated within angle brackets. Gross errors in verb tense have been silently corrected. Raised letters have been dropped.

Annotations which identify persons, places, events, etc., are to be found in the footnotes to the text. Bacot's patients at the Monticello Hospital whom she mentions by name have not been identified, but attempts have been made to track down all others mentioned in the diary; those who are not identified are men or women about whom no further information could be found. Certain well-known individuals, such as Jefferson Davis, have not been given notes. Information on the people in the text was found in census records, a report of the South Carolina Hospital Aid Association, genealogical information supplied by the descendants of Ada Bacot, and the records of Christ Church in Mars Bluff, South Carolina. In cases where the identity of a person is not absolutely certain, the note is prefaced with "probably" or "possibly."

# Acknowledgments

No scholar ever completes any work without the help of family, friends, and colleagues. First, I would like to thank Lillian Clarke James, Ada Bacot's granddaughter and a former owner of the diary. Without her information and encouragement I might well have given up before I really started; she has been a true friend. Another Ada Bacot descendant, Anita Clarke Curl, came forward with information on Ada's later years at a time when I really needed it; her research skills are the equal of those of many historians I know. Warren Slesinger at the University of South Carolina Press continued to encourage me to find a project, and enlisted the aid of Allen Stokes of the South Caroliniana Library at the University of South Carolina, who led me to Ada's diary and was unfailingly kind and helpful. Margaret Hill, managing editor at the Press, expertly guided the diary into print. Ervin L. Jordan, Jr., of the Alderman Library at the University of Virginia and Horace F. Rudisill of the Darlington County Historical Commission in Darlington, South Carolina, helped me with background information. Joanne Hutchinson and Roger Lane of Haverford College and Dorothy Twohig, William Abbot, Robert D. Cross, and Michael Holt of the University of Virginia are responsible in varying degrees for the interests which led me to this work. Carol Bleser was a supportive and helpful editor; my work is the better for her insights. Nan, Uncle Bill, Aunt Lillian, and Aunt Elizabeth inspired my interest in history with their tales of the past. My parents, Cheston and Anne Berlin, have been behind me every step of the way with love and support; their own interest in history fostered mine. My brothers, Doug, Alex, and Gordon, have supported me too, in different ways. Rebecca Anne Simpson, born during the writing of this manuscript, has brought me more joy and distraction than I ever dreamed. My husband, Brooks D. Simpson, has been a helpful and loving partner as well as a superb historian. He has pushed me to be my best; I can only hope to live up to his faith in me.

# A Confederate Nurse

# Introduction

Ada White Bacot's diary begins on September 11, 1860, with a visit to her family's graveyard on the plantation Roseville near the town of Society Hill in the Darlington District of South Carolina. As Ada walked her foster daughter, Flora McLendon, around the graves and explained who was buried there, she reflected on life and death and wondered when she would join her loved ones there. Little did she know that during the next few years bloodshed, sickness, and death would be her constant companions, casting their shadows on her state, the Confederacy, and her loved ones. At the same time, the war would bring her new work and a new family. These years would be ones of discovery and loss, joy and anguish.

Members of Ada Bacot's family were present at the opening and the closing of the Civil War; her father listened to the bombardment of Fort Sumter in April 1861 from his room at the Mills House Hotel in Charleston, and her brother Peter Brockington Bacot surrendered at Appomattox in April 1865 with Company B of the Seventh Regiment of the South Carolina Cavalry.[1] The war transformed the lives of Ada Bacot and her family in many ways. All her brothers saw military service of one sort or another, and Bacot herself served her state and country as a Confederate nurse. Her second husband was killed in a skirmish at Dandridge, Tennessee, and her father died in 1864.[2]

At the beginning of the war, the Bacots were a wealthy upcountry South Carolina plantation family. Peter Samuel Bacot, Ada's father, owned real estate worth $38,400, personal property worth $78,720, and eighty-seven slaves, while Ada herself boasted real estate worth

---

1. Peter Samuel Bacot to Ada White Bacot, April 14, 1861, Peter Samuel Bacot Papers, South Caroliniana Library, University of South Carolina; and William G. Nine and Ronald G. Wilson, *The Appomattox Paroles, April 9–15, 1865* (Lynchburg, VA: H. E. Howard, 1989).

2. Unless otherwise noted, all genealogical and historical information on Ada Bacot and her family was supplied by her granddaughter, Lillian Clarke James, or her great-granddaughter, Anita Clarke Curl.

$9,750 and personal property worth $20,975.[3] The family had arrived in South Carolina in the seventeenth century as part of the Huguenot immigration, and the "Darlington Branch," as Ada's family was known, had come to the Darlington area in the late eighteenth century. Peter Samuel Bacot, born in 1810, had many of the advantages common to wealthy young men of his time; he attended South Carolina College and went on the Grand Tour of Europe. He returned to South Carolina and married Anna Jane White around 1831. His wife was from Mississippi and was a cousin of the Rogers family, whose lands were just across the Pee Dee River from the Bacot properties; she probably met Peter while on a visit to her relatives.[4] By March 1836, Peter and Anna Bacot had been married for five years and owned twenty-six slaves and 387.5 acres of "Pine sand."[5]

The eldest of the Bacots' six children was Ada White Bacot, born on December 31, 1832. She was followed by Jacqueline Menissier Shaw Bacot (1834–?), Peter Brockington Bacot (1838–1924), Tours Loire "Pet" Bacot (1840–1882), Richard Hayes "Dickie" Bacot (1842–?), and Anna Jane White "A'Jane," "Ajax," or "Janie" Bacot (1847–1933), a boy named for his mother, who had apparently died in childbirth. Peter and Anna Bacot gave their children all the appropriate "advantages," including portraits painted by the well-known South Carolina artist W. H. Scarborough, governesses, and dancing lessons.[6] Most and perhaps all of the children were formally educated. Ada and her sister were sent to St. Mary's Academy in Raleigh, North Carolina, with their father's admonishment ringing in their ears: "I wish you to be accomplished in everything — but above all I wish your minds to be well stored with knowledge."[7] Young Peter and perhaps some of

---

3. United States Census of 1860, South Carolina, Darlington District, 381; and Tax List of Slaves, October 1860, Peter Samuel Bacot Papers, South Caroliniana Library.

4. Horace F. Rudisill, "Notes on Peter Samuel Bacot and His Family," Peter Samuel Bacot Papers, South Caroliniana Library.

5. Statement of property, March 22, 1836, Peter Samuel Bacot Papers, South Caroliniana Library.

6. W. H. Scarborough to Peter Samuel Bacot, July 8, 1836, and receipt for dancing lessons, January 18, 1845, Peter Samuel Bacot Papers, South Caroliniana Library.

7. Peter Samuel Bacot to Ada White and Jacqueline Menissier Shaw Bacot, January 30, 1849, private collection of Lillian Clarke James.

his brothers were sent to Trinity. Peter went on to attend the University of North Carolina in the 1850s and earned a medical degree from the Medical College of South Carolina. Dickie was a cadet at the United States Naval Academy at the outbreak of the Civil War and resigned his commission to join the Confederate navy.

The family's fortunes were augmented through an inheritance from Richard and Mary Hart Brockington, Anna Jane White Bacot's aunt and uncle. The Brockingtons owned an extensive plantation, Roseville, and numerous slaves. Richard Brockington died in 1843 and Mary ten years later, leaving their lands (which adjoined the Bacots') as well as other property to Ada's father, his brother and sister, and their children.[8] Peter Samuel Bacot received the house at Roseville and much of the plantation, about 750 acres, as part of his share. Even before Mary Brockington's death, Peter Bacot had moved his wife and their four sons and two daughters to this plantation.

The Bacot family had strong ties to New England. Anna Jane White Bacot's widowed mother, Sarah, had married John Angier Shaw, Harvard class of 1811, while he was working in some capacity with various schools in Mississippi and Louisiana. Shaw returned with a new wife to Massachusetts in the 1830s and served in the state legislature and tutored various young men. One of his students was William G. Russell, who later sat on the Massachusetts Supreme Court, and Shaw's friendship with the Russell family led to the hiring of Russell's sister Lydia as a governess for the Bacot children in 1838.[9] Although Lydia had returned to her hometown of Plymouth by July of the following year, she remained in close contact with the Bacots for the next decade. Her last surviving letter to her former employer, Peter Samuel Bacot, dated December 8 and 15, 1850, is signed "Your sister

---

8. Will of Richard Brockington, recorded October 18, 1843, and will of Mary Hart Brockington, recorded July 18, 1853, typescripts in Darlington County Historical Commission.

9. Charles C. Smith, ed., "Some Notes on the Commencements at Harvard University, 1803–1848," *Massachusetts Historical Society Proceedings*, 2d ser., no. 5 (1889–1890): 176; Winslow Warren, "Memoir of William G. Russell, LL.D.," *Massachusetts Historical Society Proceedings*, 2d ser., no. 14 (1900–1901): 155–62; and Thomas Russell to Peter Samuel Bacot, December 10, 1838, Peter Samuel Bacot Papers, South Caroliniana Library.

Lydia," in spite of the fact that it carried on an obviously heated debate about the immorality of slavery and the legality of states' rights. Through Lydia Russell's connections to the antislavery and transcendentalist movements, the Bacots had been in touch with leading Northern ideas and intellectuals. Coincidentally, the man Lydia Russell married in 1840, a lawyer named William Whiting, would become Lincoln's War Department solicitor during the Civil War. But such letters no longer appear in Peter Samuel Bacot's papers after 1850. For whatever reason, Bacot, who had been widowed since 1847, had begun to isolate himself from his wife's Northern family and their friends. The tenor of Lydia Whiting's last two letters to him indicate that he may have felt too deeply about sectional issues to continue contact with Yankees. [10]

Ada Bacot married her second cousin Thomas Wainwright Bacot, Jr., in 1851, and they lived at the Arnmore plantation four or five miles away from Roseville. Ada Bacot's husband had bought the plantation that same year. [11] The young Bacots had two daughters, Anna Jane and Emily Helen. Anna Jane died of illness less than two years after her birth in December 1852, and Ada's husband was killed by his overseer during an argument in December 1856. The overseer, apparently enraged by Thomas Bacot's comments on his work, picked up a post and beat Bacot to death. One account called it murder, another called it self-defense. [12] The twenty-four-year-old Ada returned to Roseville with her remaining daughter, Emily. Emily died seven months after the move, at the age of two.

At the time Ada Bacot began her diary in September 1860, she was twenty-seven years old and widowed and had lost two children. The entries in her diary reflect her unhappy emotional state. Although she had taken on a foster child, Flora McLendon, the daughter of Roseville's overseer, Flora was a troublesome ward who did not bring Ada much pleasure or maternal gratification. Ada also records in her diary

10. Lydia Russell to the Bacots, July 1839; August 9, 1840; and October 21, 1841; Lydia Whiting to Peter Samuel Bacot, May 5 and December 8 and 15, 1850; Peter Samuel Bacot Papers, South Caroliniana Library.

11. Horace F. Rudisill, personal communication, September 26, 1992.

12. Undated clippings, Ada W. Bacot File, Darlington County Historical Commission.

in agonizing detail the growing alienation between her and her favorite brother, Peter. Peter had married Elizabeth Helen Trenholm, known as "Daisy," a woman who despised Ada and drove a wedge between her husband and his oldest sister.

Bacot records in her diary on January 4, 1861, that "I have composed a letter for the Editor of the Charleston Mercury offering myself as nurse to the gallant men who are to fight for the deliverance of my beloved country."[13] From the time that South Carolina had seceded from the Union on December 20, 1860, Ada had expressed her desire to do something, anything, for South Carolina and the Confederacy. In her diary, she does not refer again to her offer of service until July 1861, when she writes that she had been disappointed in her efforts to get the advice of her neighbor, General William Wallace Harllee, about going to Virginia as a nurse.[14] Beginning in August 1861, she started planning in earnest to go to one of the South Carolina's hospitals in Virginia, but found herself frustrated by the banks and local businessmen, who turned down her requests for the cash she needed to make the journey and to establish herself in Virginia.[15] Only her father supported her, and her frustration steadily mounted: "I could cry, but what good would that do."[16] Her conviction that she could do more good nursing for the Confederacy in Virginia, the hub of the eastern theater of Confederate military operations, than she could by staying at home in Society Hill grew throughout September and October.[17] On October 13, she wrote directly to Reverend Robert Woodward Barnwell, head of the South Carolina Hospital Aid Association, who had been recruiting nurses across the state.[18] Four days later, she wrote in her diary, "I have made up my mind to start next week for Virginia."[19] On October 27, 1861, she heard from Barnwell, who asked

---

13. Ada W. Bacot Diary, January 4, 1861, South Caroliniana Library. Hereafter cited as Bacot Diary.

14. Bacot Diary, July 30, 1861.

15. Bacot Diary, August 20 and 26, 1861.

16. Bacot Diary, August 30, 1861.

17. Bacot Diary, September 3 and 20, and October 5, 1861.

18. Bacot Diary, October 13, 1861.

19. Bacot Diary, October 17, 1861.

her to go on at once, and from Kirkpatrick, her cotton broker, saying he would send her money for the cotton she had shipped him last week. "I cant discribe my feelings, I am so thankful I can go . . . Oh! that I may be able to perform my duty, Pa is going on with me, tis too delightful to be true."[20] And indeed it was; Kirkpatrick changed his mind on November 2 about sending her the money, and her father could not get her a loan, dashing her hopes once more. Ada tried to console herself with the idea that perhaps she might be more needed as a nurse at a later time on the coast of South Carolina.[21] One local doctor told her father to try to dissuade her ("twas scarcely a place for a lady"), and she reluctantly wrote to Reverend Barnwell on November 14 that she would not go to Virginia.[22] But on December 6, she read one of Barnwell's appeals for nurses to go to Virginia and decided she must go, come what may: "his request for Nurses was too earnest to be resisted."[23] On December 11, 1861, she traveled north to Charlottesville, Virginia, with Barnwell and several other volunteer nurses, and thus became a part of the chaotic Confederate medical system.[24]

When the war began in April 1861, the existing Confederate Medical Department, created and enlarged by acts of the Confederate Congress in February and March 1861, was woefully inadequate to the needs of an army involved in frequent combat. The Confederate Congress had allocated only $50,000 for the establishment and maintenance of military hospitals, and the number of surgeons and assistant surgeons to be commissioned by the government was not any more adequate.[25] Most Southern politicians either did not expect the war to last more than six months or were reluctant to say it might become a protracted struggle, and thus they made the establishment of an adequate medical force a low priority. But with each passing month in the summer of 1861, the ugly realities of

---

20. Bacot Diary, October 27, 1861.
21. Bacot Diary, November 2, 4, and 6, 1861.
22. Bacot Diary, November 11 and 14, 1861.
23. Bacot Diary, December 6, 1861.
24. Bacot Diary, December 11, 1861.
25. For a more detailed picture of the establishment and organization of the Confederate medical service, see H. H. Cunningham, *Doctors in Gray: The Confederate Medical Service* (Baton Rouge: Louisiana State University Press, 1958), 21–98.

the care of wounded and sick soldiers confronted Southerners. Concerned citizens hastily organized state and local aid associations to send food, clothing, and medical supplies to the troops when it quickly became clear that the Confederate government could not care for all its soldiers. These groups also set up hospitals and wayside care facilities in areas where the government medical facilities could not meet the demand. Unlike the Confederacy's "General" hospitals, which were open to soldiers from every state, these facilities gave first priority to men from the states which had funded them. The South Carolina Hospital Aid Association was particularly active in the Virginia theater of war from 1861 to 1862, when the Confederate government finally took over the administration of all military hospitals. The Association operated with funds donated by individuals and raised by bazaars, sales, and other efforts, and with money South Carolina's governor Francis Pickens had given to the colonels of South Carolina regiments in Virginia for the care of the sick and wounded. The surgeons and assistant surgeons who staffed the hospitals received Confederate commissions, but the nurses were all recruited on a volunteer basis, although they were paid by the Confederate government.

The South Carolina Association had several hospitals in Charlottesville, Virginia. The board of the Association had deemed Charlottesville a good location for the care of troops serving in Virginia for a number of reasons, including its good railroad connections, its proximity to Richmond, its safety from enemy attack, and the facilities and students of the University of Virginia Medical School. Reverend Barnwell and Dr. M. LaBorde, members of the South Carolina Association's board, had requested permission to establish hospitals along the line of the Virginia defenses in July 1861. President Davis and Surgeon General Moore initially refused, but the outbreaks of typhoid fever and other infectious diseases that summer following the Battle of First Manassas made it obvious that the central government could not do all that was medically necessary to care for the wounded and dying. Dr. James Lawrence Cabell, a medical professor at the University of Virginia and surgeon in charge of Charlottesville hospitals, invited the South Carolina Association later that summer to operate a hospital in a building he had leased as a home for the sick; this building became the Midway Hospital. By September the Association was encouraged to establish more hospitals, for which they would pay the rent and buy the furniture. The Association nominated their surgeons for Confederate commissions, and the surgeons in turn contracted for nurses at the government's expense. Three student boarding houses were rented, and two women were hired as matrons; the Monticello Hospital in Charlottesville was soon added as well.[26]

The first hospital, the Midway, was located in the center of the city and was supervised by Dr. Theodore Gourdin. One of the assistant surgeons there was James McIntosh, a young graduate of the Medical College of South Carolina. He boarded with Ada at the Maupin House and became a close friend of hers. The three former boarding houses — Mrs. Harris's, Mrs. Daniels's, and Mrs. Dunkum's — were collectively known as the Soldiers' Home. Formerly the main hotel in Charlottesville, the Monticello had been an overcrowded home for sick soldiers run by the Charlottesville hospital system during the summer of 1861; an outbreak of typhoid fever prevented the Association from equipping and using it until December of that year. Its opening as a hospital had created the need for staff which Ada Bacot answered, and it was in the Monticello Hospital that she would serve as a nurse. Dr. Edward J. Rembert of Sumter was the surgeon in charge as well as the director of all the South Carolina hospitals. The Charlottesville General Hospital (which was composed of several buildings), the Midway, the Monticello, and the Soldiers' Home were the four military hospitals in Charlottesville.

The women who came from South Carolina to serve as nurses in the Association's hospitals in Virginia found their actual activities in the ward restricted, as did most women who worked in Southern hospitals. The women who worked in the Monticello did not spend much time tending to the sick and wounded. Instead, the soldiers were cared for by male ward attendants and by convalescent soldiers pressed into temporary duty as nurses when the patient load was heavy. In the Monticello, the head matron was Marie Lesesne, who supervised the

---

26. For the best account of the establishment of South Carolina hospitals in Charlottesville and the rest of Virginia, see "Report of the South Carolina Hospital Aid Association in Virginia, 1861–1862," in *South Carolina Women in the Confederacy*, ed. Mrs. Thomas Taylor et al. (Columbia, SC: The State Company, 1907), 2: 93–120. See also Ervin L. Jordan, Jr., *Charlottesville and the University of Virginia in the Civil War* (Lynchburg, VA: H. E. Howard, 1988), 45–63.

execution of the surgeons' orders and the sanitary and commissary arrangements, and helped to take care of some of the patients' needs—dressing wounds, placing pads and pillows, making slings and pads for crutches, cheering up the depressed, writing letters, and discussing religion.[27] However, she was the only female who had much to do with attending to the health problems of the soldiers. Esse Habersham, a young single woman who began work at the Monticello as the dietician and laundress, was perceived to be disruptive on the wards and became instead the housekeeper at the Maupin House, where she, Lesesne, Bacot, and several surgeons boarded. Ada Bacot, who had started as the housekeeper, took Habersham's place at the hospital.[28] Bacot supervised the preparation of meals for the patients and the laundering of sheets, clothing, and other linens, and visited with the men, writing letters for them and expounding to them whenever possible on the virtues of the Bible and Christian religion.

In her journal entries, Bacot's work at the hospital often takes second place to her social life. Most of her narration centers around life at the Maupin House, where she boarded with several other South Carolinians, and it was her relationships with these people that would color her experience in Charlottesville. Her friendship with Marie Lesesne, a widow with a young son, was very warm, as was her relationship with Dr. Rembert. Bacot initially liked Esse Habersham, but soon came to think of her as shallow and flirtatious, and was relieved when Esse left Charlottesville in August 1862. As far as can be determined through biographical information, most of the South Carolina nurses in Charlottesville were "unattached" women, either widows or older spinsters. Esse was one of the few young and single women, being only twenty-one at the start of the war, and popular prejudice against a woman of her age and position working around so many men was widespread both within and without the hospital community.[29] Rev-

27. See Francis Butler Simkins and James Welch Patton, *The Women of the Confederacy* (Richmond: Garrett and Massie, 1936), 82–99, for a discussion of the role of women nurses.

28. The switch between Esse and Ada took place on January 20, 1862, shortly after their arrival in Charlottesville.

29. Simkins and Patton, *The Women of the Confederacy*, 89.

erend Barnwell and his wife and family lived in the Maupin House when they were in Charlottesville and were generally well-liked. Ada Bacot liked and respected Dr. Gourdin, but dismissed Dr. Poellnitz as a drunkard and a braggart. But Bacot's closest friend was probably the very young Dr. James McIntosh, himself only twenty-one or twenty-two. McIntosh's wife, Fannie, who arrived in 1862, was close to Ada as well. Ada also enjoyed the company of staff from the other hospitals who boarded elsewhere. Some of the Charlottesville townspeople welcomed the South Carolinians and brought gifts of food and clothing to the sick and wounded soldiers. The social narrative of Bacot's diary in Charlottesville is remarkably different from that which she kept in South Carolina. Ada Bacot in Charlottesville was a happy, committed, and contented woman, surrounded by people she liked and respected, and who, in turn, liked and respected her.

A number of themes emerge from Ada Bacot's journal, and they promise to shed light on the lives of nineteenth-century Southern women. One is the role of a deep and evangelical Christian faith in Bacot's life; through her relationship with God, both in the church and in her prayers, she sought the strength she needed for her daily life. A second is her strong sense of nationalism and her desire to do whatever she could to aid her state and advance the cause of the Confederacy. Closely allied to this Confederate nationalism is her primary self-identification as a South Carolinian; she filled her journal with derogatory references to Virginians and citizens of other Confederate states. Another theme in Bacot's diary is the expansion of horizons and opportunities which the war brought to her; new friendships and the chance to perform meaningful work redeemed her sense of self-worth. Also significant in her diary are Ada's desire for social and economic independence, her discussions of the problems of the Confederacy's hospital system in caring for the sick and wounded, and her attitudes toward hired slaves and free blacks.

Ada Bacot, an Episcopalian, was very religious. She prayed endlessly for guidance and patience and frequently embarked on courses of religious self-improvement involving meditation and reading. According to her journal, she tirelessly transmitted her religious fervor to the wounded in her charge and even to James McIntosh, when he fell ill

and she feared for his soul.[30] There can be little doubt that her religious faith was a source of strength which enabled her to function at
times of great stress and sorrow and gave her a framework within which
to make sense of her life and its losses. For many nineteenth-century
women, religion played a similar role and created the language
through which they understood and expressed their experiences.

Bacot's devout patriotism and devotion to her state remains stead-
fast throughout the course of her journal. She typified her feelings for
South Carolina as "that of an affectionate daughter for a mother, the
purest love in the world."[31] The family metaphor is particularly appropriate; Bacot's own life was bounded by the family with whom she had
spent nearly all her life and from whom marriage had not removed her.
Her belief that one owes the same duty to one's state or nation that
one owes to one's family reflects the prevalence of familial/patriarchal
ideology in the thoughts of upper-class antebellum Southern women.
Through her expression of these feelings, Bacot provides an important
key to our understanding of how these women viewed their world and
responded to it. Some historians have recently raised the question of
just how much Southern women's disillusionment with the war con-
tributed to the Confederacy's defeat.[32] While Bacot's experience can
only be considered typical of a small segment of Southern society, it is
still significant that in her journal she wrote strongly of her attach-
ment to her state and to her country and that she volunteered her services during wartime for the sometimes hazardous duty of nursing. It is
clear in her diary that Ada accepted the patriarchal structure of the
Southern plantation household and wished to do only the war work
which her society would view as "appropriate" for an upper-class
woman. Nursing was *not* for her a way to assert her power in the face of
male supremacy; rather, it was an appropriate way for an obedient

---

30. Bacot Diary, May 11 and 19, 1862, and March 4, 8, and 9, 1862.

31. Bacot Diary, January 19, 1861.

32. Drew Gilpin Faust, "Altars of Sacrifice: Confederate Women and the Narratives of
War," *Journal of American History* 76 (March 1990): 1200–1228; George C. Rable,
*Civil Wars: Women and the Crisis of Southern Nationalism* (Urbana: University of Illinois
Press, 1989).

daughter of the patriarchy to serve her country. She made the final decision to leave her family to become a nurse only when Reverend Barnwell assured her that it was a noble and suitable job for a woman of the Confederacy.[33] When Ada was described as doing her work with "quiet but unceasing devotion" in the 1861–1862 report of the South Carolina Hospital Aid Association, it was one of the highest compliments the South could pay to one of its women.[34]

Although Bacot viewed her Confederate war service as both patriotic and suitable for a woman of her class, it also greatly expanded her world. Ada's wartime experiences wrought a positive change in her. Her self-confidence rose as she demonstrated her ability to handle the dietary and sanitary needs of hundreds of soldiers in spite of chronic shortages, and her personality blossomed in a number of friendships with her coworkers. The camaraderie that developed among the medical personnel during the war and in the face of their common problems is similar to that depicted in the television shows "M*A*S*H" and "China Beach." Even after Bacot left the hospital, she stayed in touch with some of her coworkers and she saved some of the letters she received from Dr. James McIntosh and his wife, Fannie. This intense bonding experienced by Bacot and doubtless by other Southern women must certainly have had an impact on their postwar lives, forging connections between them and others that lasted over time and distance. This experience must be recognized and assessed for the effect it had.

Bacot's desire for social and economic independence was undoubtedly shared also by other Southern women. She did not want to transform the social and economic structure of the South, but she wanted to feel that she did not have to rely on anyone for emotional and financial support. As a widow, she felt she had no appropriate male to lean on because her relationships with her father and oldest brother were often stormy. She admitted the importance of family and was particularly close to her sister, her brother Dickie, and various cousins, but she still cherished the notion that she could be self-sustaining as she was fortunate enough to own her own plantation and to have the means to run it.

---

33. Bacot Diary, October 27, 1861.

34. "Report of the South Carolina Hospital Aid Association in Virginia, 1861–1862," in *South Carolina Women in the Confederacy*, 2:104.

Also significant among the themes of her diary are the day-to-day frustrations of administering a hospital for the sick and wounded and the ineffectiveness of the system in caring for those who most needed it. Supplies and personnel were always scarce, and many soldiers died who could have been saved. Civil War medicine has long been a neglected subject, and any first-hand account of the hospitals and their personnel is a welcome addition. Very few Civil War diaries kept by doctors or nurses have survived, and not many have been published; Bacot's diary is one of only two known to have been kept by any of the nurses in Charlottesville. One can gather from Bacot's diary that the South Carolina hospitals in Charlottesville did improve their medical and administrative efficiency with the Confederacy's decision in 1862 to provide more hospital appropriations and to assume direct control over all hospitals housing military personnel. At the same time, the Confederate Congress passed a law allotting a certain number of matrons, assistant matrons, ward masters, and attendants to every hospital and setting a standard pay scale for all these positions. While the staff at the Monticello seemed a bit adrift at first in the midst of these changes, with time they saw the advantages: there was no more talk of uprooting them and moving the facility to Petersburg, or Richmond, or anywhere else the Association's board might take a fancy to, and they finally had the same access to supplies as did the General Hospital. The Association still continued to provide supplemental food, clothing, and services to the former South Carolina hospitals, but turned its attention to creating wayside stations for the sick and wounded.

Of interest too for the reader of nineteenth-century Southern history is the relationship between plantation mistresses and their slaves. In fact, it has become a hotly discussed topic of late among historians.[35] While Bacot does not reflect on her relationships with her own slaves and other blacks, her journal reveals her general belief in their inferiority, her exasperation and anger with their occasional refusal to obey her orders, her

---

35. See, especially, Catherine Clinton, *The Plantation Mistress: Woman's World in the Old South* (New York: Pantheon, 1982); Elizabeth Fox-Genovese, *Within the Plantation Household: Black and White Women of the Old South* (Chapel Hill: University of North Carolina Press, 1988); and Carol K. Bleser, "Southern Planter Wives and Slavery," in *The Meaning of South Carolina History: Essays in Honor of George C. Rogers, Jr.*, ed. David R. Chesnutt and Clyde N. Wilson (Columbia: University of South Carolina Press, 1991), 104–20.

conviction that those slaves who rebel or conspire against their masters must have been poorly treated, and her overbearing sense of responsibility for those in her care.[36] Her only dramatic encounter with a black person took place in September 1862 when William, a "yellow boy" hired by the Association to help at the Maupin House, was insolent to her when she confronted him for failing to clear the dinner table. She smacked him, his nose bled, and he ran to his mother, a slave named "Old Willie," for protection. Old Willie threatened Bacot, who complained to Drs. Rembert and McIntosh. They responded by whipping both William and his mother. Both slaves were discharged, and they left the Maupin House without saying good-bye. Bacot wrote at length in her journal about these events.[37] She clearly understood that something was amiss in her relationship with Old Willie and William but could not identify just what it was; although she acknowledged feelings of guilt and distress over her role in the matter, she remained perplexed by Old Willie's desire to protect her son. While her attitudes will bring about no revision in the literature on Southern women slaveholders, she does express an underlying uneasiness that probably reflected the experiences of many others in her position.

Ada Bacot's diary is a significant document that can help students, teachers, scholars, and general readers alike understand the role loyal Southern women like Ada Bacot played in the Civil War. The contribution Bacot and other women made to the Confederate war effort, both directly through nursing and indirectly through ladies' aid associations, fund-raising drives, and personal sacrifices, had an immeasurable impact on the South's ability to keep fighting long after its resources ran short. The diary also offers some answers to the important question of how the war specifically affected Bacot and women like her. Ada Bacot's own experience would argue that many women found greater happiness and fulfillment in their expanded opportunities for meaningful work and friendships outside their previous, and sometimes narrow, social circle. What historians and students must consider is whether these women continued to enjoy a greater degree of happiness and fulfillment in spite of wartime bereavements and postwar stringencies. Reading Ada Bacot's di-

---

36. Bacot Diary, May 28, 1861; February 11 and April 16, 1861; May 1 and 3, and August 3, 1861; May 15, 1861; October 28 and November 17, 1861.

37. Bacot Diary, September 8, 9, and 13, 1862.

ary will open up for many audiences the topics of the relationship between women and war—a particularly germane question in light of the current controversy over whether to allow women in the United States Armed Forces to go into combat—and the role of medicine in war. In spite of new drugs, supplies, procedures, and training, combat medics still face many of the same problems that Ada and her colleagues did: disease, supply shortages, untrained personnel, inadequate facilities, and an unresponsive bureaucracy.

Why Ada Bacot stopped keeping a journal in January 1863 and left the nursing profession shortly thereafter is still a mystery. Eleven months after the end of Bacot's last diary entry on January 10, 1863, she had left nursing and returned to South Carolina. In November 1863, she married Thomas A. G. Clarke, a first lieutenant in the Confederate Army and a fellow South Carolinian whose sister had been a nurse at the Midway Hospital in Charlottesville. Ada probably met her future husband when he was a patient at that hospital after the Battle of Second Manassas in August 1862. Although why she left Charlottesville is not known, her homesickness and her worry about what was happening at Roseville and Arnmore may have combined with emotions raised by her lengthy visit home to Society Hill at the end of 1862 to make her return imperative. Diary entries from Ada's long trip back home dominate the eighth and final chapter of this book and show that while she was glad to be home, old conflicts had quickly re-emerged between Ada and her family. Also, the atmosphere back in Charlottesville was tense following Dr. Edward Rembert's request that Ada become the head matron at the Midway Hospital. James McIntosh adamantly opposed the move, and Ada was torn between her desire to take the new position and her desire to please her friend. None of Bacot's descendants knows why she left nursing. Family tradition holds that there was a seventh volume of her diary, but it has disappeared along with any answers it might have held. None of the letters she received after the war, still in the possession of her granddaughter, Lillian Clarke James, offers any clues either. So her journal leaves us with a mystery, but the answers it does offer to historians and general readers more than compensate for its omissions.

Chapter 1

# September 11, 1860–May 26, 1861

*". . . a half-melancholy feeling steals over me, can it be the shadow of some ill about to befall me?"*

Sep 11" 60

After twelve oclock this morning the clouds rolled away & left the sky perfectly clear, the afternoon was so charming, I could not resist the temptation to take a walk. So Flora[1] & I wandered over the fields to the grave yard, where all was still, oh! so still, even my heart seemed to stand still while there. I have not been there for many months before, not since the early spring when I went to plant a few flowers, Which have been choked by the rank weeds & tall grass which have been alowed to grow since I have been away. After satisfying little Flora's curiosity about who was buried here & there, I plucked a few sprigs from the arbivita growing between my little ones graves & a bunch or two of pretty grass which bent its graceful head to the gentle breeze. We turned homeward. There seems to be a great calm with in me ever since I left that halowed spot, perhaps 'twill not be long e'er I too will be resting there.

Nov 6" 60

I see by my last date that more than a month has passed since I have had the hart to write in my journal. I have not been in the happiest frame of mind I ever was in, & there fore avoided writing as I think I ought to give a just statement of my self. Now I am pleased to say I am regaining my usual state of feeling. Tonight as we were all seated round the table after the tea things had been removed, Sister[2] & I sewing Pet[3] writing & Pa[4] reading some article in one of the papers, we were startled by a hevy step on the piazza then a rapid knock at the door. I

---

1. Flora Cynthia McLendon (b. ca. 1852) was the daughter of a neighboring family who worked as overseers for the Bacots; Ada had taken her as a foster child sometime shortly before the start of her narrative.

2. Jacqueline Menissier Shaw Bacot Saunders (b. 1834).

3. Tours Loire Bacot (1840–1882).

4. Peter Samuel Bacot (1810–1864).

thought Mr. McLendon[5] had something to communicate to Pa, & asked Pet to open the door, he did so, & in walked four gentlemen, Dr. Porcher[6], Mr. H. Waring[7], Mr. J. Rogers[8], & a Mr. Alston from Charleston, we did not know what to make of this unexpected visit. It soon became aparent that they had come on business. Dr. P. took Pa out & told him for what they had come. Gus[9] was called & a fire ordered in the parlor, So Sister & I took ourselves off to our rooms. Tis past twelve & they have just gone, I did not learn what the object of their visit was.

Nov 8″ 60

Pa went to Charleston today he doesn't know what will be his stay. Pet is left to take care of us during his absence. Just after we had seated ourselves at dinner the butt[10] arrived, & who should get out of it but cousin Henry.[11] Eleven months ago he left home, a miserable crazy man, & now he returns a stong helthy man, perfectly restored in both body & mind, so happy to get home once more & so anxious to press those dear ones at home to his swelling heart. Tomorrow we send him up to the Hill where his wish will be gratefied.

Nov 10″ 60

After a night of wind & rain the Sun came forth in all his glory to gladen our hearts by his bright warm glow. Sister & I made our call at Mrs. McCalls[12] this morning after being so lazy about it, we found that Eugenia & her babys had left (for which I was sorry), & that Nettie had gone with her so we only saw Miss McC.[13] & Mary.[14] Down by the

---

5. Probably J. E. McLendon (b. ca. 1812), Flora's father and Roseville's overseer.

6. Dr. Edward Porcher (b. ca. 1814).

7. Probably A. H. Waring (b. ca. 1824).

8. John Alfonso Rogers (ca. 1815–1896) was a local planter and cousin of the Bacots.

9. One of the Bacot family slaves.

10. Ada uses the word to describe one of the family's wagons or buggies.

11. Henry Harraman Bacot (b. 1818), a physician in Society Hill, had a history of mental illness.

12. Probably Elizabeth M. McCall (b. ca. 1810), who was a wealthy widow with a large family.

13. Possibly Miss S. D. McCall, who was seventeen in 1860.

14. Possibly a Mary Chapman, aged fifty-three, who lived with another McCall, probably a son of Elizabeth.

branch we found some very pretty leaves the brightest I have seen this fall. We got back just at twelve & William[15] came at one. Dear little Sissy[16] she clung around her fathers neck for a long time with her little face radiant with smiles. Poor little Flora had a return of fever today which caused her to sleep almost the entire day. Randal[17] returned this morning, bringing a note from Carrie[18] & a few tokens of remembrance from her to the children, cousin Henry sent a beautiful little pearl shell to both Sister & me, some which he got in his travles.

Nov 11" 60

We have no service today Mr. Moore[19] went to Society Hill to attend a convocation. Tis the fourth annaversary of Sisters wedding day; I can scarcely realize it has been four years except when I see her three little ones. Pet killed two ducks last evening which made us quite a nice dinner in honor of the day. The papers are filled with the news of the great excitement which pervades the entire state, if the people dont take some decided measure this time I will never trust to South Carolina again. Miss Ann & Col. John spent the morning with us every one seems to be full of secession, nothing else is talked of. Many of the most prominent men from all parts of the state who hold publick offices have resigned them, & declare themselves redy for the conflict which we all expect.

Nov 25" 60

Pet left us today for Charleston where he is to take charge of a farm near the city. His negroes went off with the wagons, (filled with a variety of things necesary to their comfort, both on the way, & after they get to the end of their journey,) on Friday morning. The day was bad being both wet & cold, but there was no time to be lost so they went off. It being necesary for Pet to be down there tomorrow, & as he was unable to get off on yesterday he went this morning, depriving us of

---

15. William Johnson Saunders, an insurance agent in Raleigh, North Carolina, was the husband of Ada's sister Jacqueline.

16. One of Jacqueline's daughters.

17. One of the Bacots' slaves.

18. Henry Harraman Bacot's daughter Caroline (b. 1843).

19. The Reverend Augustus Moore (b. ca. 1815) was the minister of the Episcopal Christ Church of Mars Bluff, where Ada was a communicant.

the means of getting to church. However the day was so very cold I doubt if any of us would have ventured out if we had had the means of going. Pa had a letter from Dickie[20] asking for the particulars of our position politicaly he wishes Pa to give him the power to resign when the South may be certain of secession. He is one of Carolinas Sons who will ever be redy to stand by her.

Wednesday Dec 12″ 60

Dark as the mantle of Night is the cloud which envelops our galant little State, many are the misgivings I am forced to acknowledge, but hope is strong, & faith in almight[y] God who has never yet forsaken the oppressed makes me more at ease than I otherwise would be[.] Fear I have never yet felt I know I can live under as many privations as most people, twould be nothing new to me. Tis true I have lived in greater luxury for the past few years than ever before, & my constitution is much improved from bad health & trouble, but I thank God my powers of endurance are not entirely gone. I have thought from the first 'tis hardly to be supposed that the north will see us go out of the union, without making some effort to prevent, or bring us back. If she should there must be war. My heart does not quail, It has not yet caused me a sleepless night, or a repining. Now for the first time since my great loss am I most thankful God saw fit to take my little ones when he did. For them I would feel fear & anxiety, now they are safe & I have no one to fear for, who is dependent on me. My children[21] would have been my first care to shield them[.] Oh! how terable what anguish to have seen them suffer, but now there is no fear of that, for which I praise God. Now I can give myself up to my State, the very thought elevates me. These long years have I prayed for something to do, perhaps my prayer is now being answered. The papers are all excitement many fine speaches appear in their colloms. The South at last seems to be aware of her danger. My only fear is she will listen to some compromise. Tis said woman has no business with such matters, but what woman in South Carolina does not have the interest of her state at heart.

---

20. Richard Hayes Bacot (b. 1842) was then a cadet at the Naval Academy at Annapolis.

21. Ada's two daughters, Anna Jane Bacot (1852–1854) and Emily Helen Bacot (1855–1857).

William left us last night, he came very unexpectedly Monday morning, to see Pa on some business. Roseville truly is the place of changes, some one is always going or coming. We have sent this evening up to the Hill for cousin Henry & the two girls. They come to dinner tomorrow. Poor little Flora seems sick again tonight. Pa has at last finished Rutledge, such a time as he has been reading it. As for me I have one of my reading fits on me now, consequently I devour every thing comes in my way. Dickie spoak of resigning his place at Annapolis on yesterday or today. I am sorry yet I would not have him stay. Perronneau[22] does nothing but hunt, he is quite successful too, we had two ducks for dinner of his shooting. The weather is cold & I have been enjoying a splendid wood fire all the evening. M[a]y the time never come to me when I cant have a wood fire, tis so bright so cheerful; at times something like happiness comes over me, I begin to enjoy life once more. My health is good & I want for nothing. Surely I should be contented & thankful.

Saturday night Dec 15" 60

After a miserable night, I awoke this morning to see the ground covered with a beautiful light covering of snow, twas still snowing when I looked out of the window. Tis the first time the snow has lain on the grown for two years, the boys tryed to enjoy it by hunting but they soon returned with only one poor unfortunate cock. Carrie Hattie[23] Flora & I had a nice fire in here (my little room) where [we] enjoyed the day very much. Dear good little Carrie busied her self making me a pretty collar, sweet gentle little creature she is. Hattie is full of fun & she & Flora eat snow and amused themselves in various ways, poor cousin Henry had to go to bed with a dreadful headache we are having right merry times it some times seems like Christmas. Cousin Fannie & Cousin John[24] called yesterday morning. Twas quite amusing to hear the gentlemen talk Politics. Cousin H. is a strong union man, so of course he does not meat with much sympathy, he gets it on all sides,

22. Probably Peronneau Bacot, the son of Peter Samuel Allston Bacot, a cousin of Ada's father who had died in 1858.

23. Harriett Wainwright Bacot (b. 1844) was, along with Carrie (Caroline), a daughter of Henry Harraman Bacot.

24. Frances Mandeville "Fannie" Rogers (ca. 1815–1893) and her husband, John Alfonso Rogers.

he has to fight against us all who of course are strong secessionist, even his own family differ from him[.] I often find my self wondering what will be the issue of all the stir which has been going on for the last two or three months. I am most anxious to go to England next Summer if the country is settled, but of course I will not leave while South Carolina is in trouble.

Saturday Dec 22d" 1860

Feeling restless, & weary of the house I proposed to the girls to walk with me to pay a morning to cousin Henrietta,[25] accordingly about eleven oclock we started, the walk was pleasant the air mild & the sun just bright enough to warm us while we threaded our way through the woods & fields. Cousin H. was at home & gave us a cordual greeting. We heard the news of the Secession. The ordinance had been passed on Thursday, so realy & truly we no longer belong to the union. Tomorrow we will get full accounts. After looking at Metas[26] flowers, we walked leasurly home again. Cousin Henry is much better he will come down tomorrow. Poor Hattie & Tom[27] went home tonight, they were having such a nice time, they hated so to go, Tom realy had a fit of pouts. After tea I got my work & Dickie amused us with his sprightly talk, how I love these evenings, time pases so quickly ten oclock comes so soon. Even Pa is brighter tis pleasant to see the fond looks he bestows on our Dickie. May God ever preserve him to us as pure & fresh as he now is. Each day he seems more noble & affectionate.

Friday Dec 28" 60

I wonder why tis as I sit here all alone, a half melancholy feeling steals over me, can it be the shadow of some ill about to befall me? or is it because I have heard that Fort Moultrie has been destroyed, the spot for which so many of South Carolinas brave sons spilt their blood in the time of the revolution.[28] Yes that has some what to do with my gloomy feelings. This morning's mail brought us no news from the city

---

25. Henrietta Rogers (ca. 1810–1887) was the wife of planter Robert Rogers (ca. 1808–1882).

26. Meta Rogers (b. ca. 1843) was the daughter of Henrietta and Robert Rogers.

27. Thomas Wright Bacot (b. 1845) was the eldest son of Henry Harraman Bacot.

28. Fort Moultrie was not actually destroyed; when Major Robert Anderson and his troops abandoned it on December 26, 1860, they spiked the guns and destroyed the carriages, but left all else untouched.

dreadful was the disapointment to me, especialy as Pa was going to Town & I would be left alone with the children. I had thought to console myself with reading the papers. But none came, so I have plied my needle harde all day, indeed until just now, for I have just finished off a pair of draw[ers] for Perronneau. Both of the children are fast to sleep[.] Perronneau tryed to stay up & keep me company, he related hunting stories to me until he became exhausted, so I told him to go to bed & I would go to my room & finish my work, he is a brave little fellow, & will make a noble man some of these days should it please God he should live. My thoughts will wander to my dear Dickie, I am even more anxious to hear from him than I was on yesterday. I fear he got down too late to join Lieutenant Hamilton.[29] But fears will do no good, I can only wait with what patience I can command. Pa met Mr. John Rogers at the depot this morning & asked him to send me the news about the forts, Which he was kind enough to do about an hour or so ago. It only gave me a better understanding of what I heard this morning from a few lines written by T. Gregg[30] on a slip of paper & put into our mail bag. I suppose war will be the cry now. Where can my darling boy be? where ever he is God protect him.

Monday Dec 31 1860

No Pa tonight again, I sent this morning to the office hoping to hear from him, so this evening I sent off poor Randal in the rain, to see if he had come. He came back a little while ago shivering with the cold & without his master. Oh! I wish he had of come I am so anxious to hear about every thing, what has become of Dickie & what is doing in town, besides I am lonly, or rather not lonly but tiard of being alone with only the children. The rain has poured all day so I could not venture out. A gloomy birthday it has been, tis well I am not supersticous enough to think it is the type of what the whole year is to be for sure it would be a tearful one. I am twenty eight today, yes I can scarcely realize that such is the case, I do not now feel old, no[r] am I, but surely I ought to feel more matronly. But to tell the truth I feel younger & more girlish than I did at eighteen. My health is good & I have no

---

29. Probably Captain John Randolph Hamilton of the Confederate Navy; see Bacot's entry for May 8, 1861.

30. Probably Thomas E. Gregg (d. 1911), a neighbor.

very weighty cares. There is much for which to be very thankful, I have had my share of trouble which has not been a very light one, but when I reflect it might have been worse, I feel my heart swell with gratitude for the many blessings I daily receive. When I look at Flora & think that had my little Anna been spared to me she would have been but six month younger, I cant help a sigh, but I do not wish her back, no no, for better off is she. December of all the months in the year the most importent to me, & the most dreded, I am always glad when 'tis gone, I was married on the third, my little Anna born on the eight, my husband[31] died on the twentieth, & I was born on the thirty-first. Annavers[ar]ys of births wedding & death. May the all merciful God help me to keep the good resolutions I have formed during the day, upon him I relie entirely I cant trust myself in the least. It grows late & my fire will but just last me till I can get redy for bed. I hope to awake in the morning to find the New Year coming in with a bright smile as the old has left us weeping.

Tuesday Jan 1st 1861

1861 yes little did I think four year ago, I would live to write the year 1861. But alive I am thank God, & far better than I was four years since. Well do I remember being seated by this very little hearth raped in a dressing gown & big shawl my heart full of misry & my body weak from resent illness. But let the "dead past bury its dead" what I have now to do with is the present. At last I have heard from my dear Pa, this mornings mail brought me two from him & one (quite a long one) from Sister, Which has realy made me feel in quite good spirits all day, Especialy too as I could go out a little & take a peep at my flowers, which are looking quite as well as I could wish & have any right to expect, seeing that my pits have no glass & the poor things have been shut up from the blessed light for nearly a week. I was out all the morning superintending the puting up of the lard & making of a small quanitity of sausages there having been a few hogs kiled on yesterday. It being New years day I alowed my self a part of a holyday, & have read since two oclock, scarcely alowing myself time to eat being much interested in & amused with some of Tom Hoods letters to his different

---

31. Thomas Wainwright M. Bacot (b. 1825) was killed by his overseer on December 20, 1856.

friends.[32] What would not I give to be posessed of such powers. For any one who loves writing as I do tis a great misfortune I can write no better. I sent about noon a Newyears present of some whip to cousin Henrietta, who sent me in return some fine heads of cabbage & letuice. Cousin Robert wanted to know of the servant Gus where his present was, If I had none to send him why didn't I go myself. It has been altogether a pleasant quiet day to me, for there is nothing I like better than quiet. My dreams of last night were pleasant too though rather rambling I was cheated out of a few hours sleep just before day by a little mouse nibling at my soap. It caused me to leave one of my most delightful dreams, (for I had two or three separate ones during the night) unfinished, as I lay awake my last dream was so vividly remembered that I had half a mind to write it out when I arose this morning, but in the mean time I fell asleep again & by the time I arose the dream had almost escaped me, which I regret for 'twas quite a pretty one. I was realy rejoiced to learn from one of Pa's letters of Dickie's safe arrival in time to see Lieut. Hamilton he Dickie is out at the farm waiting for Lieut. Hamilton to make some further arrangment. Pa writes "War is imminent." He will be at home tomorrow night nothing preventing then I will get all particulars, my what a Scribe how I have written very near four pages, if I keep on at this rate my book wont last me the year, which I mean it shall.

Tuesday Jan 8" 61

E'er this I guess we have a few more states on our side. Florida has alredy seceeded & Alab & Miss had called conventions for yesterday the 7"[.] Every day we hear of one or two more forts being captured. Today I heard they were about to try Mr. Toombs of Georgia[33] for treason at Washington which was only lost by one voat, but there are so many reports now circulating which have no foundation tis hard to tell which to believe. I went today to see some of the Guards go off, we got

---

32. Thomas Hood (1799–1845) was an English comic poet and magazine editor whose work was widely reprinted in the United States.

33. Robert Toombs (1810–1885) was currently a United States senator from Georgia who would resign to serve as the Confederacy's first secretary of state and later as a brigadier general in the Confederate Army. The story of the vote for a treason trial was indeed a rumor.

to Florence about twenty minutes before the train left. I went in the cars to speak to Hannah Dyson[34] & Ida who were going down to town; Ida was with her young husband who looked extremly happy. H. was going to see hers who is now on the Island with the rest of the company. I saw & spoak to General's McQueen[35] & Harllee.[36] They said "I hear your are going to be a Florence Nightingale," I said yes but was afraid no body would send for me. Oh! how I wished I could go down with them, but may hap my time will come. When we got home we found Miss Ann who had come soon after we had left. In the morning we get the news.

Friday Jan 11" 61

Most exciting news from town this morning, the Cutter Star of the West with troops for Maj. Anderson at fort Sumpter was fired into by our troops at Mora's [Morris] Island & Fort M[oultrie] causing her to turn back—Maj. A. & the Gov. have exchanged letters, we now awate Maj. A.'s messenger sent to Washington excitement runs high, every body is looking for more news.[37] Oh! God what is to be the issue.

Saturday Jan 19" 1861

The sun look pleasant today since the heavy rains of yesterday, ver-[il]y it has done nothing but rain for weeks past. Cousin Fannie &

---

34. Hannah Dyson (b. ca. 1838), the daughter of Peter Samuel Bacot's brother Richard Brockington Bacot, was married to Archibald Dyson (b. ca. 1834), a druggist from Georgia.

35. Probably John McQueen (1808–1867), a former major general in the state militia who served as a member of the United States Congress from 1849 to 1860 and of the Confederate Congress from 1862 to 1864. He was a resident of the Marlboro District.

36. William Wallace Harllee (1812–1897) was a lawyer and a general in the South Carolina militia. He organized the Pee Dee or Harllee's Legion but saw no active service during the Civil War. He held a variety of state political posts and at this time was serving as a member of the Secession Convention, where he signed the Ordinance of Secession, and as the state's lieutenant governor. He and his family lived at the Sunnyside Plantation near Mars Bluff in the Marlboro District, and he was a vestryman at the same church Ada and her family attended.

37. The governor of South Carolina in 1861 was Francis Pickens (1805–1869). Confederate forces fired on the *Star of the West* from Morris Island on January 9, 1861. Unable to relieve Fort Sumter, the vessel turned around and left the harbor to escape damage.

John called on the bride & groom[38] today. Cousin F. look gloomy, she says she does not sleep for thinking of Bob[39] being at the Island, she wanted to know if I was not very anxious about Dickie as he is at Fort Moultry, no I said I was too proud he was there. I wonder some times if people think it strange I should be so warm a secessionist, but why should they, has not every woman a right to express her opinions upon such subjects, in private if not in public. I confes I take but little interest in any thing else but what concerns my state, I feel as eager for news as any man in the state, but I know I am not able to do any thing for her defence being a woman, still that does not prevent my being interested. My love for S. Carolina is that of an affectionate daughter for a mother, the purest love in the world. I would feel as much mortified if S.C. should disgrace her self as I would if my mother should. Each day I live I feel 'twould be harder than ever to give up my home here. No where else would be home to me.

Thursday Jan 24

Pet & Louise left us today they were to've gone yesterday but the day was too unfaverable, when will we have clear weather, the sun has not shown his face in a week, there has not been much rain today but tis cloudy & damp, all the streams are up, & the roads miserable. The weather has moderated very much, what a miserable time the soldiers must be having[.] I have had a pain in my heart for the last two days owing I suppose to the constant state of excitement I have been in for weeks past. We never hear from Dickie except through others much to my anoiance. I have an uneasy feeling all the time, looking for something, which perhaps will never come. My fears are constantly kept alive, that S.C. will not stand her ground not that I fear she will go back into the Union, as I once did, but that she will alow the Federal troops to remain at Fort Sumter, there seems to be some understanding between the Gov. & Maj. A. not known to the public I cant reconcile my self to the idea of letting Fort S. remain as it now does. Of course I dont know what is for the best, but seems to me the sooner the fort is taken the better for the State. Jim is still with us, he seems quite

---

38. Tours Loire had married Marie Louise Trenholm of Charleston on January 15, 1861.

39. Probably Robert Rogers (d. 1911).

interested in S.C. politics, N.C. seems in no hurry to join us, she certainly cant be called hasty.

Monday night Feb 11″ 61

Monday always a busy day with me. I cant say I've done a great amount of work today, but some how I find myself tiard & sleepy at a little past 10. I sent Randal off in the rain to the office hoping to hear from Pa, he only brought me the news in which there is but new, there is a letter too from Jesse[40] to his father, which I guess I will see in the morning, perhaps it may give some information conserning fort Sumter. I see the Gov's of the border states have requested Gov. Pickens not to attack Sumter yet, his reply is he cant give any direct anser but will consider the proposition. Take care he doesnt consider to his cost. I had a letter from Pa yesterday saying he will be at home tomorrow night. If there is any prospect of the fort being attacked I know he wont come.

I got through with Floras lessons today much better than I expected. My how I dread teaching her, I dont like to teach any way & she is by no means a bright child. It has been raining slowly all day, as night came on the rain increased[.] I heard Mr. McLendon say today the clouds were running up the river again, he looks for an other fresh. I find some of my young negroes have been disobeying my orders, they were found away from home with out a pass. I hope I may be able to make them understand without much trouble that I am Mistress & will be obeyed. I have never had any trouble with them until now. Even now I dont apprehend much. There is some hope of P.'s having his socks soon I have finished one & commenced the other. I think I am quite couragous. Flora & I staid in this big house all alone last night & will again tonight.

Sunday Feb 24″ 61

I realy have not had the heart to write for the last few day, besides there was nothing of importance & I have been feeling very unwell. My excitement doesn't abate & I am in constant expectation of bad news. realy my life is becoming a burden, I can't be said to live mearly to exist. I never feel lonly but I take no intrest in any thing, every thing I do is mecanical. Nothing gives me the least pleasure, I go about

---

40. Jesse McLendon (b. ca. 1838) was the son of J. E. McLendon.

like on[e] who has but a stated time to live. It seems to me that I will not live long, the idea is not unpleasant, still I pray God I may not die sudenly. I am not melancholy or am I actualy in pain. I cant be said to be in ill health, mearly weary of life[.] Having never seen but precious little of the bright side of life tis not supprising I should be weary of it. I do not mean to complain, on the contrary I feel I cant be too thankful for the many blessings I have. I spent the day at Arnmore yesterday, I felt quite well all the first part of the day. In the afternoon my head began to ache me, which got worse as night came on, which compelled me to go to bed soon after I got home. I was too much indisposed to go to church this morning am still suffering from headache. I had a letter from Sister this morning saying little Sissy had burned her face & hands on the stove. The rest were well. I also heard from Carrie she cant come owing to her health she says. I am sorry for realy dont know what is to be done with Peronneau & Flora. Dident hear again from Dickie, I expect he is too busy to write. The papers report a man of war off the Bar at Charleston The Daniel Webster.[41] Tis thought she has reinforcements for Fort Sumter. I am beginning to hope there will be no war. Were it not for the wind the day would be lovely. My flowers are begining to bloom, which is the only thing in the least cheering to me. Such queer dreams I do have last night I had quite a remarkable one.

Friday Noon Mch 15" 61

Breakfast waited for me a little this morning. I had a bad night, such dreams, then too I awoke with a terable sufficating feeling, my throat seemed it would close in spite of me. This morning I am better but have a dreadful cold. just now after Pa had read the papers to me, he said he had another favour to ask of me. Now I have for some time been dreading this very thing & made up my mind accordingly. I told him plainly I could not I would not stand his security again, nor will I. he thinks I know, that I will come over as I have heretofore, but for once he will see that I will & can be firm. Oh! why will he persist in asking me to stand his security he knows it is repugnant to me & that I have heretofore only done so because I wanted in some measure to repay him for his kindness to me. He seems determined to ruin himself

41. This piece of information, like many others Ada recorded, was false.

& me too. Now I determined to put a stop to it. I have no one to depend upon if I am deprived of my little property, I must perish, dependence is something my proud nature revolts against. I love Pa with all the tenderness I am capable of, & it grieves me to the very heart to refuse him anything in reason. I have all redy laid myself liable to an amount which it would take half of what I am worth to pay. It causes me many anxious hours. I know Pa would not for anything be the willing cause of my ruin, but there are so many misfortunes, none of us know from day to day what will happen. My feelings are indiscribable.

Sunday night Mch 17″ 61

I awoke this morning suffering a good deal with my back. went to church but felt dreadfuly all the time, just a feeling of desparation I could not controle. Tis said coming events cast their shadow before them. It has been true enough in this case. This morning Peter[42] had two letters one from his wife[43] the other from George[44] written the day after, anouncing to him the birth of a son.[45] Pa congratulated him, I did not, simply because I saw no cause for congratulation I saw he dident like it. He went to the depot this morning but returned as there was no car going down today. I suppose he felt some what anoyed at not being able to go & naturaly enough. But I see no cause why he should vent his anoyance on me, but he chose to do so. I felt hurt and told him he had no reason to be angry with me. Then there was a few more words said which is usualy the case faned the flame. Then Pa threw out one of his hints which always iritate more than any things else, because I believe he positively dislikes me, his child that I am. Oh! how they hurt my feelings, May God forgive them, a perfect sea of anguish has past over my soul this night, I can find no words to express my feelings. Pa says he considers me beyond hope, & says he wishes I could hold a few minutes conversation with Christ upon the subject of ill temper, & Peter advises me to go & read my bible that I show I know very little of it, all this I hear without a word. May God forgive

---

42. Peter Brockington Bacot (1838–1924), Ada's oldest brother.

43. Elizabeth Helen Trenholm (ca. 1839–1882), usually called "Daisy," was also the sister of Tours Loire's wife.

44. George was apparently Daisy Trenholm Bacot's brother.

45. Charles Trenholm Bacot (March–June 1861).

them for the bitter, bitter anguish they caused me, twas by the strongest effort I could scarsely restrain my tears. I got up quietly from my seat & came in here hoping to relieve my wounded heart in tears, but as I had checked them, they will not now flow, God is my judge (for he alone will judge me justly) I feel no anger, nor bear either any ill will. What is to become of me I know not. My prayer is that I may soon be released from this bondage. I have a home I see no reason why I should not go there & end my days in quiet. Some people seem born to suffer & I am one of that number. I pray God to give me patience to bear them patiently.

Tuesday Apr 9" 61

Cleared up a little though still cold, went to Arnmore, ordered The old part of the house taken down. when I returned found Pa coming across the field with a beautiful bunch of the swamp honeysucle he complained of his back, before sunset he had to send for the Dr.,[46] who got here just about tea time, took tea with me, & made himself very agreable. Dick came very late with the mail. *War* is at last declared, some excitement prevails, Pa is anxious to go to town tomorrow whi[c]h I hardly think he'll do unless very much better.

Sunday night Apr 21st" 61

The day has been very delightful Perronneau, Flora, & I went to church this morning Pa too unwell to attend us. Mrs. Harllee[47] was very much excited because the Gen. wanted to go to Va. It seems He dident tell her when he got home on Friday night that he had been offered the command of the two companys ordered to Va. On Saturday he heard that *Bonham*[48] had been elected then he told Mrs Harllee, she seemed quite rejoiced that the Gen. hadnt been elected. Cousin Henrietta seemed quite shocked at Mrs Harllee's want of patriotism. Last night & tonight, I heard the Whipoorwill, a plaintive cry but not

---

46. Probably Dr. Edward Porcher, who cared for the Bacot family.

47. Martha Sarah Shackelford (b. ca. 1819) was the wife of General William Wallace Harllee.

48. Probably Milledge Luke Bonham (1813–1890), a lawyer from the Edgefield District and former member of Congress who had accepted the command of South Carolina regiments. He was made a brigadier general in April 1861 but resigned the following year to take a seat in the Confederate Congress and then became governor in 1863. He rejoined the military in February 1865.

unpleasant to me. I took a walk through the rye just as the sun was setting.

Thursday afternoon Apr 25" 61

I did not much like having my pleasant dreams disturbed this morning, but having heard last night that my servant was worse I went to bed with the intention of rising early, though I had read until quite two this morning, to finish my interesting book, twas near three I guess before I lay me down & composed myself to rest, e'er long I was in the land of dreams, in my light sleep I went over everything I had read before I retired. The air was fresh & balmy this morning as I walked into the garden to breath the delightful perfume of my beautiful flowers before partaking of the morning meal. I thank God most fervently that I can find so much pleasure in any thing as I do in my flowers, my very soul expands with delight while I am among them & no matter what I am suffering while with them I forget all but the pleasure they afford me. The mail brought a Mercury[49] this morning, there is nothing very new. The trumpets of war sound all over the country, nothing but troops moving here & there. There has been some lives lost on the border's much propity distroyed in Maryland & Virginia, great excitement prevails, no news of Dickie. There was a letter from Jesse to his father he mentioned that the reason the remainder of the guards dident go to Va., was because of the dislight to Col. Gegg.[50] I am more than sorry Jesse dident go he cant live at Arnmore if I go, which I most certainly will if life lasts. Flora is unbearable, today she wouldent learn, she dident recolect the simplest words, she is very stubborn & I believed she dident want to say her lesson & thought she would worry me into letting her go, she made out she couldent tell what get spelt so I made her stand in the floor, to find out, when Pa came in & told her what the word was & interfeared with me about her. I told Flora to go that I would switch her for behaving so, Pa said to me twas outragous that he wouldent have a child of his treated so for anything, wher upon I told him to let me alone with Flora twas none of his business but mine[.] he said like the Yankee's he always took up

---

49. The Charleston newspaper.

50. Probably Maxcy Gregg, a Charleston lawyer and Mexican War veteran who had been commissioned colonel of the First South Carolina Volunteers.

for the opressed I said why dident he go & do it there, nothing more was said, I sent F. away from me[.] I am hartely ashamed of loosing my temper, & speaking so disrespectfuly to Pa. after dinner I went & said to him I must beg your pardon for speaking so disrespectfully to you Sir, he said he dident think of it, but I know he did, however tis past & I hope to gain by degrees a better command of myself. my health is miserable, there are time[s] when I am very nearly crazy[.] O, if I could only take a sea voiage. Tis a most lovely day the sun so bright & the air so mild. I have walked in the garden since I commenced this, I find a quanitity of beautiful strawberrys very near ripe, the rain last night has done them much good. Pa has asked me to drive to Mars Bluff with him.

Wednesday night
Roseville May 1st" 1861

Can it be possible that one year has rolled by so well do I remember every particular of the first day of May one year ago. Twas not so bright as this has been, I was far away on my way to Annapolis to visit my dearly loved Dickie[.] Now I am at Roseville where four years have passed, full of sorrow yet there has been some pleasure. I again find myself on the eve of changing my home, I hope soon, to go to my own home. There is both pleasure & pain in the change. I shall be constantly reminded of my former life there, under how different circumstances do I now go there. When first I went twas to be the mistress of the house a loving husband provided. Memory carrys me back to the happy time, & fills my eyes with tears. Now I go there mearly for my own gratification. I am my own mistress sad & alone, with no one to lean upon, no one to lavish any affection upon, all is cold, tame & worldly. O for one heart to call my own but I am selfish, I must be content with what I have my consionce smites me, I surely have no reason to complain, nor will I, so help me God. I will try to make my little home, smiling & bright where all are welcome, & where the poor may ever find asistance. I saden at the thought of going away from here, tis true I can come sometimes & see my flowers & enjoy the company of those who must ever be dear to me. At Arnmore I must necessarily be often alone[.] I have often boasted that I never knew what 'twas to be lonly, but I am punished for my self reliance, I have begun alredy to experience lonliness. I have not been well of late & am much worried by the misbehavior of some of my servants then too Jesse's coming home & not being able to give him his place again, I shall feel miserable if he is deprived of a place entirely. I must learn to take life more calmly. God I have not the slightest doubt is sending these difficulties on me for disciplin, I am in a heigh state of excitement & fear fever will ensue. I threw me on my bed for a few minutes after dinner & soon fell into a troubled sleep my dreams were peopled with strange beaings, I wandered in a magnificent building where I could not tell, as I was asending one of the splendid stair ways a negro woman came to me & implored that I would protect her that the yankees were going to shoot her. I was much excited, & when I awoke found my self quite exhausted. I have been reading all the afternoon & though fatigued find I am not sleepy owing to my nap this afternoon.

Wednesday Night May 8″ 61

About six oclock Pa & I started in Peters buggy with old Sam, to Mrs. Harllee's, Pa said as twas such a pleasant evening he would go with me & spend the evening as he owed the Gen. a visit. I enjoyed the ride so much, the air was just cool enough for a light rapping, & old Sam took us along so nicely. We arrived at Mrs H.'s just as the Gen. was returning from his ride. Mrs. H. & Miss A.B. came out to the gate to meet us, they took me to the green house to see the flowers before dark[.] I wish I could discribe my sensation of delight when I beheld the stand in the center of the green house just filled with the most exquisit of flowers, twas one of the loveliest sieghts I ever saw. After I had taken the rounds we went into the house when I had removed my hat & rapping we went into the parlor where we were soon joined by the rest of the family[.] The children each one wanted to be noticed, little Jimmie[51] the youngest, had a good many sweet sayings. He told me his aunty said he was Gen. Beauregard[52] & a good many other little speaches of the same sort. The Gen. brought me a collec-

---

51. James Shackelford Harllee (b. ca. 1857).

52. General Pierre Gustave Toutant Beauregard (1818–1893) of Louisiana was in command of Confederate forces at Charleston at this time and was overseeing the reduction of Fort Sumter.

tion of photographs to look over, among them was Lieut. Hamilton of the Navy, famous as the originator of the floating Batry[.][53] The face has haunted me ever since I have seldom ever seen a handsomer one, there were a good many fine faces in the collection[.] I think without exception Gov. Pickens one of the most repugnantly ugly men conceivable. Gen. H. is what I call an ugly man, but then he is gentle looking. After tea the mail came the papers were gleaned of all the late new's then Miss Dudly[54] was requested to play, she immediately complied, & we were regailed with some most delightful music. The first tune was the Maidens prayer, a beautiful combination of sweet sounds, then we had the enspiriting air of Dixie, then the Marseillaise hymn, one of the grandest thing ever composed. Pa asked her to sing, & The Gen. told Mattie[55] to go & asist her, at first she seemed timid, but when she thought no one was noticing she crept round & seated her self very near Miss D., so when Miss D. had finished the song she was singing she selected one which M. knew, & directly I heard a feeble little squeeky voice. I wanted to laugh so terably, but had to look as if I was admiring it very much[.] on[c]e or twice I almost lost controle over myself, but I felt that the Gen. & Mrs. H. were looking at me. I was realy glad when something occurred that I could laugh at twas such a relief. Pa dident leave until near eleven, very soon after we retired for the night. Mrs. H. accompanied me to my chamber, just oposit the parlor, a beautiful room furnished with rich mahogany there were two windows, draped with dark buff cambric with white muslin curtains under them, the carpet was of wood colour & buff. The bed was very luxurious, I felt tiard & thought I would sleep immediately, but just as I lay down Lieut. H.'s handsome face came into my mind, & I set to thinking, so twas some time after mid night before I slept. This morning the servant came to wake me quite early, I rose immediately & dressed as quickly as possible, I found Mrs. H. in the parlor, the early morning was delightful, & I found my gingham dress quite

---

53. Captain John Randolph Hamilton, formerly of the United States Navy, had invented the ironclad floating battery which had been used in the attack on Fort Sumter.

54. A local schoolteacher.

55. Martha Shackelford Harllee (b. ca. 1853).

pleasant[.] we very soon went to breakfast every one seemed in a good humor & the meal went off pleasantly. Miss D. & the children very soon had to leave for school. Miss Ann & I amused ourselves with the papers until Mrs. H. was redy to walk into the garden with us. I cant pretend a discription, I only know I felt perfectly entranced, I found that I had not seen half the beauties of the green house in the evening. Mrs. H. as she always does, promised me cuttings & roots of whatever I might wish. About ten oclock I left, perfectly charmed with my visit I was invited to spend the day to see some friends which were to've been down on yesterday but were disapointed in coming. Nothing would've been more agreable to me, but I had fixed upon today to move to Arnmore[.] I called on my way home at Cousin Henrietta's to see Mary,[56] she has a very fine infant, realy a pretty baby. M. looks well too, Cousin H. was quite unwell, just as I was driving up to the door I met Cousin John, & Cousin Fannie & Meta, the two latter were in a buggy driving themselves, M. had a lap full of beautiful flowers. I found that Pa & Peter had gone to Florence when I reached home, just as we had finished dinner they came. About five oclock Perronneau & I drove to Arnmore. Severn[57] is busy geting the rubish away as fast as possible, the little place realy looked quite pretty, I dont think I am going to be so lonly after all. I found the air quite chilly coming home. My dress was thin, & I have a little roughness in my throat in consequence. Just before dark Cousin John Rogers came in & remained to tea. Every body has retired, tis now after eleven I realy feel quite sad to think this my last night here as home at least for the present.

Arnmore, Thursday morning May 10″ 61

I was quite too tiared on yesterday to write an account of the days proceedings, so will steal a part of today for that purpos. I was up just after sunrise yesterday morning seeing the remainder of my furniture put into the wagons, then I wandered round the garden taking special leave of each little flower[.] My heart was full & I felt very sad, I had to wait for the rest of the family to breakfast, so I seated me on the front steps with my desk on my lap & wrote to sister[.] After breakfast,

---

56. Mary E. Rogers had married a Dr. Ben B. Polenitz in 1858. Their daughter Elizabeth would be baptized at Christ Church in Mars Bluff on June 23, 1861.

57. One of Ada's slaves.

Gus & I packed up some china & other little things which I was to take along with me, Pa came to tell me good bye as he wanted to take his morning ride & might not be back before I left. I couldent restrain the tears for a moment which gushed to [my] eyes, I didnt know I loved the old place so well. About twelve oclock Perronneau came round with the Butt & we started, such a load, besides numerous baskets of china & other things of a breakable nature which I was afraid to trust to the wagons, there was Flora, Peronneau & I, then Randal who drove & Dinah[58] who Pa was kind enough to lend to me for a while. We arrived safely & I went to work immediately to try & get things some what fixed up before night, & realy I succeeded much better than I expected, but I paid for it when night came I was completely wearied out, I dont think twas much after eight when I retired, but I dident sleep directly. It seemed so strange to be sleeping in my own house again.

This morning I was awake very early & had to call pretty loudly before I could make Dinah hear, she slept in the other end of the room, as soon as F. got out of the room I dressed & performed my devotions, then arranged the parlor, which answers as dining room too. Then we had breakfast, I began to feel quite settled alredy, & I dont think I am to be so lonly as every one predicts. If I am twill not be because I've not a plenty of work. I've been looking for Pa all the morning he promised yesterday he would come this morning. The wind is very heigh or there would be rain tis very cloudy.

Sunday Night May 26" 61

Flora & I were the first up this morning, though I found it hard to accomplish my exit from bed for a while, I had a pleasant walk through the garden before Pa came out to breakfast. I then looked over the papers until time to dress for church. I took F. upstair to dress her & found I had left her pantelets behind poor child she was dissapointed but I alowed her to go to her mothers[59] & she was very well satisfied. Twas terable warm riding to & from church, we had a plesent chat after church & every body seemed bright & cheerful not withstanding the war news. I was in my room from the time we reached home after

---

58. One of the Bacots' slaves.
59. Mary McLendon (b. ca. 1820).

church until dinner, then again until five this afternoon when I took a chair into the back piazza where twas shady to try & get cool after a while Pa joined me & we commenced conversing upon various subjects when Peter walked across the yard & I remarked I thought him very ugly which turned the conversation upon him, his disposition & manner[.] I then said I thought him unjust & at times unfeeling. Pa defended mearly to take the opposit side. I told him as one instance how Peter had acted toward me when I had done nothing to cause such treatment unless twas I loved him too well. We then talked of Daisys conduct towards me of late. Pa of course tryed to throw all the blame on me but my consience was too clear to allow myself to be accused of what I had never done, without trying at least to defend my self which I did. Pa chose to call it impudence in me but I had no intention of being so & told him so. I told him most people were willing to give the Devil his dues, but that he had never given me mine. I never felt less excited, I told Pa I felt no ill feeling for any one that I dident pretend to love Daisy but I was perfectly willing to live peacably with her, & would treat her with politeness. Pa said he wished I would say nothing more to him about it that it troubled him. I said I had no entention of offending him but to be {illegible} I would not trouble him again, thus the controversy ended. I sat a while then walked in the garden as the sun was nearly down, then to see old Mama Daphney,[60] poor old Soul she is nothing but skin & bone. I then went to see Mrs. McL. while there Dick came for me to go to tea. Flora wanted to stay all night & I indulged her, when we went to tea both Peter & Daisy were more courtious than usual, I think Pa must've said something to them. Pa & I have had a pleasant evening. The moon is just rising, I went to the window to get a breath of air, I could but stop to admire the field of rye, part in shade & part lit up by the moon. Tis very warm tonight.

---

60. One of the Bacots' slaves who had served as the children's nurse.

Chapter 2

# May 28–November 27, 1861

*"I hope my wish will soon be realized, & I can go to Va."*

Tuesday Night May 28" 61

Mr. McLendon came up this morning & came into the piazza to tell me of the battle fought at Harpers ferry where our troops were again victorious.[1] I could not supress my delight, God grant The Lincoln Army may soon see how useless tis to fight against such men & sue for peace. I've been realy smart today, almost compleeting a dress. After dinner I felt a little tiard & lay down on the soffa in the parlor, taking Mr. Rhett's report on Federal relations to read but I soon fell asleep. I was in an uneasy position & was much disturbed by dreams so I got up & went to my bed I slept about an hour dreaming all the time. I found it very hard to arouse my energies but succeeded after a while. I had tea very early & as Tom[2] was not in had his tea put into his room, & sent Dinah to lock the door she couldent accomplish it so I went to assist her. I would look into the plate, I directly missed a piece of the bread, I knew D. had taken it as no one else had gone to the room, she at first denied but seeing there was no chance of escape she confessed she had eaten it. I realy believe the black race cant help stealing it seems to belong to them. D. surely had no cause to take any thing to eat for she always at every meal has something of all that's on the table. She promised faithfuly not to take any thing again, but like as not tomorrow she will do the same thing. Tis rather cool for the piazza tonight.

Thursday Night May 30st" 61

Only one more day of Spring, can it be possible the month is so nearly ended. O time thou art a stedy marcher, thou dost wait for no man. The week too is more than half spent, & what have I done, so little that I am ashamed to record it, half the day I am in undress, read-

---

1. This conflict was a rumor. Virginia troops had taken over the armory at Harpers Ferry on April 19, 1861, and were developing a position there throughout the month of May; they would be evacuated on June 14.

2. Apparently Thomas McLendon, son of J. E. McLendon, who acted as Ada's overseer off and on during the course of her journal.

ing sometimes on the bed tiard with doing nothing. Though I realy need some rest for I am always up by six in the morning, & seldom ever retire before eleven at night. My mornings are always employed in housekeeping, gardning & walking around the premises. Generaly I indulge my enclinations in the afternoon. This afternoon I lay down for an hour & read I had just rizen when a visitor was announced, I hurried my toilet & went out to find Mrs. & Miss Fountain[3], they also had a little girl of two years with them[.] I did my best at entertaining for over an hour when they departed I then sent Dave[4] to Pa's for some articles he promised to send[.] I have felt an unusual excitement all the evening, why I cant tell, I hope much to get letters of the absent dear ones in the morning. It has threatened rain all day. It still continues cool thick dresses are not uncomfortable. I am sitting with closed window & doors. All are sound asleep in the house, & I can hear the breathing of each one. Although I am so entirely alone in the evening strange to say I've not yet experienced the least feeling of lonliness. All is so still that even the scratching of my pen almost makes me start.

Roseville

Saturday morning June 1st″ 61

Randal came for me yesterday afternoon about six oclock just as I was about taking my tea. Mary McCall[5] had called on her way home, & asked me to let Flora go down with her. As soon as I had given orders to the Servants I left, reaching here near Seven. Pa & Peronneau met me at the door[.] Their grave looks checked the merry greeting I was about to offer. Pa said the little baby had died about half hour before. I passed on into the house removed my things then went immediately to the poor berrieved young parents, they both spoak poor Daisy offered to kiss me & I at once drew her to me & we both wept together for a time. Peter sat pale & motionless with the little dead baby upon his knees, I never saw any face more expressive of agony, yet

---

3. Probably the widow Jane Fountain (b. ca. 1819), a planter, and her daughter M. A. Fountain (b. ca. 1842).

4. Probably one of Ada's or the Bacots' slaves.

5. Probably M. E. McCall (b. ca. 1810), the wife of wealthy planter M. S. McCall.

not even a sigh escaped him, I felt for them both from my very heart, I forgot all save that they were in affliction, as soon as I could command my voice enough to speak I asked Daisy if she would be willing to let me perform the service of dressing her darling, which alredy had been put off as long as it ought. She said she preferred doing it herself, I said she was not able, & went to order the water[.] when I returned, Peter gave up his little charge to me, & he & D. left the room. For the first time in my life I performed the office of dressing a dead body. I could scarcely convince myself twas a human being I handled, as small as I had thought it when I last saw it near a fortnight ago, twas now waisted away to the mear fraim had it lived but a day longer the little bones must have worked through the tender skin. I could scarcely manage to dress it, when I had finished I laid it upon a clean pillow then upon the bed. Daisy came in then & said she wished some of the hair if I would help her. I did so, but soon found I must do it myself. The face by this time began to change & a smile seemed spreding on it. The Dr. who was here remained to tea when twas redy I went out to attend it. The Dr. asked me a good many questions about how I like living at home again &c. I answered them as briefly as politeness would permit as I felt no inclination to converse. As soon as I could enduce Daisy to go to bed, I took my seat by the window to watch the little dead for the night. All in the house retired about twelve leaving me to keep my vigle alone. Pa insisted that one of the servants should sleep in the room so if I should want any thing, so Chloe[6] came but was soon snoring[.] I spent most the entire night in holy communion with my God, & thinking of the dear little ones I have near his throne[.] Although from time to time the tears flowed yet twas a sweet sorrow. Two or three times I lost myself in a few moments of troubled sleep, which made me feel badly so I made every endeavour to keep awake. I never like some could sleep in a sitting position with any comfort, as soon as twas day I turned the lamp out & walked in the piazza for half an hour or so which greatly refreshed me. As soon as with Chloe's assistance I could get the room properly arranged I laid the little body in his crib, thinking twould look more natural to Daisy. About eight Pa came out & breakfast was ordered. I took a cup of hot

---

6. One of the Bacots' slaves.

coffee then went to try & sleep a little. I undressed & lay down, I slept about an hour, got up & dressed. About eleven Peter came down & I took some breakfast with him. Poor fellow, he looks hagered. Daisy has come down & they are now in the room with their little one. I forgot to mention that we've had a beautiful rain this morning, but it is now clearing away[.] Daisy got a letter from her mother last night saying they had seen Dickie, he was looking thin having suffered for want of food off Santee. He was going to Savannah, & thought it likely he would find there an appointment for him from the Confederate Government.

### Night

Pa sent round to let the neighbours know that the funeral would take place at four oclock but nearly all had gone to Florence. Mr. & Mrs. McCall[7] & Mr. & Mrs. M. Rogers, Mr. Moore & Mr. McLendon were all who came, we followed the little body to the grave where Mr. M. read the usual service for the dead. Twas very solemn Peter & Daisy both felt very much, I had no control over my feelings. Just four years ago my little Emmie had left me to join the heavenly host tis the annaversy of her death & her little image seemed to lie before me all the time twas with difficulty I could keep from throwing myself on my knees by the grave, it seemed to me my child was being buried again. for a while my agony was entense. The evening has been lonly, Peter & Daisy wander about the piazza, trying to comfort each other, they came to tea but dident seem to relish food, poor young things their sorrow is but commenced. It has been raining since dark. It is only a little past nine but I am redy for bed.

### Friday Night June 14″ 61

Days succeed each other so quickly, that for me I can scarcely note time as it passes. My life is so quiet too, that it would take a more fertile brain than mine to make something interesting out of every day as it rolls away. I had endured a sort of persperation bath all day with exemplary patience, until about five oclock I thou[ght] I heard the chickens at my flowers, I got up & went into the piazza. I saw Pa coming this way, so I called one of the little boys to hold the horse. Pa called to me from the gate to know if I dident want to ride up the road

---

7. Presumably M. S. McCall and his wife.

& see the cotton. I went & was supprised to see it so good. Pa brought me up the papers, & a letter from Dickie to read, he is at Savannah, seems in good spirits as usual, dear boy may God bless him. I realy am pained to see Pa so thin & weak, he is in low spirits too. If I only could help him in some way. It realy is a queer thing Pa is always so redy to blame & underrate me, but when ever I want help, or any thing he can spare me, he is just as redy to oblige me. Now this week he sent four of his plough hands to help plough a field which wanted work very much & I hadent the means of working. I never thought of asking him to asist me, I would rather have lost the field. Mr. McL. told him about it & he very redely sent the hands. I cant make out whether Pa realy cares any thing for me or whether he mearly did it from the love of obliging. Pa staid to tea but he seemed restless. After he left I sat in the piazza enjoying the cool breze a suden joyas feeling came over me & I sang away merrily[.] When old Hannah[8] came for me to put up the milk I said to her I dont know what makes me feel so happy this evening. She laughed & said maby twas a bad signe, as suden as possible I felt a dreadful feeling of fear come over me & I thought of Pa. I hope nothing is the matter. The papers account another engagement at Bethal Church, Va, we are still victorious.[9] God grant it may last.

Friday forenoon June 21st" 61

I was too much occupied on yesterday to write. Weak, languid, & restless I contrived to get through the day without lying down. Towards evening the heat became intense & I was forced to go to my room & undress. Peronneau was very anxious to get off for Dickie, at last he went. Just after nine oclock we heard the sound of wheels along the road, then it seemed I recognised the voices, there was a whistle, yes twas Dickie. I couldent be mistaken, very soon they were here & D. was folded in my arms. He has grown some, & looks well, he isnt strikingly handsome but there is some thing so noble so truthful in the bright countenance. His figure is stoute & well put together. It took but a little while to show me he was the same dear boy as ever. Tis a real pleasure to be with him, he never talks about himself, but if asked

---

8. One of the Bacots' slaves.

9. Confederate troops repulsed a hesitant and confused Federal attack on June 10, 1861, at the Battle of Big Bethel, or Bethel Church, Virginia.

any thing is redy to answer & does it with so much courtesy[.] I dont think there could be another boy of his age in the country who would kiss his father, I saw D. walk up to Pa & kiss him good night as naturaly as if he had only been five years old. We dident retire until after eleven there was so much to tell & hear. The papers came too, There was some little altercation in the papers concerning the capturing of the regiment. They were not captured as we heard but routed, took to their heals & threw away arms & bagage in their flight. The girls[10] dident come up as was expected, I cant say I was very much dissapointed. Peter is looking miserably, very thin & pale.

Night

This has been one of the warmest days I ever felt, not a breth of air stirring. I lay down in the bed & fell into a troubled sleep, such dreams & such heat I longed for ice & drempt I had found a cool spring of water. I dresed just before the sun went down & walked out into the rye field where the boys were looking at Perronneau's chicken coop. I was taken with severe pain in the bottom of my stomach, then a faintness came over me, Dickie supported me back to the house where I was much revived by smelling camphor. The nights are lovely the moon being very near the ful.

Sunday after dinner June 23d″61

Last night will long be remembered as one of the warmest nights on record in this part of the world, twas impossible to sleep with any comfort. Flora rolled, talked & whined almost all night. I cant say I slept until just after sun rise there was a cool breeze coming in one of the end windows & I lay in it. No one except Pa & I seemed enclined to go to church today. D. complained of a pain in his chest from a strain, the other two are never very fond of church. F. went to see her sister who leaves this morning. Mary P.'s little baby was baptized today it behaved very well. Mr. M. only read the service everyon[e] was suffering with the heat. We heard through Gen. H. that Gen. Beauregard had taken Alexandria, the news came by the express two oclock this morning. Which is very good if true.[11] Miss Dudley invited me to her examina-

---

10. Daisy Trenholm Bacot's sisters.

11. The information proved to be false.

tion on Friday next, her term ends then, I will go if nothing prevents. I think we will have rain it thunders.

Sunday night after the rain,

I was seated in the parlor this after noon reading & fell asleep in my chair, Pa came in which awoke me, I then went up stairs but couldent sleep again. When I went down I found Jesse had gone over to see Dickie. They were talking over their adventures on the islands about Charleston. There has been two or three fine showers this afternoon cooling the air a little. Some hail fell but not enough to do any injury. We had for supper a box of salmon which was very nice. Dickie said he only ate it to help get rid of the supply of yankee articles in the county. I never have seen any one more strongly opposed to yankee traid than he is. Like me he is affraid that as soon as the war ends the traid will go on as ever.

Arnmore

Tuesday morning July 23d 61

Several days have past since last I wrote, my mind has not been in any state for writing or indeed any thing. I am some what calmer this morning, but still some what excited. Sunday we all went to church but Pa. The day passed slowly to me for my heart was heavy. I helped Dickie to pack up. After tea a discussion took place (I dont know how it arose) about Charleston. Daisy got pretty warm & I think angry with me, for giving my opinion about Charleston. I have noticed that when ever I thought proper to join in any conversation she was ingaged in she has seemed offended & alway's makes it a point to appear perfectly indifferent or to make some insulting reply, or talk to some one else. Now I have tryed ever since she came up to be sivil to her, I realy feel sorry for her for she certainly has no politeness & cant help venting her spleen on me when ever the opportunity offers she seems to try to treat me with contempt, she treat[s] me with contempt, tis laughable, she has succeeded in making my brother hate me he who but little more than a year ago I would have gladly died to serve, for often have I prayed to die that he might have the little I have. I thank God from my heart now he dident hear my prayer, though I had rather have died than that I should have lived to feel what I now do, my brother is lost to me forever, never again can there be even the least feeling of friend ship between us. After the discussion at the tea table was ended we all went into the piazza. After a while Dickie made some remark about some paqulier phrase used in the low country, when Daisy turned to him & said do you too hate the low country so much after having staid there so long last winter, she then said something about the ancient critics, about their being spiteful. I dont remember exactly how she said it but I knew in a moment she ment it for me. So I said Daisy if you mean that for me you are very much mistaken about my feelings in regard to Charleston[.] I never fail to take up for it, but I never could bear for any one to hint at me, if they have any thing to say why let them say it out. She took no notice of what I said but pretended to be talking very earnestly to Peter all the time. After Dickie left & the two girls[12] had gone up stairs Pa & Peter were in the yard, Daisy went into her room for the purpose of going to bed without daining to say good night to me, I felt terably excited & tryed to compose myself but I went to the windo which opens in to the piazza & said to her I wished to speak to her she put on the most tragic air & said she wished to be excused, she would be obliged to me not to speak to her. I told her I mearly wanted to ask her one question, no she would not be spoken to by me. When she said that I was determined I would speak, so I said I was not angry with her but I mearly wanted to know if she never intended that we should be friends, she said how should she be when I had insulted her before her sister's, now the idea of my insulting her, I cant see what I said to insult her, so I said, God have mercy on you Daisy, & left her as soon as Pa came in I went to him & told him what had taken place, I cant discribe my feelings. It isent that I care the least for Daisy for I know no one whom I have a greater indifference for, but I think it very wrong to have misunderstandings with any one, & very unpleasant, Pa went to Daisys door & called her & asked her to come out he had something he wanted to say to her she waited a few minutes then came out, went up to him and asked what he wanted, he told her he was very sorry we couldent understand each other & was about to continue, when she turned upon her heal in the most hauty manner tossing up her head & walked out of the room saying I thought twas a matter of importance you wanted to see me about, Pa told her to stop, she said she['d] rather not, but Pa told her he though[t] it of im-

---

12. Two of Daisy's sisters who had finally arrived for a long visit.

portance, not only to her but to us all, she assured him she did not, then related the greater part of what I have said & speaking of me with the greatest contempt[.] I told her I felt quite as indiferent tords her as she did me, but that we were both communicants of the church & that was the only reason why I had wished to speak to her, she said then she thought we had labored or such, I told her I thought so, Peter then drew her away & told her twas no use speaking to me any more, that he had a perfect contempt for me, I said they should not be troubled with my presence again, they said they would be very glad, & shut the door, I couldent help saying as he did so, you puppy. the idea of my own brother saying he had a contempt for me. I went to Pa told him good night, & said I couldent come to Roseville again as long as Peter & Daisy remained, I then went up to bed, I was the last to retire[.] I read, then told the girls good night saying I should be gone in the morning before they were up & asked them if they felt any inclination, to come up & see me, I then put the light out & knelt by the open windo where the moon was shining brightly & wept & prayed long.

Saturday Night Aug 10″ 61

I am weary tonight & my head aches, but I must make a record of the days prosedings. I was up quite early though I had spent the greater part of the night in reading the papers, Pa sent the butt this morning for me, this was the day we had appointed to organize our society for the relief of the soldiers. We met about ten o'clock at the Goodwin house. Mr. Robert Rogers was good enough to organize the meeting, Mrs. R. Rogers[13] President & in my opinion there couldent be a better. They honored me with Vice President, Meta Rogers Secretary, very good, Nettie McCall,[14] Treasurer, also good, Mrs. Porcher,[15] Mrs. M. Rogers, Mrs. Moriss,[16] Mrs. Waring[17] & Mrs. Gamble[18] Managers.

---

13. Cousin Henrietta.

14. Unidentified, although possibly E. E. McCall, the twenty-four-year-old wife of twenty-seven-year-old planter James S. McCall, Jr.

15. E. A. Porcher (b. ca. 1815).

16. Rosa Morriss (b. ca. 1840), wife of planter Levi Morriss (b. ca. 1834).

17. Hannah P. Waring (b. ca. 1836), wife of planter A. H. Waring.

18. Probably V. M. Gamble (b. ca. 1838), wife of hotel keeper J. W. Gamble (b. ca. 1815).

All went off pleasantly. After making some arrangement for sending for the cloth needed to make up garments, we dispersed. Nett asked me to dine with her, which I did. The heat has been very oppressive all [day]. There was watermellon handed soon after I got to Mr. McC.'s which was very refreshing. Eliza Johnson is staying with Nett a few day's Miss Martin[19] came in just as I was leaving. She told me she had contemplated spending the day with me, but just as she was about starting her cousin told her he thought it likely I belonged to the Society. If she had come up she would've had a very warm ride for nothing. I have kept the Butt that I may go to church tomorrow.

Wednesday Night Aug 21st" 61

Twas very refreshing to see the sun again. This evening about two hours before sundown it cleared away, & Pa came, I was winding the wool when he came, so had to change my dress as soon as possible. I was as glad to see him as if I had been from him a month. He brought no papers, but brought a letter from Sister, she seems to be having a nice time[.] Pa & I are thinking of going on together to Va. in the capacity of nurses. Pa Flora & I walked up the road to see the cotton. The evening has been delightful. The moon shines beautifully bright, I could see how to wind thread in the piazza. I hope my wish will soon be realized, & I can go to Va. But I am afraid to hope too much. God direct my doings, our Society meets again tomorrow, Pa gave me five dollars for it this evening.

Thursday Night Aug 22d" 61

I am at Col. Warings tonight having come with Hannah this morning from the Goodwin house after the Society ajurned. We accomplished more today, Cousin Hannah brought her piece of flannel which she succeeded in dying a sort of purple, which will answer much better than the red. The papers tonight say Congress had adopted the tax.[20] There is a goodeal of grumbling about it, I havent any thing to say. I have thought all along that we must [be] taxed pretty heavily, I

---

19. Perhaps M. M. Martin (b. ca. 1836).

20. On August 16, 1861, the Confederate Congress had passed a war tax of one-half percent on the value of all real and personal property, exempting the property of the state and local governments, churches, and individuals whose net worth was less than five hundred dollars; Jefferson Davis signed the bill creating the tax on August 19.

would rather pay every cent I have in taxes to our own government than have to submit to the Black republican rool. I have spent a very pleasant day. H. & Col. W. are both so kind. They have put me in this sweet little room for the night all so nice & clean. The room is not large, but quite roomey enough for one person. The furniture is a pine cottage set, painted white, ornamented with bunches of grapes & gilt. I am tiard & sleepy last night I slept but little & was up early this morning.

Monday Night Aug 26" 61

Pa came up quite early this morning & offered to go to the village & see Mr. Woods[21] about getting the money from the bank for me. He wrote the note & we signed it together[.] I felt self condemned as Pa put his name down as my Security without my asking him to do it, I have so many times refused to do it for him. Nothing can exceed his kindness to me. Oh! why is it I so little deserve his goodness. But I do love & honor him more than I ever did in my life before. My spirit has been humbled, & I now feel willing that he should exersize the controle over me that belongs to him, what I never felt before. I waited in great impatience for Pa's return, striving to persuade myself all the time that I was to be disappointed about getting the money & tryed to be contented if I should not. At last Pa came[.] He couldent do anything for me, but Mr. Woods said if I wished he would write to the bank for me & perhaps they might be willing to accomodate me. In spite of myself I was terably cast down. But I havent yet lost all hope. I feel sure if I cant get the money twill be because God thinks it best I should not go. I have earnestly prayed that he would do for me what is best.

I got Pa to write and ask Mr. W. to write to the bank for me, which he did & I sent it up immediately. Isaac[22] has returned & Mr. W. says I have neglected to sign the note, so there *will* be another days delay tommorrow I send [it] again. I am too restless to sleep so will commence the book Meta R. lent me on Friday which has been highly recomended to me. It is The Initials, translated from the German.[23]

---

21. S. A. Woods (b. ca. 1816) of Darlington was a wealthy merchant and banker.

22. One of the Bacots' slaves.

23. *The Initials: A Story of Modern Life* by Jemima M. von Tautphoeus went through several editions in the nineteenth century.

Tuesday Night Sep 3d″ 61

Pa sent me the papers this morning, & a note from Cousin Fannie asking me to go with her on thursday to the Society. I accepted the invatation. There seem's to be a general opinion that there will be a battle soon, I feel like there will & have alredy begun to feel for the wounded. The wish to go on to Va. has returned with all its former force. I thought I had abandoned it & settled down to my quiet mono- tonus life with all due composure but I find to my distress I have not. O that there was the smallest hope of my wish being gratified. Tonight after prayers I was walking in the piazza singing & thinking of the sol- diers, when I heard the gate open & saw some one walk rapedly to the door, then stop pull off his hat & make a bow. I couldent distinguish whether twas a white man or a negro, when I saw him coming to the house I thought twas Thomas,[24] but when he stoped at the door I thought twas a servant, & asked sevral times who twas, but got no an- swer I was just going into the house to call Thomas, when I hear a laugh, & found twas Thomas, he had tryed to frighten me, & he suc- ceeded better than I alowed him to find out. As soon as I found out who twas a weakness came over me & I was obliged to sit down, I won- der if there realy any danger could I defend myself. Some times I think I could then again I fear not, I fear I am nothing more than a weak woman at last.

Tuesday Night Sep 17″ 61

Our Fair is over & we have been much more successful than we ex- pected, every thing was disposed of and most of the articles sold very well. I helped Hannah Waring & Mrs. Porcher with their table at which we made $75[.] I met a good many of my friends & had a very nice day. Tonight my head aches & I am dreadfully tiard having stood most of the day. Gen. Harllee told me he expected an attack on the co[a]st very soon, & if my services were needed as a nurse he would let me know. He advised me to stay at home & keep myself in rediness for home duty instead of going to Va. I saw Julia Ashby's little girl[25] today,

---

24. Thomas McLendon.

25. Julia Porcher Ashby, Edward Porcher's daughter, had married Thomas Ashby on May 6, 1860; her daughter was Julia Elizabeth Ashby, baptized on November 17, 1861.

tis a sweet plump little thing very like Julia. One of the Manassas he-roes, Col. Pawley & a hero of Bethal, Jonnie Williamson, were present. Every one seemed to be in good spirits & the day passed pleas-antly. The dinner gave general satisfaction.

Saturday Morning Sep 21st" 61

Another lovely day only a little warm again. All are well, Pa is alone again I heard from him this morning. He sent me the Mercury[.] Peter & Daisy left last night. I feel disapointed that they went away without seeing me or leaving a message for me, I did not think they hated me quite so much. Now I suppose we will never meet agin. Perhaps it is as well. God knows I forgive them. I hope they may yet be brought to see how ill they have treeted me. I received my books this morning from Russell & Jones. Just in time for this is now out.

Later

I am looking for the butt every minute to take me down to Roseville for the night. I can scarcely believe I am to go down again, but am glad I can. I wonder what I am to fill my next book with. I feel some great changes are to take place in my life before as many months roll around as it has taken me to write this volume.

Arnmore Sept 22d" 1865

Read over a portion of this book today many many changes in my life since it was written

AB Clarke

I have read a portion of this record

J. H. C.[26]

Roseville

Saturday night Sep 21st 61

Again I am at Roseville exactly two months tonight since my dear Beloved Dickie left us. Twas moon light then too a much brighter night than this oh! memory what a wonderful thing is memory. There are some things I wish I could forget. I felt so strange when I drew up to the door, all rushed to my mind in a moment what I had suffered this very night exactly two months ago. But let it pass.

---

26. Probably James E. H. Clarke, Ada's future husband, or possibly his brother Joseph Clarke.

We didnt sit down to tea until quite late, every thing was very nice, & Gus has the house in good order. After tea Pa asked me if I had heard of Mrs. Witherspoons death. I had not. Gus it seems had heard of it & told Pa, but didnt tell him any thing about what he had heard was the cause of her death. He was in the room so I asked if he knew what was the matter with her, he said he had heard but didnt know if it was true that she had been smothered in her bed, That he had heard that some of the servants were in jail. Terable, I cant get it out of my mind. We none of us know when we are safe. I have some about me that I fear twould take very little to make them put me out of the way. I dont mean any of my house servants for I think they are very fond of me. It is quite cloudy & has rained a little. It is very dry here & rain is much more needed than at Arnmore. Pa has had my old room fixed for me but it dont look natural with the big bed, & small wardrobe. If it should rain much I am likely to get a shower bath.

Sunday fore noon Oct 13″ 61

I never saw a more lovely morning, so clear so bright & the air delightfuly bracing, not a cloud to be seen. The folage still green & glossy no untimely frost has niped the tender buds. Here & there a bright turned leaf may be see[n], the only indication that winter is not far distant. Oh! the beautiful Sunny South The home of my birth my childhood & of my womanhood, could I leave thee, could I clame another home[.] Ah! no, Thou art dearer to me than all else earthly. As long as I live let it be on Southern Soil & when I die let my remains be covered by her warm & genial Sod. Truly I am a child of the South, I love her as a fond Mother. I couldent survive in a colder less genial clime.

Night

We had just finished our cold Sunday dinner when Pa drew up. I had put on my bonnet to strole among the trees a little while, before seating myself for the afternoon reading. Pa brought me a letter to read from Dickie. He was at Brunswick when he wrote. He also brought a letter from Caroline saying she would come any time this week she was sent for; & the package from Town containing Floras dresses. Pa & I took a walk through the fields, found the sun rather warm. I wrote to

Mr. Barnwell[27] today relative to my go to Va. Pa took the letter down for me. The night is as lovely as the day has been.

Sunday Night Oct 27" 61

Where shall I begin, how shall I discribe the events of this delightful day. Although so delightful it has not been without its troubles. I am at last almost sure of my trip to Virginia, I had a letter from Mr. Barnwell this morning asking me to go on at once, also one from Mr. Kirkpatrick[28] saying he is quite willing to alow me the proceeds of the cotton I sent down last week. I can't discribe my feelings I am so thankful I can go, God has heard my prayer. Oh! that I may be able to perform my duty. Pa is going on with me, tis too delightful to be true. Every one at church today seemed to be glad for me, they seemed to think I was going to do something very noble. I only feel I am about to do my duty—I cant see that I am going to do any thing so wonderful. Most people wonder I am willing to under take it they say to me, just think of the hardships you will be obliged to endure. If I were not willing to endure them I can see no virtue in my going. I am not going for my own pleasure. Mr. McLendon came over while we were at dinner to tell me that Thomas had come down to let him know that two more hogs had been killed the night before. The rogues however were not fortunate enough to carry off their booty. That makes more than a dozen they have taken from me since January. I went to see Mrs. McLendon, after dinner she has a very fine child & is doing very well, while there Dinah ran over to tell me Cousin Henrietta had called, so I hurried home. Cousin's H. & R. staid until twas quite dark. We had a nice call at Cousin Fannies after church, I know no one who can make them selves more agreable.

Friday Night Nov 1st 61

The beginning of another month, I can scarcely believe it. I hope today hasent been a specimin of the month. It comenced to rain soon

---

27. Reverend Robert Woodward Barnwell (d. 1863) was a deacon of the Episcopal Church, a professor and chaplain at the University of South Carolina, and head of the South Carolina Hospital Aid Association. It was at his exhortations that Ada and other South Carolinians went north to Virginia to nurse in the Association's hospitals. He and his wife would die of typhoid fever, probably contracted in the course of his hospital visits, six months after the end of Ada's diary.

28. Probably Ada's cotton broker.

after nine this morning & hasent stoped once since. I have been near having the blues today. Again no letter nothing but wait wait, well I hope to hear some time. Pa got me to patching of his old shirts (now as the iritable Man used to say in the Home Guard "If there is one thing I dislike more than another" tis mending old shirts.) But I have managed to get through with them. My how the rain pours, tis considerably warmer too, so I suppose there will be rain again tomorrow, not withstanding the almanac say to the contrary. I think Pa is getting as anxious to be off as I am. I must write & let Mr. Barnwell know I will be with him as soon as possible[.] I dare say he is wondering what keeps me.

Saturday Night Nov 2d 61

It has been a cloudy gusty day, quite cool tonight & every indication of a heavy frost. It has cleared off beautifully & the sky is studed with stars[.] Just at twilight I was out walking I never saw the evening star more magnificent, she was shining alone, lighting up the sky with her soft mellow light. That beautiful co[u]plet of Wadsworths came into my mind "When night draws her mantle round & pins it with a single star." I compleated a soldiers shirt from half past eleven to half past five. I've felt almost perfectly well today.

I received my expected letter tonight, my disappointment is compleet, Mr. Kirkpatrick wont advance the money, but advises me to apply to the banks. That I have alredy tryed with no success. I scarcely know what to do next give up my hope of going to Va. I will not[.] God will not forsake me, though he may see fit to try me a while longer. Pa has kindly offered to go to Darlington for me on Monday to see what he can do. Pa has headach tonight.

Tuesday Night Nov 5" 61

I slept late this morning & only bounced out of bed upon hearing Pas step in the passage. I took my time over my toilet however, Pa had walked out, so I had to wait in my turn for breakfast. Oh! I'm getting horrably spoiled, this inactive life is wearing me. I can well imagine how the soldiers feel. They grumble more about having nothing to do, than they would if led to a fight every day. I've read the entire day, tonight I've finished my book. The Mercury came tonight, nothing different of the mighty fleet yet. The gale on the coast seems to have been very terable, much affecting the Armada, providence still favors us. The protestations against the President & indeed against the whole administration, grow louder every day. The whole Confederacy seems to me given it self up to ill humor. I see that even Beauregard is not exempt from an attack, one of the Richmond papers assails him. Why cant every thing go on smoothly. But that would not be in human nature.

Wednesday noon Nov 6" 61

"A little more sleep & a little more slumber" I said to my self this morning. O how I hated to get up. At last I opened my eyes tumbled out of bed seated me on the rug before the fire, & fel into a doze. It required no little courage to arouse myself & dress. Tis a mild fitful gusty day, trying to the nerves, & to me very unpleasant. After breakfast, I went to the garden to look for some violets, I never saw the plants more luxuriant but they bloom little[.] I love the little modest blue flower above all others. Pa has gone off to the election. The Gen. has no opponent but his friends are desirous of giving him a full voat. The woods are in their fall dress of bright & varied colors. Tis the season I love best. I wish I could see Dickie today wonder where he can be.

4 oclock

Pa has just returned with the inteligence that there was heavy firing off Port Royal[29] on yesterday also at Tibee, & about fifty sails off Charleston bar. There is considerable movement of troops Clinmans Reg[30] went down today & Maj. Ramseurs batary[31] goes tonight, quite an excitement prevails. Pa is very anxious to go down tonight. What I ought to do now is not very clear to me, whether I am most needed in Va. or on the coast. Oh! God direct me. Perhaps this may be why I have been dissapointed in going before.

---

29. The Confederate ships in Port Royal Sound in South Carolina were fired on by four United States naval ships on November 5, 1861.

30. Probably Clingman's Regiment; Thomas Lanier Clingman, later a general in the Confederate Army, resigned his seat in the United States Senate in March 1861 to accept the colonelcy of the 125th North Carolina Infantry, which saw action in North and South Carolina through the spring of 1864, when it went north to Virginia.

31. Probably the Ellis Light Artillery, a Raleigh battery commanded by Captain (later General) Stephen Dodson Ramseur, who was killed at the Battle of Cedar Creek in 1864.

Cousin Fannies

Sunday night Nov 10″ 61

There was quite a thunder storm last night which has not cooled the air as expected. It has been cloudy all day, not withstanding there was a fuler attendance at church, I could not help being amused as I looked around in church to see the long faces & downcast looks of all, strange to say I do not partake of the feeling I am still very hopeful. I know if we trust in God & not in our own strength that we will yet turn the enemy to flight. Now is not the time to endulge in gloomy forbodings but cheer our brave men on to the victory. I feel as if I could do any thing endure any privation give up any thing for my countrys good. I expect I will be peniless before many weeks roll round. If I could only have paid my debts I would not care, for thank God I have only myself to provide for, no Husband no child to be uneasy about[.] I will exert myself for any one who may need my help. Miss Ann & Meta have spent the evening here, they are both very patriotic. Cousin Fannie has been amusing us all, declaring if cousin John goes she will follow she is going to cover her a wagon & take every thing necessary to camp out. She is too funny.

Roseville

Monday noon Nov 11″ 61

I have just now time to write I returned here from cousin Fannies hospitable home about ten oclock. I was in the garden getting some flowers for cousin F. when Leah[32] said her master was come, I ran in & beheld Pa, he had come last night expected to find the butt there for him but I had heard there was no train & did not send it. He saw Peter & Tom they left for some port on the coast they did not know exactly where, on Friday night. They were both well. He did not see or hear from Dickie, all water communication is cut off to Charleston. Beaufort has been shelled & burned the people bearly escaping themselves, their negroes refused to come away from three to four thousand have fallen into the enemys hands.[33] I realy feel sorry for the poor wretches they have an idea they are free now & will not be obliged to work any

---

32. One of the Bacots' slaves.

33. United States forces captured the city of Beaufort from their base at Port Royal on November 9, 1861.

more[.] We have not learned whether the planters had time to burn their cotton or not, I fear not.

night of same day

I dressed with a great deal of care, & was all redy to start when I noticed that one of the horses (Henry) was sick. I had to give up my visit to Mrs. Harllees. Tis quite a dissapointment, Pa offered to take me down in the buggy, but I knew he was tiard & would not accept the offer. I have given up all idea of going to Virginia, Pa mett Dr. Chisolm[34] who told him to try & disuade me from going, That twas scarcely a place for a lady. Tis a bitter dissapointment to me, I had hoped to be able to do something for my country, now my dream of usefulness is banished what can I do now, I cant give up I hope yet to be able to do something my own state may need me. Oh! how gladly would I sacrifice my all for her. Mr. McLendon came in this evening to ask Pa the news, he told me that on Friday afternoon Mary saw a man dressed in uniform on horseback ride up here he went back almost immediately. I have enquired but can hear nothing of him from the servants. I cant imagine who it could be. Pa tells me he came up with Mary Chisolm, she was on her way to her fathers to be confined. Her husband was not with her as he belongs to some company on one of the Islands. She bearly had time to get to Florence whear a little daughter was born to her, Dr. Chisolm & his wife were with her. They sent for her father who had arrived before Pa left. What am I to do with myself this Winter, I must have some occupation. I suppose I am to stay here, I dont like it but have no other alternative. Oh! if I could only do something, well I must not give up until I find something, I never in my life felt such a spirit of perseverance.

Wednesday night Nov 13" 61

About eleven oclock Pa asked me to go with him to Brockington.[35] Twas so lovely out, & I had nothing to keep me at home so I redely consented, I fixed us a simple lunch, gathered up my knitting & off we

34. Probably John Julian Chisolm, a surgical professor at South Carolina College, who was currently heading a Charleston laboratory making medicine for the Confederate Army and whose 1861 book, A Manual of Military Surgery, was widely used during the war.

35. One of Peter Samuel Bacot's properties.

went with Sam in the buggy, twas a pleasant ride along the lake bank
I got Pa to get down & gather me some haws I saw on the cool side. I
have a childish liking for all sorts of fruit. The lake is still quite full &
mudy, but within the banks. The hands had just brought the cotton up
to the gin house to be weighed before getting their dinner, Mr.
McLendon was there, overlooking, & as Jack called out the weights he
set them down. I went up into the gin house which is a two story one,
I had a good view of the plantation from one of the upper windows,
from the other I could see almost the whole of Mr. H. Charleses &
Mr. T. Fountains,[36] both join Brockington but are not considered as
good, as they are more subject to overflow. I was amused at the con-
trivance for getting the cotton from the upper story to the gin. There
is a hole about two feet square in the floor just over the gin a funel
made of cotton baging is suspended from it to the top of the gin,
through which the cotton is conveyed, without the trouble of going up
& down the steps with it. Tis very simple but saves a good'eal of trouble. We seated ourselves under the trees near old Jacks house on some
of his rude benches Pa read the paper to Mr. McL. while I knitted,
when all the news had been extracted from the paper we had our
brunch. Then Pa took me round to see the plantation as I had never
seen [it] only just around the houses, we first went to the lot to see a
mamoth hog. I never saw one so large they expect him to weigh at
killing time 400 lbs, we then got into the buggy & road through the
cotton tis very fine & so beautifully white we then went through several old fields very near to the river about two hundred yds. of the line
fence between Pa & Mrs. Witherspoons plantations. I was rather too
tiard to go down to where GrandPa used to have a landing on the
river, so we turned homewards. Pa complained of being tiard & weak
in his back. We got home just in time to enjoy a brilliant sunset. I love
such a day now & then, I believe Pa is glad to have me with him again.
I hope I may be a comfort to him.

Wednesday afternoon Nov 27" 61

Flora has come poor child she was so delighted to see me. She
sprang into my arms radient with smiles, as soon as she was helped
down from the buggy. Twas amusing with what promptness she deliv-

---

36. Thomas E. Fountain (b. ca. 1815) was a well-to-do farmer.

ered the messages Mrs. DuBose[37] had charged her with, twas so like a child. I think her quite improved & am delighted to see her in good health & spirits, she tells me Mrs. DuBose is very kind to her. I will feel myself fuly repaid for the trouble & expense I am now undergoing for the dear child if I can only see her a well educated christian.

Night

Pa road over to Cousin Fannie just before dark he dident know whether he would stay to tea so Flora & I had seated ourselves before the fire after we had returned from our walk & I had taken up a book but Flora seemed to wish to talk to me so I was listening to her, when I heard a tremendous knock at the door, I got up & opened it, & was just in the act of shuting it again as I dident see any one, when Mr. Moore steped forward, he came in & we had a very pleasant evening. I consulted him about helping the low country people to find places for their negroes, he has promised to let me know if he has any other applications.

---

37. Ada had apparently sent Flora to the Salem Female Academy, where Mrs. DuBose may have been a faculty member; she was still attending the school in 1864.

Chapter 3

# December 6, 1861–January 19, 1862

*"I am enjoying myself so much that realy I can scarcely realize I am here on so sad a mission."*

Friday Night Dec 6" Springville
I had an early start this morning & reached the Hill about ten oclock was fortunate in being able to transact the business I went upon. Stoped at Cousin Marys[1] before I went into the village to let her know I would dine with her, they were all so astonished to see me, Caroline met me at the door with Why Cousin Ada I thought you were in Virginia, when I said I hadent been she was surprised indeed. As I was returning from the village I met Mrs. Evans who told me her husband had returned. Old Mrs. McIntosh died last evening after a very painful illness of some days.

While I was at Cousin M.'s Mrs. Martin called, I have not seen her for a number of years before. Had a pleasant day, saw an address of Dr. Barnwell's before the Christian Association in behalf of the Hopsitals in Va, I think I will have to go back with him, his request for nurses was too earnest to be resisted.[2]

Arrived here safely just after dark the horses came back much brisker than they went[.] Feel quite fatigued.

Roseville
Saturday noon Dec 7" 61
Awoke this morning with one of my visiting headaches, on my way down met Pa about three miles from home, told him of my intention to go to Va., he dident seem in the least surprised but asked how I had heard from Mr. B. I said I had merely see his address in the papers & had determined to go with him. He then showed me a copy of a letter

---

1. Mary Elizabeth McIver Bacot (b. ca. 1822) was the wife of Henry Harraman Bacot.

2. Of this address given on December 2, 1861, one Charleston woman recorded that he said, "But, what was needed was the presence of the ladies themselves, not so much as nurses, as to superintend the different departments, to read to them & in fact to supply all the charms of home to soothe the sick beds of our noble soldiers." John F. Marszalek, ed., *The Diary of Miss Emma Holmes, 1861–1866* (Baton Rouge: Louisiana State University Press, 1979), 101.

which Meta R. had sent to me to read from Mr. B. asking her if she couldent get one of the ladies belonging to the Florence Society to go with him as nurse. It made me more desirous than ever of going. So when I got home I wrote to Mr. B. that I would go on with him. I called at Mr. R.'s to get Miss Ann to come & asist me with some work she was not there, so I hurried home without seeing any of the family. Mary McLendon is kindly helping.

Night

Mary & I have realy been very smart we have made a double gown since one oclock & I have cut & fixed some other work. There was quite a budget of letters tonight, two from Dickie[.] Caroline sent Perroneau & me the Palmeto ornaments they are very pretty. It must be near twelve.

Monday near Sundown Dec 9 61

We were up early & worked hard got my work nearer done than I thought, I am off to the Depot in a few minutes.

Night

I had to return Mr. Barnwell dident come, I am not very much disappointed, perhaps I may see Sister tomorrow I am very tiard.

On the boat at Wilmington two in the morning Dec 11 61

I was fortunate enough to meet Mr. B. last night & have started with him he has twelve others along[.] Boyd Brunson got on board at Mars Bluff, he came & conversed with me until we got to Marion where he left me, he looks very well & was quite pleasant. A great crowd came on tonight the weather is delightful.

Wednesday Goldsboro eight oclock

After we crosed the river at Wilmington our party found great difficulty in getting seats our party got divided & Mr. B. has just been here to tell me that he lost me last night & was delighted he had found me. We dont get out here to breakfast. There are crowds going on from here. Mr. B. tells me he is afraid my trunks have been left at Wilmington he has telegraphed on to know. There are any quantity of men moving about in uniforms. I hear we are to stay at Weldon all day.

Weldon one oclock

We have arrived safely but too late to make the connexion, so we stay over here until twelve tomorrow. Mr. B. dear good patient man has at last succeeded in getting four rooms for the accomidation of his party. I am to share a room with two other ladies from Charleston. I consider myself fortunate to have two such nice companions.

night

We have been amusing our selves with a party in the next room who have come over here from Va. to get married we hear it is a runaway match but I hardly think so. They seem too easy. There is a perseptable change in the weather.

Thursday morning Dec 12″ 61

The party were not married last night. I hear they are to be as soon as the cars come, which will be at twelve. The girl is realy quite pretty but too boald looking. Her hair is very light & is cut short. The groom elect is very young, he cant be more than twenty[.] There are two other ladies & one other gentle man (evedently an officer from his dress) in [the] party. We are in a miserable little room with positively nothing but two beds in it. The two ladies who are with me, one a Mrs. Lesesne[3] & a Miss Habersham,[4] a niece of Lieut. Habersham of the Navy.

Night Richmond

We found out that Dr. Thompson[5] would have to stay a day here so Mrs. L., Miss H., Eddie L.[6] & I asked Mr. B. to let us remain with him. Just as we were going to get into the cars at Weldon this morning we met Mr. B. going into the hotel again, he said he had been asked to marry the young people, & had consented to do so as they explained the circumstances to him. It is not a runaway match they only went to Weldon because her guardian objected to her marrying the young man he not being of age. Mr. B. told us their names were Willie Reed of Georgia who is an officer on Gen. Coopers[7] staff & a Miss Nonnie Manard of this place. The others of the party were her brother & his wife & her sister. they are very nice looking people. The party came

---

3. Marie Lesesne (b. ca. 1820) was a widow from Charleston.

4. Esse Habersham (b. ca. 1840) was apparently the daughter of a Beaufort planter.

5. Dr. William Thompson of Greenville, South Carolina.

6. Edwin Lesesne (b. ca. 1847), also known as "Nonie," was Marie's son.

7. Samuel Cooper (1798–1876), a West Point graduate and former adjutant general of the United States Army, had been appointed general in the Confederate Army and served as adjutant and inspector general throughout the war.

on with us today. I have had a most delightful day. Mr. B. has divided the party sending six of us here to the American under Dr. Thompsons care. Three of the ladies go on in the morning while we remain until Saturday morning. Tis realy cold but I dont feel it much. Three of us are to sleep in one bed in a very small room too small to walk in. When my trunk gets in I realy dont know where we will dress. As usual my trunk has been misplaced & I cant get it before morning. This is a terably fussy place.

Friday Noon Dec 13" 61

Last night saw a dispatch stating that a fire had broken out in Charleston & a great part of the City had been [burned] & that groops of people who had been burned out were standing about the streets.[8] It makes my heart bleed to hear of the terable suffering. Nearly all of the handsomest public buildings are gone. I have no doubt twas the work of Yankees in the City or of Negroes who have been put up to it by them. We went out this morning to make a few purchases & see something of the City. We walked about the Capital grounds & saw the Presidents house & grounds. We walked poor Dr. Thompson down then we came in. We find a great deal to amuse us, we laughed a great deal about our jaunt last night. I have been awake since four oclock this morning tis the fussiest place I ever was in in my life such a passing up & down stairs, & ringing of bels.

Night

I have written three or four letters this afternoon & feel greatly relieved. Mrs. Lesesne got up an acquaintance with a Georgia lady the wife of Gen. Hennenson who is now staying here, she has been very kind to all of us, she & Miss Habersham find they know a great many mutual friends, so we had quite a general conversation. There was whist later in the evening which I dident participate in. I have had a very pleasant time but feel some what anxious to get on to Charlottesville. I fear there is to be some trouble about our passport, Mr. Barnwell was to have sent it back to Dr. Thompson but it hasent come, I

---

8. A widespread blaze destroyed most of the business district of Charleston on December 11, 1861, dealing a further economic blow to the city already reeling under a blockade and threatened by a United States force at Hilton Head Island.

dare say he has forgotten he left us here. Mrs. Hennenson has given us a blank one she had dated Aug. which I fear will not answer the purpose. Though we appreciate the kindness. We leave very early in the morning & It is very late now.

Saturday 5 oclock in the morning
Dec 14″ 61

About four oclock there was an alarm of fire. Mrs. Lesesne was the first to wake up. I hear some noise in the street but was too sound asleep to know what twas but the moment I was called I sprang from the bed & began to dress. Then Dr. Thompson came & beged us not to be a minute dressing so we went at it with renewed vigor, as soon as we were dressed we got to the window & looked out, found it was a two story brick house at the end of a side street just by the Hotel. If the wind had been in the proper direction there would have been no posible chance of saving the Hotel. Soon we found the danger had passed, & it was too early for the cars we sat in our room all redy. The fire presented a most splended appearance. Tis the first large fire I have ever seen so near. The night is surpassingly lovely & the great colams of elimanated smoke & spark from the wood work of the house was splendid, but it made me feel very dreadful as I heard piece after piece of heavy timber fall with a terable crash on the floor beneath.

Charlottesville
Saturday Night Dec 14″ 61

At last we have arrived in safty [after] various difficulties about the transportation & passports. We were rather a more silent party than the day before as none of us had slept since four in the morning. Mr. B. couldent go to the Depot to meet us so he sent Dr. Lafar.[9] The abominable man to think that I should be thrown in such close contact with him. He walked up to the house with us which is only a little way from the depot where a nice looking yellow girl met us & showed us a room, a nice comfortable room with a little dressing room ajoining, Which Mrs. Lesesne has appropriated, Miss Habersham & I have the large chamber together. I realy feel quite at home alredy every

---

9. Dr. T. A. Lafar was a member of the Executive Committee of the South Carolina Hospital Aid Association.

thing is very nice & comfortable we have a nice fire place which will add very much to our comfort. Mr. & Mrs. Barnwell[10] called to see us this after noon & took us over the stoar which is the same yard, & over the House which is being prepared for the reception of patients on Wednesday.

Sunday Night Dec 15" 61

Realy I am quite charmed with my situation, so home like so comfortable, Mr. & Mrs. Barnwell move down tomorrow. Some of the gentlemen are particularly pleasant who are staying in the house. I find James McIntosh[11] here, he came up to me & spoak saying he had reconized me but dident know if I did him, at first I did not as I have not seen him since he was a boy, Dr. Rembert[12] is here also the brother of my friend Lou, then there is Dr. Gourdin[13] all of dear old S.C. We attended the Episcopal Church this morning, Mr. Quimby[14] politely showing us the way. Dr. Thompson walked with me & realy exerted himself to be entertaining. After service we met Mr. & Mrs. Barnwell, Mr. B. asked us to walk up to the Midway hospital with him, we did so & found a young Fowler from S.C. he is suffering with Chilblanes in his feet which confines him to bed. We then went to Mrs. Robinsons[15] for a little while, then came home, I suppose the walk there & back must have been three miles. Dinner was so late that we declined going to Church this after noon. We sat in the dining room by the fire where Dr. Rembert came & we had a nice talk. Tonight after tea we again sat

10. Mary Singleton Barnwell (d. 1863).

11. James McIntosh (b. ca. 1838) of Newberry, South Carolina, was a graduate of the Medical College of Charleston and an assistant surgeon at the Midway Hospital in Charlottesville.

12. E. J. Rembert (b. ca. 1825) of Sumter, South Carolina, was physician for the Monticello Hospital and director of all the South Carolina hospitals in Charlottesville, although he held only the rank of assistant surgeon.

13. Theodore Gourdin (b. ca. 1829) was a physician from Charleston who was in charge of the Midway Hospital.

14. An employee of the Association, Quimby may have been the chaplain for some or all of South Carolina's hospitals.

15. Probably Susan Robinson of Charleston, one of the matrons of the Soldiers' Home complex.

in the dining room where Mr. Quimby Dr. Gourdin & after a while Dr. Thompson [joined us], I had a very pleasant evening. It is all so different from what I expected.

Monday Night Dec 16" 61

I began my duties as a housekeeper today. I dont think I ever saw a house in a more filthy condition. I have been sweeping & dusting but nothing looks clean yet. This afternoon I had time to run over for a few moments to see how Mrs. L. & Miss H. were getting on. They were getting the bunks redy for the men who are to come on Wednesday. After tea we gave up the parlor to the Gentlemen & we sat in the dining room but we soon had all of the gentle men with us, James McIntosh came in & had a nice talk with me. He told me of a young Harllee[16] who is very ill here, I go to see him tomorrow. I am suffering very much from a cold & can scarcly make myself heard all of the gentlemen seem to try to see which can do most for me. One brought me some Honey & Soda, & another an Orange. They noticed my indisposition so much that realy I got fidgety. Dr. Thompson told me today with the brightest face possible that he was going to stay in Charlottesville. I am enjoying myself so much that realy I can scarcly realize I am here on so sad a mission.

Tuesday Night Dec 17" 61

Dr. McI. went with me this afternoon to see Lieut. Harllee[.] I think [him] very ill & have written to His Uncle, or rather to his Uncles wife, I think it better they should be in some way prepared for his death, for I have no idea he will live. I take him to be a man about thirty. He is very large & Mrs. Coats[17] the old lady who has been nursing him says he is hard to move up. I got Mrs. Lesesne to walk into the street with me just before sundown to hunt up a bonnet. I succeeded in getting one but I dont much fancy it, however it will do for this place. The weather is perfectly lovely. Poor Savary's[18] trunk hasent come to light yet.

---

16. A nephew of William Wallace Harllee.

17. A nurse at the Farish House.

18. Savary was Ada Bacot's slave. She accompanied her mistress to Charlottesville and assisted her with housekeeping duties.

Wednesday Night Dec 18" 61

I succeeded in getting off from my household dutys about eleven oclock then went to Lieut. Harllee's room at the Farish House to relieve good Mrs. Coats. I received a message from her while at breakfast, to please go to help her. I remained until five this afternoon when I came home as I was afraid to remain until dark & walk home alone. Mr. & Mrs. Barnwell with their two little ones have now come to stay with us, which is very pleasant. We have had a very pleasant evening down in the dining room, every one seems to avoid the parlor. I dont see that my cold gets any better.

Friday Night Dec 20" 61

Went this morning with Dr. Rembert to visit the upper hospitals, found several poor men very sick, but perfectly in their minds, they seemed much gratified to see a lady & received what I said to them very kindly. There was one poor man at the Harris House, now kept by Mrs. Robinson, who has Typhoid fever he is very deff from the effect of it when you would ask him any questions, was almost impossible to make him hear, when he did he would scream out his answer at the top of his voice. Dr. R.'s manner is very kind & considerate, tis a pleasure to go with him to see the sick. I saw about a dozen in bed some not much sick, others again very ill[.] great pains are taken to render the men comfortable. I dident see one who complained of his condition, all seemed grateful. I couldent get round to see Lieut. Harllee until four oclock this afternoon. I sat with him until six he seemed anxious to converse, I indulged him a little, but he is too weak to talk much. The Dr. seems to have hopes of his recovery. Dr. McIntosh went for me & accompanied me home. Esse H. seems to be making quite an impression on some of the gentlemen in the house. She is certainly a very sweet girl. The evenings here are very pleasant. Mrs. B. has been to[o] much indisposed to come down today. Quite a change in the weather. Mr. Q. got back today, we have quite an amazing character in the house for a day or two. Dr. Thompson returned today with the Trent glorious news from England.[19] They demand our commissioners,

---

19. The British had presented their demand for the release of Confederate commissioners James Murray Mason and John Slidell, captured by Federal forces while sailing under a British flag, to the United States government on December 19, 1861.

to be placed again under the protection of the British flag as when they were taken, or war will be declared. I am only affraid the Yankee government will be cowardly enough to give them up.

Sunday Night Dec 22d 61

The weather is raw & disagreeable. Both Esse & my self had quite a fright last night, we heard a terable knocking at the front door so E. got up opened the window & looked saw a man who said he wanted Dr. Gourdin. She directed him where the Dr. was to be found, soon after we went to sleep & I was awoke by a queer noise in the sheet. I dont know what it was, I slept but little afterwards, Esse & myself went to church this morning, just as we were going to sit down to dinner Dr. Gourdin came in, saying forty men had arrived at the Monticello & they wanted food & drink. We went to work to get what they wanted, sending all the food we had in the house & beging some from some of Mrs. B.'s rations. The Tea & Coffee were soon redy I made it in large pitchers & sent it over by the young gentlemen. I went over to see some of the men late this afternoon when they heard we were from S.C. they seemed gratified. It seems they were under the impression that the Va. ladies had gotten up the Hospital. I asked if they were comfortable, they said yes very, so different from what I expected. It is raining quite hard & is groaning quite hard.

Monday Night Dec 23d 61

When I came down this morning the trees were hanging with icicles & twas bitter cold, fortunate we got the men in on yesterday. I heard just about dinner time that Frank Law was one of the patients at the Monticello. I went to see him this afternoon, he was much gratified to see someone from home, he has a wretched cough I have sent him some syrup[.] called to see Lieut. Harllee for a few minutes he is improving rapidly. He brightened up when I went into the room. Dr. McI. tells me he is much gratified that Mrs. Coats & myself attend him. Dr. Gourdin told me his resignation had been accepted.[20] I am truly sorry, he will be quite a loss to our party. Had three letters today, one from Dickie at last, Essie Dr. Rembert & myself have had quite a frolic at our room door. The Dr. is very full of fun.

---

20. Dr. Gourdin's ill health and his fear of the approaching winter's effect on his condition led him to resign his commission and return to South Carolina.

Wednesday Night Dec 25" 61

There was service this morning but I dident attend[.] Mr. B. got back in time for our Christmas dinner, which went off charmingly. We had the Dr.'s cake for desert[.] Just before dinner Dr. Gourdin came into the dining room where I was sitting & placed a small package in my hand saying twas a present for Miss Habersham he asked me to open it & pass opinion upon it[.] I never saw a more ludicrous thing[.] It represented a Christmas tree hung with desirable articles[.] A man was at the bottom trying to reach them but was unable to do so. I saw the point immediately, Mr. Quimby has shown a decided preference for Esse, but evidently is afraid to venture to address her. The Dr. asked me to take charge of it, so I brought it up & when Esse came gave it to her. I had promised the Dr. not to betray him, so I had to be very quiet, Esse suspected Dr. Thompson, & said she knew I had something to do with it. I said Dr. T. hadent given it to me, we all had a good'eal of fun over it. I fear Mr. Quimby suspects that we are none of us very partial to him. Poor man Tis a pity he wouldent go away. I shall be hartily glad when Christmas is over. It has been almost impossible to get a servant to do anything today. Virginia Negroes are not near so servile as those of S.C. I find housekeeping any thing but pleasant here. We had quite a merry time at tea.

Friday Night Dec 27" 61

I have been able to get more time this morning for myself, so I am over to the Monticello for a little while. Mr. Law is improving, he relished the lunch I took him. Tis a gratification to be able to do any thing for the poor men, they are so greatful. One man beged me to sit a while with him he was so lonly. He seems to pine for his mother & sisters. Found Lieut. H. alone when I called to see him. He complained of not being so well today as yesterday. I think him decidedly better he is beginning to feel his weakness now the fever has left him, his eyes are very red from trying to read. Lieut. Maning came in while I was there. Two or three of the men are very ill at the Monticello. One by the name of Davis has been dieing all day. Esse came into our room just before tea laughing with a small package in her hand & said she had had an adventure. She has been noticing young Franklin (one of those who was detached as a nurse for the men of his company who are at the Monticello), a great deal carying him little dainties & oth-

erwise noticing him. Mrs. Lesesne & myself both told her she had better be careful that the young men might not put the right construction
upon her motives for paying those attentions. This evening just as she
was coming over for the night Franklin stoped her & put this package
into her hand beging her to accept it. Esse refused, but he entreated
her to keep it, which she did. Mrs. L. & I scolded her for her imprudence, she is in great trouble about it & I think she will be more careful in future. I love Esse she is very affectionate. After tea Mr. B. asked
me to do some copying for him, when it was done he complimented
me upon the performance. Mrs. B. had a present of two Gallons of
beautiful oysters today, she has just treated us to a supper of them. Mr.
Quimby has been quite sick all day. My cold is better, I have been remarkably well all day notwithstanding the terable attack of cholramor-
bus I had last night.

Thursday Night Jan 2d 62

Compleetly wornout tonight have crossed the street at least a dozen
times today going back & forth to the Monticello House. Esse went
with me to see Lieut. H., she commenced her cooking today for the
sick, she has a nice little room with a stove & all sorts of nice little
cooking utensils[.] I paid her a visit about twelve oclock & beged for
some soup for Lieut. H. Mrs. Jackson (the widow of the hero)[21] sent
her a donation of jelly & custard today. Lieut. H. complimented me
very highly as I was leaving him for the night, by saying he was sorry I
was going for he found me a very agreable companion. Tonight, Mr.
Barnwell has had us to coppying reports for him, I spoiled so many
sheets of paper that I concluded twas labor lost & stoped for the night.
I have realy felt perfectly happy today tis such a gratification to feel I
am doing some good. Tonight Mr. B. wanted to find out when we arrived here, none of us recolected the day of the month so Esse proposed I should get my journal & tell him she ran up here for it & I
looked out the date. Dr. McIntosh pretended he was quite curious to
know what I wrote. I know there is going to be some great joak about

---

21. The widow of James T. Jackson (the owner of the Marshall House Tavern in Alexandria, who had killed Colonel Elmer Ellsworth of the United States Army when he
removed the Confederate flag that Jackson was flying from the tavern's flagpole) had
fled to Charlottesville in May 1861.

my poor journal among the gentlemen. Dr. McI. said he was quite curious to know what I had written about a week ago. I cant imagine what he means, Esse is beging me to leave off writing & go to bed, so I will oblige her.

Saturday Night Jan 4" 62

The ground has been covered with ice all day. Twas very amusing to see people sliping & sliding as they walked along some fell sprawling I went over to the Monticello about noon & had four falls before I reached the steps, but fortunately got off without a bruise. Dr. McIntosh got two falls, & Dr. Thompson had one at full length, he hapened to look round before he got up & there were two girls near by laughing immoderately, he jumped up & asked them what amused them. When he came in to dinner he told us he had goten so many falls, that at last he had written a lable, with "Glass this side up with care," & pined it to his back, he is very amusing. When I went to see Lieut. H. this morning he beged me to perform Mrs. Coats duty for him. I hesitated a good while, but he beged so hard that I consented at last when I found that he couldent realy use his hands[.] when I had finished washing his face & combing his hair, he thanked me so politely that I felt I had realy confered a favour. I visited my other patients this afternoon they welcomed me with smiles, about eighteen new patients come today, poor creatures they were almost frozen when they reached here. They were soon made comfortable. Tis very pleasant to hear the men express them selves so much pleased with their treatment. Mr. Barnwell made us roar with laughter at the tea table, I never saw any one who had a keener sense of the ridiculous than he has, he told us that Mrs. Osborn came very near being burned to death today. Mrs. L. oft said that she supposed that Mrs. O. had been burning inside so long that it was not astonishing that she should catch fire outside. Mr. Quimby came down to tea. Tis bitter cold tonight.

Thursday Noon Jan 9" 62

Went over to the Monticello about eleven, call to enquire after Harllee first, he is very bright & very happy this morning. The Dr. has promised him a furlo of thirty days. I soon left him & went to see the other men I am in the habit of visiting all [who] are better. The Dr. called my attention to a very sick man, I forget his name, poor fellow, I hope to do something for him. Tis sad to see so much misery, but I am glad to have it in my power to do something to eleaviate it. I am much better today. The Sun is out but the street is very sloppy, not so cold today.

### Night

I ventured over to the Monticello again after dinner but was in constant teror of sliping in the mud all the way across. Went to see a poor man in the old part of the building, who I am convinced will die tonight. There are sevral others very ill. Esse came over very early with a nervous headache. Tonight just before we were seated at the tea table Mr. Quimby brought up a most disgusting subject of conversation. Shows the man has no delicacy. I was so sick I thought I would have fainted, I couldent make up my mind to eat my tea. Dr. McI. remarked my want of appetite, but of course I couldent tell him the cause of it.

Mrs. Lesesne, Esse, Nonie & myself had a little supper up here tonight. It rains. I dread the condition of the streets in the morning.

### Thursday Noon Jan 16″ 62

I feel as if I wanted to go out & wander all about every where this beautiful bright morning, but the streets are too shocking. I've been enjoying the splendid prospect from my window all the morning, Mrs. Barnwell asked me up to her room to see the view from her window, I wish I could describe it. The bright Sun shining on the ice causing it to look like large ponds of clear water. Tis too dazzling to look upon long but I could not force myself away. I've never in all my life seen any thing like it.

There was another death at the Monticello last night, quite a boy, a melancholy case, he was very much frightened, & I'm told wept nearly all day yesterday. I am so very sorry I did not know it, I would have gone to him & tryed to ease his last moments. I havent a doubt he was some mothers pride, & perhaps her only prop & stay in this world tis too sad. Dr. Rembert tells me that pneumonia is taking off hundreds. It is even more fatal than Typhoid fever. Tis too too sad.

### Just before Tea

Went over with Marie to the Monticello about four oclock, saw Peter Harllee who has returned from Manassas with his brothers bags he told me his brother had gone out, so I went to see some of the men in the other part of the house & Marie asked me to take a look at her Laundry, every thing is working beautifully. We were seated in Esse's room paying her a short visit, Mr. Barnwell came in in the best spirits possible & gave us a pretty little wine glass apiece he said to give medicine in. When we were returning home just now I looked up at Harllees window & saw him, he saw us too, threw the window up & we had a few minutes conversation, he tells me he is going home on Sunday. I've just been telling Marie that I am in too high spirits, I fear something dreadful is going to happen, when ever I feel so very happy I always prepare myself for something disagreable after it. There goes the tea bel.

Maupin House Friday Noon Jan 17". 62

How can I discribe the horable scene we have passed through in the last ten or twelve hours. We had but a few minutes finished our Tea & gathered around the fire when a negro boy came in & asked for an axe, twas a strange request to be made at that time in the evening & in the dining room so one of the gentlemen asked for what it was wanted, we soon learned the Monticello home was on fire, all the gentlemen ran over immediately & we ran into our room to see from our window. We soon found we must pack our clothes which we did very quickly & sent the trunks down out of the way. My whole thought was for the ill men where ever scattered all over the house. I could see them pouring from every door & the beding flying from every window, almost everything was saved. Dr. Carter[22] came up to our room & insisted upon our going to his house with him. We beged hard to be alowed to stay until there was a greater danger, but we were hurried off. on the passage just by the front door we met Mrs. B. raped in a large comfort from hed to foot, she was an object to behold, I went into the parlor saw a poor old man by the name of Powel lying on the soffa he was a good'eal exerted, I dont think he can possibly live. Dr. McIntosh was standing on the porch looking very white from the fatigue he had just undergone, helping the ill men from the scene of danger. A little way from the gate Lieut. H. came up to me, said is this you, I am so delighted, & offered to take what I had in my hand, but I asked him to take care of my dear Marie, he went with us as far as the Hotel where he was to

22. Charles Carter was an elderly practicing physician in Charlottesville. Formerly a surgeon during the War of 1812, he was in charge of the Midway Hospital for a few months and was hired as a contract physician for the Soldiers' Home.

spend the [night], we then followed dear old Dr. Carter on to his Hospitable house, where we were received by his sweet wife in the most affectionate manner. Soon there was a room in readiness offered us. When we retired to our room for the night I could but remark how comfortable & homelike it was. This morning the servant came in to light the fire, we asked if it was time to rise, "she said we could do so when we liked, but breakfast was not redy" I laid in bed for a few moments longer enjoying my liberty, when we went down we found our old friends alredy seated at the table, how sweetly every thing looked. As we came in Mrs. Carter said we would have waited for you, but thought you would prefer the Dr.'s eating his breakfast as he had to go to the Hospital. We all said we were very glad they had not waited. The meal was most exelent, the coffee particularly delightful. We finished off with snow & cream. Mrs. C. let us come off a little while after we had finished our breakfast as we were anxious to see what damage had been done. Lieut. Harllee came out to say goodby as we passed the Hotel, he went home today. We met Mr. Barnwell & Dr. Lafar at the corner of the street, & went with them over the part of the building which remains. Even it is a wreck for the doors & windows were nearly all pulled down, & even parts of partitions toarn away. The floors look as if nothing would ever bring them clean again covered as they are with mud & water. Mr. B. has just been up to consult with us about the arrangement of the building, he has carpenters alredy at work puting things to rights, & is now trying to make arrangement for carying on the Hospital. Nothing has yet been fixed upon.

### Night

Mr. B. has not rested all this day he has been working both mind & body trying to right up every thing. Of course we are all greatly fatigued & feel the loss of sleep. I have written a long letter too to Pa.

### Saturday Night January 18" 62

It has rained all day greatly impeding Mr. B.'s opperations at the Monticello. Two other houses have been hired in the upper part of the town for part of the men who lost their places. Mrs. Becaes & Mrs. Bremer have been brought here for several days until their appartments can be fixed for them. They are both in bed one with mumps & the other threatened with pneumonia. Mrs. Barnwell & the children are still at Mrs. Patens where they went the night of the fire. Mr. B. has determined as far as I can learn, that only Mr. Jones & Mr. Jackson are to stay in the Hospital, all of us are to remain as we have hither too at this house, Mrs. Lesesne & myself are to take the three wards at the Monticello between us, Miss Reynolds[23] keep the house, & attend to part of the nurishment. Esse is to take my place here in housekeeping & prepare the other nurishment. I hope it will all work well. Am willing to do my part. I greatly fear something will turn up to brake up our little circle, but will hope for the best. The wind howls terably, every one is out of spirits, my patience has been greatly tried twice today, but I have been able to command myself. I thank God for it for I have heard so many ill natured remarks of late, & seen such exibitions of temper that I am thuraly disgusted.

Sunday Night Jan 19th" 62

I was too unwell all the morning to think of going out to church which I regreted. Tonight I had two invatations one from Dr. Rembert the other from Dr. McI. to go round to hear Mr. H. I would gladly have gone but the streets are in too miserable a condition to walk. Capt. Taylor[24] called just before tea, he is very pleasant quite military in appearance. Dr. Rembert paid us a short visit in our room tonight. Poor Esse seems to've had something very disagreable to anoy her, for she has been venting her spleen upon Mrs. Lesesne & myself without the least foundation acqusing us very unjustly, & all together showing a good'eal more temper than was agreable. I took no notice of what she said further than to ask her if she dident feel ashamed. I took a little supper of cold meats to Drs. R. & McI. room for them tonight. This being my last day in the housekeeping department, It being turned over to Esse now, & I was determined to retreat in flying colours. We are all faged & got to bed earlier than ususal, tis now eleven.

---

23. An assistant matron and dietician at the Monticello Hospital.

24. Probably Bennett Taylor, then a captain in the Nineteenth Virginia Infantry, Co. F or I. He was promoted to major in July 1863 after he was taken prisoner at the Battle of Gettysburg and to lieutenant colonel in October 1864.

# Chapter 4

# January 20–March 31, 1862

*"Dead tiard worn out cant write Too tiard to talk, want sleep."*

Monday Afternoon Jan 20 62

Turned the keys over to Esse this morning, awoke with a miserable headache[.] Esse disturbed me several times in the night, first she roused me out of a sound sleep to ask if I was asleep. I told her I was awake, then she said she was sorry for what she had said to Marie & myself before retiring, I told her I thought nothing of it, but please to let me go to sleep that I felt sick. A short time after she again woke me by getting up opening the door & going into the passage. I called after her to know what she was after. Twas nine oclock before I went down this morning. Mr. B. hurried Marie & myself over to the Monticello to get the bunks arranged we succeeded very much better than I at first anticipated. It has been raining hard all day, so much so that we have not gone back this after noon[.] I am suffering from a headache, couldent eat my dinner. Mr. B. & I settled up my housekeeping accounts this afternoon, he complimented me much more than I deserved. I hope I may please him as well in my new position, I surely will make every effort. God help me. We find that nearly every thing in the way of beding & clothing has been saved. Things are constantly turning up which have been paked away. Some of Mrs. Sweets articles of clothing came to light this morning, I dont know if the teeth have yet been found. Mrs. Becaes eyes (as she calls her spectacles) & her keys have not yet been found & I doubt if they will be. Twas raining when we came over to dinner, Ladies here mind the rain & mud less than any where I've ever been, I saw a good many out today.

Tuesday Morning Jan 21st" 62

I couldent go down to tea last evening my head ached so terably, about eight oclock Dr. Rembert came to the door to ask me to go up & put a blister on Mrs. Bremers side. Marie was up here with me, so she went the Dr. walked in & sat a while with me. I know he was laughing at my invalidish appearance, I was reclining with my head on the back of the chair afraid to move for the slightest motion made my head worse.

I am quite well again this morning the weather still very bad, went over to the Monticello, but only staid a few minutes. Mr. B. said there was but little to do & we had better not expose ourselves. I think the Monticello when compleet will be a modle hospital. The men beg us to hury & get redy for them we can take 75, wish the weather would clear. The weather is quite as changeable as in S.C. yesterday too warm for fire, today quite cold.

Thursday Night Jan 23d 62

Dr. McIntosh refused our assistance this morning saying twas useless to go up in the cold unless there was something to work upon, which was all very true. I went over to the Monticello & had the fires made expecting the men to come in today but they did not, no sun again today, the weather very cold & dreary[.] Mrs. Barnwell has been too unwell to come down today. Mrs. Becaes goes to Westland tomorrow, Mrs. Bremer still in bed. Marie & myself had a small Oyster supper for ourselves tonight, sent Dr. Rembert & McIntosh some, over which they were very merry judging from the laughter we heard in their room. Poor Esse was so provoked because we dident tell her of our entention of having the supper, that we could scarcely enduce her to eat any thing. I am sorry to see she is extemely sensitive, she is particularly so about the Monticello, Mr. B. has thought it best to take her from there entirely, which she seriously objects to, but I think Mr. B. is perfectly right, Esse is too unstable to be in a Hospital. Marie & myself walked up Main Street in search of some flannel, I got some, for I find I must have it here. I never heard of such exorbatant prices as are asked here for every thing.

Charlottesville. Maupin House
Monday Night January 27" 62

My duties at the Monticello as Hospital nurse actualy begun today. I have been all day runing up & down stairs, attending to poltices, giving medicine & answering questions. The men are generaly polite & genteel looking. My ward is now full, five new ones came today, some I fear quite sick I am thourely sick of the sight of men, & would gladly get away for a time to rest, but I know these are not the right feelings and will suppress them.

Dr. McIntosh asked Esse to go with him to hear the Wood Ministrels tonight, she went not withstanding the threatning state of the weather. Dr. Rembert asked Mrs. Lesesne & myself, we both declined, Esse is a wild one, with very little sense of propriety. I dont think she enjoyed what they heard or saw much they said very little about it when they got back. Esse feels she did something not exactly right, for she said to Marie & myself, I see you ladies look disaproving, which neither of us did that I know of. So it must have been her own concience which told her she had committed an impropriety. The weather has again moderated.

Tuesday Night Jan 28" 62

Had a glooming morning to begin with, got up feeling low spirited & out of sorts, was at the Monticello all day until about five this afternoon[.] Marie, Esse & I walked to see dear old Mrs. Carter. She was at home & received us in her warm kind manner. The walking was very bad, the snow just melting making it wet & slopy. Heard tonight Frank McQueen[1] & Mr. John McClenaghan came today. Dr. McIntosh went round to see them at the Farish House. There he has just come, tis very late, Esse says I must put out the light & go to bed. O my to think of getting up early in the morning & going among men, I am so sick of the sight of them.

Charlottesville

Friday Night Jan 31st" 62

One month of the new year alredy gone. Tis almost impossible to note time here[.] every thing is done by clock work, each hour having its appointed duty. I paid Mrs. Barnwell, who is still confined to her room, a short call this afternoon[.] Mr. Barnwell & myself had quite a discusion about Mrs. Becaes & Bremer, I took Esse's party & told Mr. B. that I thought it very hard she was to be complained of by the Mrs. B.'s after the efforts she had made to please them. He seemed to think they had been very badly treated by all of us, which I protested against, I fear they will yet cause some disturbence in our peaceful household. Frank McQueen came in after tea & spent the evening. He is decidedly handsome & particularly agreable he has promised to come in again to an egg nog before he returns to camp. Dr. Lafar had a dispatch tonight from the Telegraph agent saying Gen. Beauregard & staff will breakfast at the Central Hotel (which is just at the depot,) at half past

---

1. Frank McQueen was probably the son of General John McQueen.

six tomorrow morning. Esse says she is going down to see him. I should like to too but cant make up my mind to face the crowd. I know there will be no ladies present at that time in the morning. Esse, Dr. McIntosh & myself had a funny talk tonight about marriage, I said I could not admire the two fashions which have crept into society with in the last few years. That of marrieng for money, & that of a woman marrieng a man younger than herself. they both agread with me, but not entirely. I say I have a contempt for a woman who will do either. I regard marriage as so holy a thing, that one cant be too careful before entering into it. I predict another bad day for the morrow, I hear the rain patering out side now. Had a letter from Sister today, all well at home, for which I am thankful.

Charlottesville<br>
Saturday Noon Feb 1st" 1862

Esse went off this morning with Dr. Rembert to the depot through the rain to see Beauregard, she was the only lady present, I have never seen the General but could not make up my mind to face such a crowd. Then too I have no fancy for going to see men I would certainly have looked at Beauregard if he came in my way, but I wouldent run after him or any great man.

Night

Just before the desert came on table Nonie ran over to the office & brought in the letters. He handed me one I looked at the direction but couldent make out the hand writing I broke it open & was still more puseled so I turned to the signature & found twas from Lieut. Harllee, I am much gratified that he should have recolected me. Dr. McIntosh must have seen something peculiar in the expression of my face while I was reading the letter, for he began to tease me immediately, he first asked me if twas a poetical efusion[.] I said no, told him twas a very plane mater of fact letter, but he dident give up. Tonight I got down late at tea, I had bearly taken my seat before both Dr. Rembert & McIntosh they began [to] run me hard, one pretended to know the difference between the hand writing of an officer in camp, or one discharged, or one on sick furlough. The other said he reconized the hand writing across the table. Of course I dident believe any of it so dident commit myself.

Charlottesville
Monday Night Feb 3" 62

Was supprised to find the ground covered with snow this morning twas snowing fast untill mid day Marie & myself wraped up & went over to the Monticello, just as though it was the most delightful sunshiny day. We found that Mrs. Becaes & Mrs. Bremer had proseeded us & had taken a grand snow balling on Mrs. Lesesnes ward with some of the men. Dr. Rembert went up & put a stop to it immediately cant imagine how any lady could think of snowballing in a hospital. Tonight after Mr. Barnwell went up stairs we got Esse to give us some cold Supper[.] when we got just in the midst of it & enjoying it heartily down came Mr. Barnwell, I dident care the least, but some of the others did, I offered him some of all we had but he would not take any thing. I answered Harllees letter tonight. Marie says my answer was just the thing. I hope it is. I entertain a very kindly feeling for him, but nothing more.

Charlottesville
Tuesday noon Feb 4" 62

Esse felt too badly to get up this morning so I volunteered my services to act in her place until twas time to go over to the Monticello. But three of us appeared at the breakfast table. Eight breakfasts were taken up to the rooms. The snow is melting & the streets are sloppie beyond measure. Found Northcut something better. Young McKinney is a treasure of a nurse. Tis a real pleasure to go over & find that Matilda has finished up her rooms & swept up all clean & nice.

Night

I hurried through with the tea at the Monticello, that I might get back here in time to fix my little Supper. I was rather later in getting through than usual, & bearly had time to dress myself before Frank & Capt. McClenaghan came, I entertained them until some of the others came and then went & prepared my oyesters Sallard, & egg nog. The gentlemen appeared to enjoy the vian[d]s very much. The evening passed of[f] very quietly, Mr. Barnwell monopolized the conversation mostly. Capt. McClenaghan said he thought it worth being sick to be able to mingle in society again. After supper had been dispatched conversation became more general. Esse feigned horseness, or rather loss of voice for she whispered all she said, I cant immagine why

she did so but I am sertain she could have talked if she chose. She
retired as soon as the gentlemen left. Dr. Rembert, Dr. McIntosh,
Mrs. Lesesne & myself had a pleasant little talk after all were gone. Dr.
Rembert got to teasing me about that everlasting letter. McIntosh declared he was going to make Riley bring all the letters to him before
they were taken to the office, that he might see who I wrote to. I told
him that would do very well if he wasent the day after the fair, that I
had alredy answered the said letter.

Charlottesville
Wednesday Noon Feb 5" 62

Dident get down to breakfast this morning, twas near two when I
retired last night. Went to the Monticello at eleven oclock found that
my ill men had not had any soup for breakfast Dr. Rembert came to me
very much woried about it. It realy seems that if I am not present to
tell them what they are to take up to the wards, every thing goes
wrong. Thank heaven every thing has been righted & I have had the
satisfaction of seeing every thing go up looking beautifully. Have a
wretched cold & head ache.

Night

Dead tiard worn out cant write Too tiard to talk, want sleep.

Charlottesville
Saturday night Feb 8" 62

Couldent make up my mind to get up in time for breakfast this
morning. Esse sent it up to both Marie & myself. Went to the Monticello earlier than ususal, gladened some of the poor men by sending
them something besides soup. It realy gave me pleasure to hear how
they enjoyed it. Dr. Thompson came to see me this morning at the
Monticello we had a very pleasant half hour together. He dined with
us here today. After dinner we were all seated around the fire, Marie &
Dr. Lafar on the soffa, after a while the papers were brought in & ev-
erybody seized one. I said to Dr. McIntosh, that the papers contained
a good'eal about the Hospitals, he asked me to give him the amount of
those entered & of those which had died, he & Dr. Rembert immediately began to make a calculation, soon after I heard them laugh[.] I
thought directly twas about some thing but they kept on with the calculation. Marie had gone out of the room in the meantime. Tonight
Dr. McIntosh asked me at tea if I knew what the laugh was about, I

said no but I dident think twas about what they were doing. He then told me that as Marie got off of the soffa they caught sight of Dr. Thompsons hat perfectly crushed, Marie had been sitting on it. Dr. Lafar gave one of his queer looks & said "alas poor Yorick" which made them laugh so. Then too the expression of Dr. Thompsons face was a perfect picture when he saw his hat. Dr. Rembert has been spending the evening with us & Marie got Esse to let her show him her love letter, I never saw any one enjoy any thing half so much[.] I thought we had laughed all we could about it before, but we found enough more to laugh at when Dr. Rembert read the letter out. I had a nice long letter from Dickie today. Tis now very late I must retire for it wont do for me not to be at breakfast again tomorrow morning. Dr. McIntosh has just come in from a supper at the hotel given by Frank McQueen & Capt. McClenaghan. I hear great laughing going on, he must have brought back something funy to tell. I'm sorry I laughed so much my throat aches from it.

Charlottesville
Tuesday Night Feb 11″ 62

The morning was bright & lovely every body began to say we will have a good day. But alas for human hopes, by noon twas snowing fast which continued for two hours. The news this morning was moor gloomy than that of yesterday. Elizabeth City has been shelled & burned & the enemy is now advancing on Edenton.[2] A telegram was also received from Missourie, To the efect that we have gained a brilant victory.[3] I hope it may be true for God seems to have forsaken us for a time. Dear old Mrs. Carter called to see us this afternoon, Esse says Capt. & Mrs. Taylor called this morning. Tis pleasant to be remembered but we realy have no time to visit. Dr. Rembert had a beautiful daguerrotype taken of himself on yesterday, Tis one of the best I ever saw in my life. He has promised to give each of us a photograph of himself. Today while we were all seated around the fire after dinner,

---

2. United States naval vessels destroyed the remains of the Confederate "Mosquito" fleet at Elizabeth City, North Carolina, on February 10, 1862; they would go on to capture Edenton, North Carolina, on February 12.

3. There were several minor skirmishes in Missouri at this time, but nothing that would qualify as a major victory for the Confederacy.

Dr. Rembert insisted that Dr. McIntosh should bring down one he had. It was brought down & given to Marie to look at[.] I was near her so had a look at the same time. Both of us shrieked with laughter, tis the funniest looking object I ever saw, nothing like Dr. McI. you could tell twas taken for him, but nothing more.

One of the men on my upper ward is very ill. Dr. R. told me when he came into Tea, that he was worse tonight, so I concluded I would go over about 9 oclock to see if he had all he would want for the night. I was glad I went, I found I could do several little things for him. I feel satisfied now, I hope the poor creature may yet recover.

Charlottesville

Friday Night Feb 14" 62

No sun to cheer up today, consiquently I've been the dullest of the dull. I could scarcely get up a laugh when Esse got her valentine, I never saw any one more completely fooled in my life. She was sure twas from Franklin, she said she reconized the handwriting. Dr. McIntosh did imitate it admirably. Have worked with renewed spirit at the Monticello today, Dr. Rembert told me when he went round he found all the men better. I find a Mr. Calhoun in my upper ward a nephew of John C. Calhoun, I hear. I did not see him until yesterday he has not been on my diet list before, & I never go into the rooms unless there is some one in bed, or I have nurishment to prepare for any man in the room, then I always make a point of going to see it delivered once a day at least. Matilda is such a nice servant I can trust her with the cleaning up of the chambers. I should be very sorry to leave the Monticello now, I have become so interested in the men. Tis more gratifying to me than I can express, to be able even in this slight way to be of some use to my country. I thank God more & more each day that he heard my prayer. The Papers contain encouraging news from the west today. Dear Marie is quite unwell tonight & I've come up to sit with her. The gentle-men all seem in a meditative mood tonight. Dr. R. received orders to go to Richmond & stand his examination for full surgon, so he is studieng hard to refresh his memory. He goes the first of next week. Dr. McIntosh is to be in charge at the Monticello during Dr. R.'s absence. I can but hope the Dr. will be successful & that he may be ordered back here. I should be very sorry to loose him, our relations have been very pleasant thus far.

Charlottesville
Friday Night Feb 21st" 62

Although it has been a bright day outside, It has been one of anxiety to me. Dr. McIntosh has been worse all day not very ill but quite
too sick to be out of bed.[4] I was in to see him about the middle of the
day then again at tea time; & I've just left him. The Dr. swabed his
throat & gave him a pill, I bathed his head & rubed his temples until
he slept. I hope he will be better by morning. Dr. Rembert has brought
in news that the report of Prices victory is confirmed.[5] He also said he
saw Frank McQueen he has returned here quite sick. I will have my
hands full, of course I will have to attend to him. I would not be willing to have any one else do it. This morning about ten oclock there
was great comotion in the street[.] Soldiers runing backward & forward
men women & children grouped about in the streets, shouting & Hur-
raing going on, & there was a general stir up. We soon found out that
a Reg. of Tenesee Troops were returning to protect their capital. They
were in high spirits poor fellows. They had been alowed an hour to
come up into the town to breakfast. Soon the whistle blew & they
were racing back to the depot. In short order they were all aboard,
some inside & others on the top. The cars moved slowly off. The brass
band struck up a lively tune & the shouting comenced again. Twas to
me a sad sad sight.

Charlottesville
Sunday Night Feb 23d 62

Another dreary day has alredy passed. The night too is dark &
gloomy. Not even a star visable. No Service to night, Mr. Hogg is too
unwell. I'm sorry to miss two Sabbaths in Succession. Dr. McIntosh
has been sitting up nearly all the afternoon, I went in to see him about
a half hour ago. I saw Walter Gregg[6] this morning. If I had not known
he was in Charlottesville, & had not seen him in Dr. McIntosh's

---

4. In addition to his cold, James McIntosh had contracted erysipelas, a deep skin in-
fection that leads to the inflammation and red coloring of tissues and makes breathing
difficult if it settles in the nose and throat.

5. This report was erroneous; General Sterling "Pap" Price was not involved in any
major military action at this time.

6. Walter Mack Gregg (d. 1896) lived near Ada in the Darlington District.

room, I should not have know[n] him. I realy dont know what to make of Esse she acts very strangely, she is deeply in love with Dr. McIntosh & she knows he is engaged. I'm in constant dread lest she will betray herself to him or Dr. Rembert. I must say I feel disappointed in her, again so much for forming hasty attachments. How different it is with my dear Marie; every day I find somthing new to admire in her. Heard today of Lieut. Harllees return to camp, Tis very strange I thought he was obliged to return here to report.

Monday Noon, Feb 24" 62<br>Charlottesville

I never saw a more terific wind. It whistles & sigh's mournfuly around the house, & through the ruins of the old Monticello, one of the tallest slenderest chimneys of the ruin has become its victim, about eleven oclock it was seen to sway back & forth, looking as if every fresh puff would bring it against the end of the house. Directly there was a crash, bricks & durt flying in every direction, but fortunately there was no injury done. If we could only hear that the enemys boats had suffered. I've just been in to see Dr. McIntosh he is worse again today he took fresh cold last night, & is suffering terably with his eyes. He has permitted me to nurse him a good deal, & realy seems to like me to wait on him. I told him to let me take Lous place, that I would gladly do what I could for him.

Charlottesville<br>Monday Night Feb 24" 62

Had a nice long letter from Pa after dinner. The wind has continued very high all the afternoon & tonight, keeping up the greatest {cavatina} with the winds, slamming & banging about. About a half dozen men left the Monticello this morning, discharged for camp. None very ill there now[.] Dr. Lafar returned today from Richmond. He says the enauguration passed off quietly without excitement of any kind, he says there is no dispondency there at our reverses. They are felt, but cause no discouragement.

The papers today say that twelve or thirteen thousand of our troops surendered to the Yankees at fort Donelson.[7] I cant believe it, I will

---

7. General Simon Bolivar Buckner surrendered Fort Donelson unconditionally to General Ulysses S. Grant on February 16, 1862.

hope it is not true. Dr. Rembert is indignent to think that Southern men would comit such folly so am I. There must have been some very good reason for the surender or the men would never have alowed them selves to be given up to so contemtable a foe.

Dr. McIntosh has been very sick all day, I have been with him almost incessently since one oclock. This afternoon I went in & found Walter Gregg sitting with him, I was about to retire, but W. insisted so much upon my going in & sitting with them that I did so, & realy had a very pleasant time. I am formaly established as the Dr.'s nurse, no one else is called upon to [do] any thing for him, I am delighted he will alow me to nurse him. Mr. Jones is very ill, Dr. Rembert asked me if I wouldent go to see him tomorrow, of course I will do so with pleasure, am always glad to do what I can to relieve the suffering of any one, & especially of one who has made himself so beloved & respected by his acts of kindness & attention to his fellow creatures. Mrs. Barnwell came down to tea tonight for the first time in some weeks. The wind has some what lulled. Tis a beautiful night, clear, cold, & the sky studded with stars.

Charlottesville<br>
Tuesday Noon Feb 25″ 62

How delightful & charming to see a bright day & to feel the warm sunshine, I could enjoy it to the full, but for my uneasiness about my friend. Dr. Rembert told me when he came down to breakfast that Dr. McIntosh was a good deal better that he sleped well, I had sent him up some gruel early in the morning which he drank & was about to send him up something more at breakfast but Dr. Rembert thought I had best not. I inferred from what he said that Dr. McIntosh was up, when I went into The room at eleven oclock I found him in bed with his eyes still covered with the cloth's & very much swolen. His noze too was very red & quite swolen. I washed his face & hands comed his hair then gave him the hominy & butter & a glass of milk. Dr. Rembert came in just as he had finished, looked at him & pronounced him very sick. I am over to the Monticello, gave the punch round & went to see all the men came back here & went in to see Dr. McI. I found him a good deal worse, Dr. R. has just steped in to ask me to stay with the Dr., he thinks him quite sick & needing constant attention so I am going in now to stay the rest of the day I have just written to his sister telling her of his sickness.

Night. Dr. McIntosh's room<br>Charlottesville

How quiet it is not a sound except the measured breathing of my invalid friend. I've not left him except a few minutes at a time, since noon[.] Tis a pleasure to do for one who receives all that is done so patiently. The swelling is increasing, & I fear by morning will entirely close the othe[r] eye. Dr. Rembert has gone up to Nonie's room for the night, & I am to keep watch. Walter Gregg came in this afternoon & sat an hour or so. I had a letter from my dear boy today. Mr. Barnwell dident come & Mrs. B. is so frightened about little Singleton that she sent to ask Dr. Rembert to go up & see him, the Dr. thinks him quite an ill child. Dr. McIntosh seems quite frightened about himself, since he has found out he has Erysipilis. I've tryed in every way to southe his mind. He has taken his night draught & now sleeps. I cant say quietly for his breathing is loud & difficult being entirely through the mouth. There was quite an accident about three oclock today, Lieut. Hester, who is rather a trifling character I fear, was lying drunk in the street, some man came by & tryed to get him up, when the Lieut. cursed him, blows followed & the Lieut. was badly cut up. He was taken to the Monticello & put on Maries ward. Poor Marie I fear she is too much worked she has had my wards today in addition to hers. I forgot to mention this morning that Mr. Jackson came in to breakfast with us & brought our Charactures they are exelent.

Dr. McIntosh's room<br>Charlottesville<br>Wednesday Morning Feb 26″ 62

The night is passed, & I thank God my patient is more easy this morning. The swelling is still spreding. He slept soundly most of the time[,] once he awoke & growned, I was by his side in an instant he complained of being weary, I rubed his hand which soothed him almost instantaneously. He said, "Mrs. Bacot you dont know the obligation I am under to you,["] I beged him not to think of it, but to call on me for what ever he wished, soon he was asleep. I feel dreadfuly, dont think I ever was more used up by a night watch. My face pains me, I dare say I am to be the next down.

Night, My own room

I've had a few hours repose late this afternoon, Walter came & sat with my friend while I slept. When I awoke Marie wouldent let me get up but called Dr. Rembert in to tell me to stay in bed. He has forbiden me to sit up tonight, I however got up after he left the room, dressed & went in to see the Dr. he is better & I hope he may rest through the night. Walter sits up the first & Newton the latter part of the night.

I told Dr. McIntosh Dr. Rembert had prohibited my sitting up again tonight he said he was glad but that Walter & Newton couldent come up to me. Tis gratifing to know that he liked my nursing. Mr. Barnwell did not come again today, Dr. R. told me he saw General McQueen this afternoon, he is here to see Frank, who isent actualy in bed but has a tendency to Typhoid fever. Dr. Rembert received a telegram from Lieut. Harllee today, his cousin Armstrong H.[8] is very ill in camp. Dr. R. had of course to run me a little, he never looses an opportunity to do so. My face is quite swolen on the left side, I suppose by morning I will be colour de Rose, with Erysipilis. Twelve oclock.

Charlottesville
Friday Morning Feb. 28" 62

I feel a good deal rested by my naps & greatly relieved to hear from McIntosh that Dr. Thompson had performed his office of nurse so well. I confess I was a little uneasy for fear he would not. I cant say I think the Dr. better for his mind wanders more than on yesterday. Every noise seems to effect him. Tis a bright but wild blustering day. Mr. Barnwell has just been in to see Dr. McIntosh, on his way to church, Tis fast day & every body has gone to church even Dr. Rembert. I of course cant leave my friend, Mr. Barnwell says I am confining myself too much, That if I am not very careful I will take the same disease, & declared he could see no necessity for my staying about the Dr. so continualy. I of course said nothing, but felt that Mr. B. knew very little about what was necessary as he said he dident think the Dr. so very ill. I only wish I dident know he was so very ill. My face still pains me a great deal at times I am convinced tis mumps, fortunately the swelling

8. Robert Armstrong Harllee, son of Dr. Robert and Melvina Cannon Harllee and nephew of William Wallace Harllee, had been confined to the Charlottesville Hospital in November and December 1861. He died on February 28, 1862.

keeps in bounds & I am not so much disfigured by it as I feared. I am dreadfuly woried about Marie she had both her own & my work to attend to at the Monticello, she tells me my men enquire very particularly after me every day.

### Night

I am very weary tonight from the constant standing & bending over to attend to my friend, twas too pitiful to hear him speak of all those so dear to him, imagining them near him. Then he would call to me & beg me not to go. The very sound of my voice seems to southe him. I've had to stand by & talk to him. He knows he is delirious. He is dreadfuly worried about the state of the country. Our late reverses seem to have made a great impression upon him. Walter will stay with him the latter part of the night. I can always stand it very well until two oclock, then I begin to want sleep. Dr. Rembert is very much worried about Dr. McIntosh & Jones. He thinks them both extremely ill, he says their life hangs in a balance but hopes to bring them through. If prayers will avail, I know their lives will be spared, I've been an age writing this, I have to jump up every 2 minutes.

### Monday Morning Mch 3d" 62
### Charlottesville

I was realy ashamed of myself for sleeping so late this morning. Poor Walter had to wait for me until ten oclock, I never saw any one look more relieved than he did when I made my appearance at the door. My friend is so very much better this morning that the Dr. has ordered custard for him. I think it rather early to begin to give it but will make it & if he likes he can have a little. It doesent rain but it is dark & cloudy & bitter cold, I am glad I can stay in doors today. Marie is out though & I fear will make herself sick. Mrs. Barnwell has been very sick for several days past. I hear she is to go home before long. As sorry as I will be to part with her, I think it the best thing she can do.

### Night my own room

What a relief to both mind & body to be able to sit quietly in my own room. The Dr. is very much better so much so that I've written to Lou that there was a decided change for the better. I feared tonight he was going to be quite sick again, the custard he ate in the middle of the day seemed to disagree with him in some way, but it is passing off & I hope he is going to have a good night. I have just been in to take Dr.

Thompson (who sits up tonight) some coffee, he has put some comforts down on the floor below the fire to lie on, I fear he will either
take cold or the fire may pop onto him. The wind is blowing a perfect
gale. Dr. Rembert has been in & had a talk with us about our going
home. He declares nothing has troubled him so much in a long time,
he says nothing will go on right if we go away. Mr. Barnwell is talking
of winding up about April. Then I think we must go. I will realy be
very sorry to brake up here. It has been so very pleasant. It makes me
sad to think some of us may never meet again.

Charlottesville<br>
Monday Night March 10″ 62

Every body was up bright & early to see Mr. & Mrs. Barnwell off, I
declared it was right sad to see them go off. I like them both very much
& it was pleasant to have them in the house. Dr. McIntosh was up &
dressed quite early. I quite missed my usual morning attentions to him,
for three weeks past every morning I've bathed his face & hands. I am
very very glad to see him able to help himself once more, but am sorry
I will have nothing more to do for him. Not withstanding the wet
morning we have had a beautiful day. Tis lovely out tonight, bright
moonlight with here & there a star. Mr. Miscaley went down to Gordonsville with Mr. Barnwell, intending to go on to Manassas & from
there to Warren Springs to look after some stores belonging to the association.[9] But he could get no further owing to the communication
having been cut off, the track is torn up. The army has fallen back
from Centerville & Manassas to Winchester, & now they are falling
back from there to the Rapahannack where it is believed we will make
a stand.[10] The accounts Mr. Miscaley gave us of the confusion at Gordonsville was heartrending, hundreds of sick soldiers lieing about on
the ground & damp planks without any thing to protect them not even
a blanket many of them, & nothing under their heads, & worse than
all nothing to eat. Car loads of women & children come up here today

---

9. The Association had been forced to close a hospital at Warren Springs, Virginia,
on March 7, 1862.

10. Confederate General Joseph E. Johnston was retreating from Manassas and its vicinity in the face of General George McClellan's superior forces; Johnston planned to
fall down to a more strategic location where he could make a stand.

& the streets are alive with officers & men who have run up here for a few days until they can find out where they are to go. All of our men who were discharged to camp come back they dont know where to find their companys a dreadful state of things exists, let us hope it is not for any length of time. Esse went down stairs after we had come up & heard a man playing a banjo, so she asked Willie[11] to go & call him to play under our window. Of course he came, & such music[.] Dr. Rembert came down to listen, so he Marie & myself enjoy a good talk while Esse & Nonie were entertained at the window by the minstralls. Directly I heard them both shriek out with laughter & run away from the window, what they saw I dont know, for they wouldent tell us. Esse got very much provoked with Marie because she told her she thought it improper to be looking out of the window at the negroes, seems to me Esse looses her temper quite frequently of late.

Thursday Night March 13″ 62

Charlottesville

Bad weather has set in again. The air is damp & raw & I would not be supprised if by morning it snowed. As soon as I saw poor Bently this morning I knew he would not live. Tis terable at any time to see any one die, but doubly so when they are in a strange land far away from all you love or who care for you. Dr. Rembert is still in bed. I went up after dinner to see him, he talked & laughed a good deal, when we spoke of coming down for fear of his talking too much he said "no I would like you to stay until tea time" of course we couldent do that. As usual he had to tease me about the Dr., he said my friendship for Mc (as he calls him) was a sort of {fad} with me. That I was redy at any moment to defend him. It worried me some at first until I talked it over with my dear little friend Marie. She of course put it all right. I had a beautiful Note from Miss Higgins[12] today thanking me for letting her know of the Dr.'s illness. I had also a letter from Dickie & one from Caroline Bacot. Mrs. Singleton[13] called to see us this morning.

---

11. Willie, "a yellow boy," and his mother, Old Willie, were slaves hired by the Association for the Maupin House.

12. Fannie Higgins (b. ca. 1838) was James McIntosh's fiancée.

13. Probably Mary Lewis Carter Singleton of Richland County, South Carolina; she was the mother of Mrs. Barnwell.

Esse went out with her to take a walk. The war news is incouraging today a dispatch was received here today announsing a great victory to us in Missoury.[14] Both McCulloch[15] & McIntosh[16] are reported among the killed. The Yankees are down upon Mr. Welles since the success of the Virginia.[17] Edward[18] speaks of returning to camp in the morning, we all regret it. When I went my rounds at the Monticello this afternoon I found Bently still breathing but there is no hope for him, I called to see if the wine I caryed Mr. Campbell in the morning had agreed with him, he said it did agree & would like some more[,] that he had relished it more than any thing he had tasted since his illness. I ran over here for some & took it to him. Poor creature what a pleasure to be able to do any thing for him.

Monday afternoon Mch 17″ 62

The weather is beautiful & spring like. Too pleasant to stay indoors. I was at the Monticello from ten to half past twelve. Newton Fowles went off to camp this morning. Twas realy affecting to see Miss Reynolds take leave of him she shuck his hand a long time while the tears filled her eyes, she said God bless & prosper you, then raising his hands to her lips she bade him farewell. I too was sorry to see the poor boy go. I saw Frank McQueen & Hanford McQueen[19] for a few minutes this morning. Dr. Rembert & Dr. McIntosh road out to Monticello just before dinner on horseback. They got back about a half hour after we had dined, looking quite faged. They were so much pleased with their visit that they have invited us to go out with them tomorrow. I hope the weather will be fine, I should very much like to go. Mr.

---

14. Actually, the Confederates were defeated at Pea Ridge, Arkansas, on March 8, 1862.

15. Brigadier General Benjamin McCulloch (b. 1811) was killed at the Battle of Pea Ridge, Arkansas, on March 7, 1862.

16. Brigadier General James McIntosh (b. 1828) was also killed at Pea Ridge.

17. Gideon Welles was Lincoln's secretary of the navy; the Confederates had raised the former U.S.S. Merrimack, a frigate, and refitted it as the ironclad C.S.S. Virginia although it was still generally known as the Merrimack. It had some success ramming Federal naval ships in March, and the crew acquitted itself well in the Battle of the Monitor and Merrimack on March 9, 1862.

18. Edward McIntosh, James's brother and a soldier.

19. Probably the brother of Frank McQueen and son of General John McQueen.

Jones came in & dined with us today, he is delighted to get out once more. I have just had a funny scene with the little yellow boy William who waits around here. He came to the door to tell Esse Nonie was in the Store. He said Nonie with out puting the Master before it so I told him never to let me hear him say Nonie again. His eyes flashed with anger, & he said I cant call him Master Nonie when he isent my master. I never saw a more stuborn little villan than he is, I have not the slightest use for a Virginia negroe.

Charlottesville<br>Tuesday Night March 18″ 62

All things pleasant like every thing else must have an end. So is this most delightful of days now at an end. But the memory of it will live forever in my mind. Every thing seemed to conspire to make it as agreable as possible for us. The Sun was bright & clear, the sky was the deepest blue, & the air as mild & spring like as could be. The day was all the most fastidious could have desired. We hurried through at the Monticello & were redy to start at eleven oclock, precisely at that hour the carriage was announced, in a few minutes we were all bonneted & cloaked. The gentlemen met us in the hall & packed us away in a nice open carriage, we started off in heigh spirits. The very idea of a ride was exhilarating, when we got as far as the railroads we found the cars hadent passed so we had to wait a few minutes. While there we heard that our late reported victory in Arkansas was confirmed by telegraph.[20] The enemy met with tremendous loss. But we have losed McCulloch. Dr. Rembert got the conductor to move back & alow us to pass, soon we were splashing & plunging along the miserable roads, which leads out to Monticello. Marie was perfectly terified she caught & held my hand & several times comanded the driver to stop & let her get out, but he kept stedely on, presently we came to a gate at the head of an avenue which wound through a beautiful farm to a magnificent house belonging to Mr. Alexander Reeves.[21] Never have I seen anything more beautiful. The landscape was perfect, for miles around there was a succession of hills some covered with young wheat looking

---

20. See entry of March 13, 1862.

21. Possibly Dr. Alexander Rives, one of the surgeons at the Charlottesville General Hospital.

like mounds of green velvet dotted here & there among others whose bright coloured earth had just been turned up redy for grain, while others still remain covered with gray grass, all lending to the picturesqueness of the scene. The road ran just at the base of the mountain I saw a little mountain stream come trickling down through its bed, & a little further on just under a clump of trees by the side of the road a cool spring of sparkling water gushes out employing itself through a rustic spout the whole effect is beautiful, soon we found ourselves near the enclosure containing the tomb of Jefferson, we got out of the carriage & walked up to it, the gentlemen opened the gate for us & we went in. A more neglected desolate place one could not imagine. The toom which is of comon brown stone spiral in form is mutelated & defaced in every possible way. I picked up a few fragments which had been chiped of[f] by some rude hand, & gathered a few seed from the scotch broom which seems to grow wild over the place. Dr. Rembert, Marie, Esse & myself walked up to the house by a ruged path. The first thing which strikes you is the want of care about the place. The first thing we saw was the entrance to the underground tunnel through which it is said Jefferson escaped during the revolution. It is nearly filled up now, only a small appature being visable which is kept open I suppose mearly to show visiters where it is. We then entered the yard which is covered with a soft green grass, pleasant to the eyes. The trees are large & extend over the whole yard, a few stunted cedars are scattered here & there, there are also some clumps of hawthorn which still retain some of their bright orange berrys. The gentlemen hunted up the old lady a Mrs. Wheeler (whos husband leases the place,)[22] she soon opened the door for us & we walked in. The porch is not very large with stone steps & large stone collums which support the roof, in the cealing of which is fasened a cumpus, against the wall just over the door is the face of a clock. You enter through double doors a sort of hall or rotunda. A few portrates & ingravings are strung around, & the clock whose imense waits hand down on either side teling the day of the week as it unwindes. We saw the ladder which was used to get up to the clock to wind it. There is very little that was owned by Jefferson

---

22. Joseph or Joel Wheeler was the caretaker of Monticello; his stewardship led to a decline in the estate's condition.

now in the house. The modle of the ship which Levy,[23] the present owner of the house, now commands, the (Vandalia) ornaments one side. Near by sat an antique table with a war club said to have belonged to some indian chiefs, there was also another wepon composed of wood & sword fish teeth very curious, we each beged a tooth which the old lady granted. We then went over the house, I never was more disappointed. There isent a large room in the whole house. Every door way has two doors, one of wood the other of glass excepting the chambers which were both of wood. The parlor is a very pretty room partly octagon in shape with two large mirors built in the wall, the floor was of wild cherry & mahogany & as slipery as glass. The dining room is very small its chief beauty being a very curious mantlepiece, there was a nitch at one end for the sofa & a small cubard in one end. Just off this opened a small room with nitches in the wall for statues. It must have been very pretty, but is now filled with dust & dirt. The chambers are very small, with little recesses in the wall for beds which put me in mind of the burths on bord ship. The ball room which is the largest room in the house is quite too small, & in the thurd story, the ceeling runs up almost to a point & on the top there is a small sky light at one end just over the back porch is the wine closet for the ball room all very convenient. I dont see what could have been the idea of having a ball room on the top of the house & with stairs so narrow it is impossible for more than one person to go up at a time. To be sure hoops were not worn in Jeffersons time, but they [are] even too narrow for the gourd dresses. At each end of the passage is a sort of door in the roof with steps leading up to it, out of which I got on to the top of the house, where I saw the country for fifty miles around. Charlottesville was laid out before me like a panorama, there was the river winding through this lovely vallee. It was a scene to see but not to discribe. After going over the house we found twas time for dinner, so we selected a sweet spot on the lawn near a fallen tree, where we spred the cold vian[d]s we brought with us, all except Marie & Dr. Rembert seated ourselves on the grass where we enjoyed the good things of our basket. When we had dined we walked about to enjoy the fresh air &

---

23. Uriah P. Levy (1792–1862), a United States naval officer with a controversial career, had purchased Monticello in 1831.

see the covered ways which run from the kitchen to the house. The
gentlemen went back into the house to see what they could find in the
way of relicks, before long they came out to where I was sitting, Dr. R.
puled out a shoe lase out one pocket & a cup out of the other. I re-
monstrated but he said Mc has a cup for you, by that time Mc came up
with the cup in his hand saying See Mrs. Bacot what I have for you. I
did not like to refuse nor did I like to accept, I felt I was encouraging
a very bad habit & said so, but the Drs. agreed that we might as well
have what we could get as the Yankees. I said nothing more, so Dr. Mc
told me he had a piece of one of the old mahogany chairs belonging to
Jefferson for me, that I could not refuse. I declare it was very kind in
him to think of me. While Esse & Marie were diging up some roots of
flowers on the other side of the house I gathered some evergreens, Ivy,
perywinkle & hawthorn. The ride home was delightful. I was not in
the least tiard, I dressed a glass with the greens I had gathered & put it
into Dr. Mc room. It seems the gentlemen have enjoyed the day as
much as we have. I have been to see poor Campbell since my return he
is I think graduly waisting. So it is the world over, while some enjoy
themselves others are dieing.

Charlottesville
Sunday night Mch 23d. 62

We started out this morning intending to go to our own church but
just as we got by the Presbyterian church we saw crowds of people coming from that direction, & several of those whom we knew to be Epis-
copalians entering the Presbyterian church so we concluded there was
no service at our own & entered too. Esse & Nonie went on when we
returned we found them waiting for us, they found there was service at
our church they say the church was crouded so was the one we attended. Quantities of strangers are here. tonight we went to hear Mr.
Hogg again I was very anxious to hear the conclusion of the subject of
which he only gave us a part this morning. Walter took tea with us &
went with Esse, Marie & Dr. Rembert, & Edward & I went together.
Twas decidedly the best effort I have heard Mr. Hogg make since I
came here. His language was realy chas[te] & beautiful.

After we all returned Esse gave us a little cold supper which the gentlemen seemed to enjoy. Dr. McIntosh did not eat any, he looked
badly & there was a dark circle around his eyes I feared he was sick

again Marie came up stairs before we had the supper. Some how or other Mrs. Osborns name was mentioned by Esse, which set both the Dr.'s to talking about her. Dr. R. defended her & said Mr. Barnwell had been too hard on her, he refused to take her home with him & had scarcely furnished her with money enough to bear her expenses. Dr. McIntosh said he dident see that Mr. B. had been so hard on her, that he would not take her home that she had not acted in any way to command the respect or attention of a gentleman & that he wouldent feel himself bound to show her any. Dr. R. contended that she was a woman & therfore entitled to the protection of many the only thing I said was that I thought if a woman did not behave as a woman ought she could not expect consideration from any one. Dr. McIntosh fully agreed with me. Then all of the others who Mr. B. had brought on at the same time with us came in for a good share of ridicule, I realy was disgusted & said nothing Esse said a good deal. So when Walter left I got up & went to the fireplace where Dr. R. was standing saying as I did so, well we have had enough scandle for one Sunday night. It was just what I felt, Dr. R. I saw was offended[,] imediately I was sorry, but made no appoligy because I did not mean it any more for him than the others, when we came up stairs Esse said to me she thought Dr. McI. was going to be sick again so I thought I would go down & find out If he was & what I could do for him. He says he is quite well that nothing is the matter, I am glad to hear it, but I fear he will think me trouble-some always asking so particularly after his health.

Charlottesville
Wednesday night Mch 26" 62

Ten men came to the Monticello today on the mid day train. They were equaly divided between Marie & myself. One by the name of Lawson from Darlington. Twas sad to hear them tell of the hardships they underwent before they got here, for some weeks past they have been without tents without comforts of any kind, they were sent to Orange Court House, & had to lye on the floor, they had only two meals a day, with no attention & not able to attend to themselves. When I told them I was from Carolina & would attend to any of their wants, twas realy pleasant to see their hard thin faces brighten up, & one said why Madam it makes me think of you like kin folks. Miss Rey-nolds came in to our room this afternoon & gave us a most amusing account of some of Mr. Hicks[24] poor family. I hear he has begun to lay down the law in fine stile there all redy. We have dubed him my Lord Hicks. Our evening down stairs passed off even pleasanter than usual. A report came in today that Jacksons army has been dreadfuly cut to pieces.[25]

Charlottesville<br>Saturday noon March 29" 62

I did not retire until near one oclock, waiting for the Doctors to come in. It occured to me that if any thing was the matter with either of them they would not be brought over, so I determined not to sit up any longer. We were all down at breakfast this morning, even Marie. Both Dr. R. & McI. looked the worst for their late hours. One of the first things we heard when we went down was that both Campbell & the wounded man had died in the night. Tis a great relief to me to hear that Campbell is at last relieved from his suffering. I think he was a good man. The other poor fellow I fear has left this world of suffering for a worse, I hear he was very dissapated that for several weeks past he has been under the influence of liquor he was at the time was why he fell. That too it is thought was the cause of his death. There was a down mail this morning. I hear we are to have none from the south for some weeks. There is a great change in the weather, about ten oclock It rain sleeted & snowed. A troop of minstrells came in this morning. Esse has just given me some nice coffee & a roll for lunch. Marie hasent come over yet, I left her still fetching about the Monticello. Mr. Hicks is very busy about looks very consequenchal.

Night

This has indeeed been a changable day, sunshine, sleet, snow, Rain, thunder & lightning. A most shocking kind of day. Just before we went down to dinner we were attracted by a terable cry in the street. We soon found it emenated from the little carrie all which was standing at

---

24. The Reverend G. W. Hicks, a member of the executive committee of the Association, had been in charge of the hospital at Warren Springs until it closed. By November 1, 1862, he was the chaplain at the Association's hospital at Petersburg and went from there to the Manchester Hospital to serve in the same position.

25. Stonewall Jackson's men acquitted themselves well at the first Battle of Kernstown, Virginia, on March 23, 1862, but were outnumbered by Federal forces and suffered large losses.

the hospital gate with some men in it. We at first thought it might be one of the soaldiers which they were moving down from the upper hospital for it sounded very much like the raving of a delirious man. Nonie came rushing up, so we stoped him & made him tell us what the matter was, he said they were bringing down a black man who was deranged from one of the upper hospitals where his master had been staying & who was now trying to make arrangements to send him home to S. Carolina. I hear he was a most faithful servant but dreadfuly homesick, which it is thought has caused the poor fellows present trouble.

Dr. Rembert was called round to the Hotel to see some officers wife & child who is sick there, he heard some terable news about the Yankees advancing on Warrenton,[26] which would make it necessary for us to fall back from here. I saw something was weighing on the Dr.'s mind all tea time, about nine oclock we came up, soon after Dr. McI. came, then Dr. R., he came to our door asked if he might come in saying he had something to tell us, we admitted him, he has been advising us to go home, he thinks it best as there is danger of our having to evacuate the place & he thinks it best we should go while we can do so without trouble. Of course, we consented to go at any time he might think best, I dare say it is very well, for although we do dislike going as long as we could be of any use here, still now that Mr. Hicks has come down to the Monticello, I have lost interest in it, I fear he will make it very disagreeable for us. This evening he came into the dining room while we were there, & said he saw Miss Reynolds had entirely too much to do. She told him it was strange he should make the discovery when she had not done so. Why he said it is now six oclock & you have not tea on the table. She told him she was quite redy for it when it was redy to be brought in. That shows you have too much to do said he, you are helping with the diet in here when you ought to be in the kitchen hurrying the servants. Now Miss Reynolds does not help with the diet, she mearly keeps the soup pot boiling. Marie told him she dident see that Miss R. had any thing too much to do that we were perfectly satisfied with Miss R. & she with us, that she thought twas his business to push up the servants & see that the meals were brought in at the

---

26. Although Jackson's men were retreating up the Shenandoah Valley in order to divert Federal troops from McClellan, Warrenton was not attacked at this time.

proper time where upon Mr. Hicks went off highly disgusted with the whole affair.

Charlottesville

Monday night March 31st" 62

About noon it cleared up so beautifuly bright that Marie & myself determined to go out after dinner to pay some visits, we went about five oclock. Mrs. Singleton came for Esse to walk Marie & I went first to Mrs. Hornseys[27] neither of the elder ladies were in[.] Miss Lizzie is rather a pretty young girl, with brown curls, but wants polish. We then went round to see a Mrs. Tom Taylor who some time ago call[ed] at the hospital to see us, she was not in, & we then went on to Mrs. Patens where we had a charming time, she is a realy pleasant person, told us she was packing up & arranging her effects so as to move at a moments warning. Dr. Guin of this state came in just before we left he is one of the Confederate Surgeons. Mrs. P.'s little cottage is beautifully situated on a slight elevation, which commands a view of the country for miles around. I could not help sighing as I stood at the door when we were leaving, to think the Yankees very soon [will] be in posession of this lovely land. Just after we got back Dr. McIntosh taped at the door & handed me in a beautiful little ruler he had made for me of the piece of mahogany he got at Monticello the day we were all out there. After a while Esse came in with an invitation from Mrs. Singleton to us to go round after tea & spend the evening with her, we entended accepting, but while we were at tea a dispatch came for Dr. Rembert, saying a special train was on the way with 30 sick men for our hospitals, we of course had to go to work immediately at the Monticello to get beds redy for them. Marie & myself went over first but could find no one we wanted. Mr. Hicks, Mr. Jones, Miss Reynolds & all the servants were off we came back again for candles & Dr. Rembert went over with us, twas some time before Mr. Hicks could be found, when he came he was in a great passion to think Dr. R. would take the liberty of bringing sick men into the house before he had said he was redy to receive them. Of course we were only amused at him. I never knew a more consiquential man. We were very nearly redy when the poor creatures came in. I never have seen a more wretched batch come in at any

27. Probably Mrs. C. C. Hornsey of the Charlottesville Ladies Aid Association.

time. They tell a dreadful tail of suffering & privation without tents, often without food & no bed to rest their weary bodies upon. As soon as they were comfortably in bed we had food given them which they ate eagerly twas a sad sad sight. I cant bear the idea of going home now & leaving them to the care of others. Dr. Rembert told Marie & myself tonight that he dident now see the necessity of our going so soon that if the government was sending so many sick men here they could not apprehend danger for this place soon. Dr. Cabell[28] who is the Surgeon of the post, has been ordered to get redy accomidations for double as many men as he has ever had here, which will be about eight hundred or a thousand men. Over 150 came tonight at the same time ours came. I hear a great many deaths are occuring at the Delevan[29] at this time. We did not get through at the Monticello until half past ten, Esse had some supper for us which we enjoyed, I am so tired I can scarcely move running up & down the stairs at the Monticello is no easy work.

---

28. James Lawrence Cabell (b. 1813), a professor of anatomy, surgery, and physiology at the University of Virginia, was the surgeon in charge of the Charlottesville Hospital.

29. The Delevan was one of the buildings which made up the Charlottesville General Hospital.

Chapter 5

# April 1–June 20, 1862

*"We see the worst feature of the war."*

Charlottesville
Tuesday night Apr 1st" 62

I've been as busy & as happy as the day is long. All the morning I was imployed at the Monticello. I realy felt quite in my element again making punch & preparing nourishment. Dr. Rembert is complaining again. After dinner Dr. McIntosh asked me to go round to the Dagonian gallery with him to take my choice of likenesses we went about four oclock he gave me three to choose from, for some time I could not make up my mind which I liked best, at last I took one. It is realy a handsome present too handsome for as I told him I did not care about the case in the least. As we were about leaving I saw the man had made up his mind that we were something more than meare friends, so I said dont you think my brother & myself very much alike, he looked at me for a while then said yes maam I would take you for brother & sister, the Dr. enjoyed the joak.

When we had goten through at the Monticello Marie & myself thought we would take a walk, before coming in. We stroled down by the depot a little way off we saw a beautifuly green yard which we went up to[.] A servant was standing at the gate & we asked if we might go in & look at the flowers, he opened the gate & invited us in very politely. the flowers were indeed beautiful Hyasinths, crokasses, lillys, & heartsease were in great profusion. The man gave me a beautiful heartsease I felt a perfect thrill of joy as he handed it to me. Dr. McIntosh has gone out to call on the young ladies at Capt. Taylors, Dr. Rembert has been amusing him self teasing me about my letter I was writing down Stairs after tea. He came in here for a few moments Marie has just been in to fix him off for the night, he has pain in his face & a terable cold. Just as he was leaving our room he said I declare I cant let you ladies go home, you have spoiled us this winter we cant do without you.

Charlottesville
Friday night April 4" 62

Another charming spring day, I longed to wander among the hills so green & fresh, gather wild flowers & listen to the birds. As we started along to church this afternoon the sweet air faning our cheeks I dreamt of home. I have for the past few days had an intense longing for home. Yet I would hate to leave this lovely country. The flowers are beginning to bloom in profusion & the trees are puting out, I cant bear to think of snow again. The streets were filled with ladies this afternoon, a good many Marylanders among them. Dr. Rembert is beginning to be sorry he said any thing to us about returning home, he told Marie & myself today he could not do without us. Mr. McMaster[1] had a letter from Mr. Barnwell today, he speaks of coming on shortly, & says something of dividing his force between this place S. Carolina & the West. Marie & myself have bespoken a place out west.

Charlottesville
Saturday night Apr 5" 62

Rained a little this morning remained cloudy all the fore noon. Dr. Rembert had a telegram this morning early saying 70 sick had been sent to him, none of them S. Carolinians, we had every thing redy at the Monticello by half past nine, the train got in at ten, eight were sent to the Monticello. I have six of them, mostly Georgians, some quite sick. They say they have been without food for four days & without medical attendance, their clothes have not been changed for three weeks. First I had the sickest shown to their beds then took them Soup, & as soon as possible had warm water & soap for them to have a wash & change their clothes. One poor fellow a Missippian beged me for liniment to rub his side[.] I told him I had none but the Doctor would soon be round & give him some. I was very busy all the morning with them getting them comfortably fixed, the more I see of the suffering of our brave men the more wicked & unrighous I feel the war to be. Miss Hamsie Miss Singleton[2] & Mrs. Miner called after dinner,

---

1. G. H. McMaster was a member of the Executive Committee of the South Carolina Hospital Aid Association.

2. Probably Rebecca "Decca" Coles Singleton, daughter of Mrs. Singleton and sister of Mrs. Barnwell.

Esse had a boquet of lovely flowers sent her this afternoon. It cleared off beautifully just before sundown, I have been in a perfect glee all the evening. After tea Dr. Rembert got Mr. McMaster to sing My Maryland for us. As soon as we caught the tune, we all tried it. The tune is pretty enough but too tame for the words. We sent to ask Mr. Jackson to come & play it on the flute for us, he came & obliged us, Marie & Esse have been singing My Maryland ever since they came up. I have just asked them to spare me, & save it for another day. I am perfectly convinced I will be sick of it in a little while.

Wednesday night April 9" 62

Never in my life have I seen an April day rain, sleet, snow, all three in quick succession. The mud in the street ankle deep, obliged to be at the Monticello almost the whole day, found it dreadful coming from one house to the other, wonder I dont take my death of cold. Did not know until today that poor Chandler is from Darlington. I scarcely expect to find either he or Gatling alive in the morning. The latter raves like a madman, he has refused to take his medicine all the afternoon. I got him to take a dose for me. I never have seen kinder & more attentive nurses than some of the men have proved themselves. Young Sloan & Mr. Lawson have done their duty faithfuly. Dr. Rembert told Sloan he deserved a medal. The train came up today but brought no mail.

Charlottesville

Saturday night April 12" 62

The work goes heavily on, & I am very well & happy. The first thing I heard when I went to the hospital this morning, was that poor Gatling was no more. He had died at dawn. Martin the man in the same room with Gatling I am told that when he heard G. was dead he sat right up in bed & looked at him, then laid down quietly, without a word. They do not seem to feel any fear or distress for one dieing in the same room, unless he happens to be from their company. Montgomery was something better this afternoon, I dressed his blisters for him this morning, they were as raw & red as a piece of beef. He almost fell asleep while I was dressing them. Marie & Mr. McMaster plaid chess until after eleven tonight. They both play very well. Dr. McIntosh sat by looking very wistfuly, I hear he is a good player. Marie has promised him a game on Monday night. Dr. Lafar came in from Capt. Taylors where he had been to tea with the news that fort Pulaski had surrendered.[3] It is too sad, that one after another of our forts should be given up in this way.

Charlottesville
Sunday night April 13" 62

This has indeed been a day of work, instead of rest. There was so much to do this morning that I couldent get to church. Marie was too unwell to get down to dinner, I came up directly after I had finished mine to try & get her to take a cup of hot coffee, which she did, soon after I went to the window upon hearing the car whistle, I saw Dr. Rembert a little while after coming this way with a sick soldier, a perfect stream of them followed some looking very weak & scarcely able to move along twenty of the worst off were taken to the Monticello. 16 have been put on my two wards, some of them very ill, we did not know they were to be up today so nothing was redy for them, however it did not take long to make beds for them as every thing was at hand & every one redy to help[.] Good kind hearted Miss Reynolds soon had plenty of good soup & bread in rediness, & helped us distribute it to the poor hungry creatures. Then there was punch, poultices, & plasters to be made & put on I did not rest from 1/2 3 until 7. I told some of the young men whom I have been nursing, that they must help me now that I had so much to do. O, yes maam they all said in a breath, we will do any thing for *you*. We can never do too much for you. Tis very gratifing to me to hear all this. I thank God I have been able to do any thing to relieve the sufferings of any of our brave soldiers. Not one of the men who came in today was a South Carolinian. Though I am glad to do what I can for the men of other states I am sorry that our own men should suffer for attention. I have no doubt there are many Carolinians suffering for the very attentions we are bestowing on these men from other states. Our men are out of our reach here having fallen back from these lines. More rain tonight, Marie & myself took our tea up here, we were to[o] fatigued to go down when we got in.

Charlottesville
Monday Night April 14" 62

Was at the hospital by half past eight this morning, made punch & took it round first thing, dressed some dreadful looking blisters, have

---

3. Fort Pulaski in Georgia surrendered on April 11, 1862.

ten ill men on one ward & eight on the other. tonight when I went round on my lower ward, one of the patients a boy about eighteen, was making considerable fuss about his blisters. I told the girl who waits on them, to dress the blisters, but he would not alow her, said he did not wish any one except the doctor to do it[.] I went to him & asked if he would not alow me to do it for him, while I was removing the old dressing he cryed like a child, I felt sorry for him, he looks so young & delicate. Mr. Hicks asked Marie & myself this afternoon if we wouldent go to the Delevan hospital to see two South Carolinians who were very sick there. The old man was very anxious to be moved to one of the Carolina hospitals. Mr. Hicks & Marie went up to see them (I had too much to do to leave). They found the son had died on yesterday morning, the old man had come on a short time ago from home to nurse him & himself took sick, tis a very sad case. Mr. Hicks got a carriage & had him brought down to the Monticello, & gave him a part of his room, where he will be well attended to. Twas very kind & thoughtful of him. Dr. Lafar & Mr. Jackson went off this morning to see after our Carolina soldiers, & make arrangements necessary for hospitals, now they are cut off entirely from us. There is some little talk of moving our hospital to Petersburg if our troops continue on that line.[4] I should like very much to go there. Heard today that Mrs. Barnwell has another little boy. Mr. B. is expected very soon. Marie & Mr. McMaster are at chess again.

Charlottesville<br>Tuesday night April 15″ 62

The old man which was brought down on yesterday, enjoyed his comfortable quarters but a short time, he breathed his last this morning about nine oclock, I saw him but a short time before he died, he was perfectly colected & was very greatful for all that was done for him. I've had very hard work today, dressing blisters is no easy task. The little boy who came in on Sunday has some pretty tender ones, he

---

4. Ironically, the Association's hospital at Petersburg, which opened later that month, was never as full as the Charlottesville hospitals during this time; although it had facilities for 450 soldiers, it was usually filled with North Carolinians because there were not enough South Carolina troops in the area and it was deemed too difficult to move wounded soldiers there from other facilities.

wept all the time I was dressing them, poor child I learn he is but six-teen. I am very weary too much so to write. It has rained all day.

Charlottesville
Thursday night April 17" 62

The heat has been oppressive today, almost like a may day in Caro-lina. I was so faged last night that I could not sleep. The moon light streamed into the room lighting it, was up very early this morning & was down stairs before breadfast, one side of my face was a good deal swolen from a sensitive tooth. Dr. Rembert told me all my men were much better today & that he found every thing in perfect order on my wards. This morning as I dressed an old mans blisters he shed tears they were so soar he said he could not help it. I go through many pain-ful scenes. This evening just as I was about to leave my upper ward it occured to me to go into one of the rooms again & ask after the men, they were all better except one who said "my head ache is coming on again, & my blisters pain me very much, if you could dress them for me in the morning I would thank you very much." I told him if he would like it I would do it for him then, poor creature the most greatful ex-pression lit up his face in an instant, I of couse dressed his blisters, he was profuse in thanks. Got over just before tea, Dr. Walker[5] took tea with us, very warm tonight[.] I am so sorry I cant attend the services at our church which take place every morning this week at eleven oclock, I have so much to do at the hospital that I cant spare a half hour during the morning. Had a short nap after dinner today which refreshed me very much.

Charlottesville
Friday night April 18" 62

Another bach of poor weary soldiers came in this afternoon, only three were taken to the Monticello, they were put on my ward, none of them very ill. The heat was over powering all day just before sun-down there was quite a thunder storm, which cooled the air some what, but did not last long. Mr. McMaster had a telegram from Dr. Lafar today stating that he has rented a building for a hospital in Pe-tersburg. Mr. McMaster & Dr. Rembert were both amazed, for neither of them had been consulted about it before Dr. Lafar left, he was

---

5. R. E. Walker of Beaufort was a physician at the Soldiers' Home.

mearly to go & see about some place of safety to remove our stores to if there should be a necessity for doing so. Tonight after Tea Mr. Mc-Master invited Dr. Rembert & Dr. McIntosh over to the store to cokus over Dr. Lafars action. I think Dr. R. is a good deal put out that Dr. Lafar should have done so important a thing without advice from other members of the assosiation. I fear there will be some little disturbance about the matter yet.

Charlottesville
Monday night April 21″ 62

Such a day to be obliged to go out I would not look out this morning for fear I would not have the courage to venture. Marie & myself had our breakfast sent up to us as we wished to go immediately to the hospital. I couldent put on a clean dress to drag over those dirty stairs in, nor could I go down to breakfast in the one I wished to wear over there, found two more of my convalessants in bed this morning, the weather I suppose has effected them. I have another case of ——[6] on my lower ward, God grant I may escape again, the poor man seems anxious to have me do for him, & likes me about him. I feal no fear & can only hope there is no danger. I went over to the hospital in a pouring rain this after noon, I dont know how I kept dry, I had no umbrella. Miss Reynolds good Soul had some nice cakes for me[.] one of the men asked me if the hospitals were moved to Petersburg, if I would not go along too. I am thankful they like to have me do for them, poor creatures. The rain seems to be over, the stars are all out. Mr. McMaster had a telegram from Mr. Barnwell tonight telling him to send on supplies to Richmond for Petersburg as soon as possible. The papers have full accounts of our great victory as the Yankees them selves acknowledge they were badly whiped.[7] Heard tonight that we had an Army of 75 or 80 thousand men at Yorktown, more than were wanted, some have been sent to reinforce Jackson. Hear the mortality at the Delevan is very great, five died there today. Am afraid Jacksons army will suffer greatly falling back in such dreadful weather. Dr. Rembert has been joaking me about my journal again tonight declaired I prom-

---

6. Bacot left a long blank space in her journal instead of naming the disease.

7. Bacot may be referring to the Battle of Shiloh; there were no decisive Confederate victories at this time.

ised to let him see it one of these days, we all live here just as one family so very pleasantly together, will be too sorry to break up.

Charlottesville
Tuesday noon. April 22d" 62

The sky began to clear & I thought we would have a bright day, about half past eleven Marie called me to the door to look at an enormous black cloud in the west, e'er long it came up. There was a flash of lightning & instantly after a terable clap of thunder. The hail poured in torants for at least fifteen minutes, covering the ground & every thing like a carpet. It was soon washed away by the rain which followed. It cleared up before it was time for us to come over.

Night

The air is very cool, a heigh wind is blowing, a telegram came after tea to Dr. Rembert that 70 sick would be sent from Gordonsville to-night on a special train. Dr. R. cant take but 18[,] 4 at the Monti-cello[,] 14 at Midway, the rest go to Dr. Cabell. Dr. Rembert is quite unwell, Dr. McIntosh has gone down to the cars which has just come in to receive the sick. Dr. R. has paid us a visit in our room since tea, only Marie & myself were up here when he came in. He got talking about Esse, I am glad to see he understands her so thurely. It seems Esse has complained of Marie & myself to Dr. R. I am sorry for I thought we were very particular in our attentions to her. The weather has been so mild for some time past that Mr. McMaster alowed our wood to get very low today it gave out entirely. Fortunately we pro-cured a small load just before night. Jackson went to Richmond today to see about getting cars to take our Stores to Petersburg. Tonight Mr. McMaster got a telegraph telling him it was impossible to send supplys by Gordonsville, the cars are not runing down from there, but were runing up from Winchester. There will be an effort to get them off in the morning. Some twenty wagons belonging to Jacksons Army came in today they seem to be bringing all the surplus bagage away from Staunton. It looks rather Suspicious, I hear he is being heavily rein-forced.

Charlottesville
Wednesday night April 23d" 62

Last night I did not retire until twelve oclock, no sooner had I got comfortably in bed, than there was a great wrapping at the door, I went to the window & found it was Miss Reynolds wished to get in I went down & opened the door for her. I had a miserable night was very sick, had to get up twice, vomited quantities of bile. Have been in bed nearly the whole day, attempted to get up & dress as usual this morning but came so near fainting I was forced to go to bed again, went to the Monticello about ten, couldent stay[.] Dr. Rembert has been in twice to see me, he has proscribed a blue pill, but does not think there is much the matter. Old Mrs. Carter came in today the dear old lady is very sad, her daughters are being scattered in different parts of the country, & it is likely she may never see them any more. She told Esse that a young Mrs. Preston had just returned from Richmond & told her that a young lady there had received a few days since, from a young friend of hers now living in Washington City, a present of a simple pincushion. It struck her as being so simple a present to risk so much to send it, that she suspected it might be for some purpus, so she riped it, & found a letter written on fine French paper, teling her that she had learned from some officers boarding at the same house with her, that it was not the purpose of McClellan to attack the peninsula with his whole force, but to attack us at the same time at Gordonsville & force his way to Richmond. The letter was sent immediately to the War Office. I hear that eight Negroes deserted last night. Tis thought they have gone over to the enemy. Times look squally, Jacksons waggons still continue to come down in numbers, at least forty have passed through with in the last two days[.] One of the teamsters told us today he was going down to Gordonsville for provisions for the army. He reported the panic in Staunton as terable.

Charlottesville
Tuesday night April 29" 62

This has been a genuine April day Sunshine & rain alternately. This morning directly after breakfast I went up Main Street a little way to settle an account I left partly settled yesterday afternoon. The prices asked for goods here are perfectly fearful, I got me a dress, for which in ordinary time I would have paid about three or four dollars, I gave eight, pins of the commonest kinds 40 cents a paper & 50 cents for common soap a cake, calico we used to give 12 1/2 cts" for is now 62 1/2, I wonder the people are not ashamed to tell the prices. Mr. Barnwell came today, he was delighted to see us all, he is full of the Petersburg hospital, but says the Surgeon General seems to think we had better continue these here for some time longer, as one of our Carolina Regiments has been sent some where on the Fredericksburg road & all of their sick will have to be sent here. Mr. Barnwell is staying with Mrs. B.'s aunt Mrs. Southhall.[8] I am very sorry for we would have him to talk to us after tea if he staid here. Dr. Rembert & McIntosh are both a little blue about not going to Petersburg. The Surgeon general doesent seem disposed to let them go yet a while at least. Marie & myself both bid to stay where ever they are.

Charlottesville<br>Wednesday Night. April 30″ 62

The weather does not encourage cheerfulness, therefore I feel at liberty to indulge in a fit of homesickness. Mr. Barnwell said if we would volunteer for the war, he would give us furlough, I thought of course we could get them at any time we wanted them[.] Marie told Dr. Rembert this morning we wished to go home for a few weeks, but he said we could not be spaired, I felt it was asking a great deal, but I am so anxious to see them all at home, then too I want to know what is going on, neither Pa or Sister tell me any thing I want to know when they write which is very seldom. Dr. Walker was invited down to dinner that he might be present at the caucus which was held after wards. From what I can learn it is decided that all of our hospitals here shall be kept up until the Surgeon General orders them closed. They are to go on the same. It was decided we should stay here. Dr. Rembert confessed himself much pleased, & I am sure we are[.] Dr. Lafar came in from Richmond while we were at dinner. He gives a glowing account of the buildings he has secured for the hopsitals, he say the people are very kind & attentive, much more Southern in their feelings than these here. Mr. McMaster is to stay here to superintend these hospitals, I hear Mr. Hicks is to go to Petersburg. The Store is to be given up, & The gentlemen who have been sleeping over there are to occupie rooms in this house. Mr. Barnwell asked all of the servants if they would be willing to go with us if we had to leave here, they all say they are perfectly willing to go. Matilda & Annie both said they would follow me, Mr. Barnwell was giving us a bit of the prices for articles of

---

8. Possibly the wife of James C. Southall, a local newspaper editor.

food at home, Tea $8 a pound, coffee not to be had at any price, Ham $1 a pound, butter 60 cts", chickens $1 a pair, Turkeys $3 a piece. Sugar 25 & 30 cts a pound, I cant see what people are to live on, even salt one of the greatest necessities of life $20 to 30 a sack.

It has been raining nearly all the afternoon, I went to tea feeling very gloomy & homesick, I noticed Dr. McIntosh ait nothing & looked sad. I wondered what could be the matter when we got up from the tea table he left the room, Dr. Rembert wrote on a slip of paper & handed it to me, "This was to be McIntosh's wedding night you must excuse him." As soon as I read it I felt as if I could have wept, poor fellow, he feels it deeply. I left the little party down stairs to come & write him a note of sympathy. It had escaped my mind that this was the night fixed upon for his marriage until Dr. Rembert reminded me of it. I showed Marie the note, she laughed & made great fun of my thinking of writing to the Doctor; but said she would take him the note, which she did. Mr. Hicks sleeps in the house tonight he came in after we had finished tea. Tonight ends another month, who can tell what the history of the next may be. Mr. Barnwell drew up a gloomy picture of the state of affairs as they now exist at the dinner table to-day. Davis seems to have lossed every friend he had by his obstinacy & self will. Mr. B. even said he thought it would be a na[t]ional blessing if Davis were to die. I firmly believe God will deliver our beloved country yet. A hard strugle we will have for our independence but I believe he will cary us through. Both Marie & Esse have retired, & the light is anoying them, so I must make redy to follow them.

Charlottesville<br>Thursday noon. May 1st" 62

May has come at last, alas how different from the old May days of my childhood. Then all was bright & lovely, every vase was decked with beautiful flowers & we were robed in white dresses & alowed to rome about at will among the flowers, or in the woods. I remember too with what delight we helped ourselves at lunch, to the lushus bright red strawberrys & cream my dear old GrandMa[9] always had redy for us, when we paid her our accustomed visit. Even after I grew up I went to

---

9. Probably Mary Hart Brockington, whom the Bacots referred to as their grandmother.

May parties to see other children enjoy themselves. It seems so strange to sit here watching the rain come drearly down & see a fire on the hearth, no flowers in the room, & a thick winter dress still on. I have not so much as heard of a strawberry here yet, I see but few spring dresses yet. The fruit trees are just blooming here. Their white & pink flowers look beautifuly & add much to the landscape. I admire the view from my window more every day.

Night

I had often heard that variety was the spice of life. Mr. Barnwell has seen fit to give us a little variety today. It seems he was very much vexed with Dr. Rembert for having his servant whiped. Dr. R. heard that Mr. B. was very much vexed with him, so he came to him immediatly to have a explanation. Dr. R. has been telling us all Mr. B. said to him he did not alow any one to punish his servant, & said a great deal that was realy insulting to the Doctor. Mr. Barnwell had alowed the servants to come to him with complaints against the Doctor, & had believed them. Dr. Rembert acted with a great deal of prudence & good feeling & at last succeeded in pacifying Mr. B.

After tea the Doctor was telling us of all this & said he would vote for some different regulations in the Society, where at Dr. Lafar saw fit to get in a terable passion, & flew at Dr. Rembert without the slightest provocation, to the amazement of us all, for Dr. Lafar is noted for his good nature. Dr. R. kept very quiet & soon convinced the Doctor that he was exciting himself unnecessarily, as he ment nothing personal, That so far from condeming him about what he had done in reference to establishing the hospital, he comended him very much, & thought now that he had learned that he had not done so upon his own responsibility (as was first thought) that he had worked wonders. Things are working smothely again much to the satisfaction of all.

Charlottesville<br>Sunday Morning May 4" 62

I've just run over for a few moments. I feel too badly to go to church having taken fresh cold last night. About eleven oclock last night we had a delightful treat, we had all retired & some were asleep, when I heard very near by the sound of a violin. I awoke Esse, she got up & raised the sash so we could hear better. Oh! I dont know when I ever heard any thing so delightful, I think there was two performers, they plaid perfectly together. I was too sorry when they left off. We have another beautiful day a little cooler than yesterday but that is no objection. All have gone to church but myself. The holy communion is to be celebrated today at our church. Old Poston died a short time after I went to the hospital this morning he spoak to me & seemed perfecly in his mind. I hear he has a wife & seven children. Such cases are not unusual.

### Night

Just after I had sent up the dinner to my lower ward Annie came to me & said Mr. Dychs wanted me to write a letter for him to his mother, but did not like to ask me to do it, as he feared I might think it bould in him. I went up to see him & told him I would write but thought he had best wait a few days as it might frighten his mother to hear he was so sick[.] He agreed with me, but said he thought he would like so much to see her before he died. I tryed to calm him for he began to weep poor man I could but think how much more likely the chance was that he would die, than that he would get well. Dr. Rembert was very late going round this after noon Marie & myself had both goten through before he went. Dr. McIntosh asked me at tea to go to church with him, much to Esse's disappointment, I saw she had set her heart upon going with him. She got almost vexed with me for accepting his invitation. As we were going Dr. McIntosh steped on one of the planks causing it to tilt up just as I was about steping on it & it struck me on the ankle, causing a good deal of pain, we got to church in time to secure a good seat. I liked Mr. Hogg better than I have yet. When Esse & Nonie got in Esse went in & seated her-self in the dark in the parlor. Marie Took the candle to show Dr. Lafar the flowers & found her there.

### Tuesday Night. May 6" 62

I have been as light & joyous as a bird today. The bright sunshine & sweet Spring air, always makes me feel light hearted. The men are all better too, except poor Douglas who has been here for so long, I fear he will die in spite of all our efforts. Dr. Rembert found at the depot a man who had been wounded in a fight on Sunday, he had been brought down on the mornings train from some where near Staunton, & laid on the platform at the Depot. The Doctor with his usual kindness had him brought up to the Monticello, where he now lies, all blue in the face, & suffering terably. A Roman Catholic Priest has been to see him & anointed him. The men were very much amused at the ceremony. There has been quite a change in the house hold arrangements, Dr. Rembert & Dr. McIntosh have taken the room above us, Mr. McMaster has the one next us which the Doctors used to occupie & Mr. Jones & Mills have the one Mr. Barnwell used to have. I went out to shop a little this afternoon[.] Met Mrs. McCall, Dr. Walker came in to tea & to say Adieu he leaves for Petersburg in the morning. Not so cold as last night, still we had fire.

Wednesday Morning May 7" 62

Found the wounded man still alive when I went to the hospital. he is more quiet, & has spoaken, he may live. Two ladies came down from the Delevan Hospital this morning & asked to see the sick we took them round, they were very much pleased, said they liked our small rooms better than the large one at the Delevan. They were Missipians. We are getting quite an abundance of milk now[.] I saw the girl who brought the milk with some bunches of asparagus, she told me she asked ten cents a bunch, & it took four bunches to make a dish full. These Virginians know how to make money if any body does. We have news of a reported victory at YorkTown on Monday, took some cannon & a number of prisoners.[10]

Night

Dr. Rembert seems very much conserned at the state of things at the hospital. No management, the nursing bad & things going wrong generaly. Marie is quite unwell. The moon light is beautiful now.

Monday Night. May 12" 62

I was very busy the whole morning did not get over until two oclock, three men came in before dinner a Captain among them, he was wounded in Thursdays fight[.][11] about four oclock this afternoon more men came in, we had to go over & get them in bed as well as we could. The hospital is dreadfuly crouded. I think the most of them are

---

10. The action at Williamsburg, Virginia, on May 5, 1862—with General James Longstreet and General A. P. Hill leading the Confederate troops, and Major General Joseph Hooker and General Philip Kearny those of the United States—was essentially a Federal victory with heavy casualties on both sides.

11. The Battle of McDowell, Virginia, on May 8, 1862, involved Jackson's men, who repulsed Federal forces under the command of Robert Schenck.

the illest men we have yet gotten in, they certainily are the dirtiest. I had warm water & soap brought as soon as possible, their faces & hands washed, & clean clothes put on them. Mr. Darnell was indefaticable, he arranged every thing in the shortest time & most approved way. When I took the supper round, the poor creatures caught at the milk eagerly. They thought the gruel was very nice & enjoyed it. Mrs. Smith came into the hospital late this afternoon to offer me milk & bread, which I accepted, she soon brought it[.] The sick enjoyed it very much she seems to be a very kind woman. We did not get over until very late just before the tea bel rang. Dr. Carter took tea here tonight. Marie & I had ours up here, we dressed & went down about half past eight. We had a little singing by way of enlivening us, I have seldom been more weary.

Tuesday Night. May 13″ 62

Savary awoke me this morning at half past five, I got up at six & went to the hospital in a half hour. I arranged all of the breakfasts sent it up, then went rounds to see that each man had what he wanted. Some of those who came in last night are very ill[,] one I fear will not be alive more than a few hours longer. I had Capt. Sanders moved into Mr. Darnell's room last night. This morning when I was returning to the hospital after breakfast Miss Smith met me with a beautiful bunch of flowers in her hand she stoped, gave them to me & asked that I would distribute them in the hospital. I took them round myself. I gave Capt. Sanders some of them, he was profuse in his thanks, he left in the town train this morning, when he was leaving his brother in law sent for me to thank me for my kindness he said to his brother, & said they both would remember me with pleasure. After they had left I found the Captain had taken the flowers off with him, I learn he lives in Louisa County about 25 miles from here. He has a wife & three little ones, he was wounded through the th{igh} a painful but not a dangerous wound. I am worn out with the encesent runing up & down stairs & standing up. I could not eat my tea tonight I was so weary. It is very warm tonight, I sat in the parlor alone for nearly an hour after tea by the open window the fresh night air faning my parched brow. The moon light streamed in filling the room with a soft mellow light. I fancied I heard the sighing of the wind among the pines.

Charlottesville
Monday night May 19″ 62

Found that Ma——had died in the night last night, his feet burst a few minutes after he died. He was a great sufferer, I found Montgomery very much exhausted this morning from coughing last night. He told me he thought he would have died in the night, but that he still had hope, I tryed to make him comprehend his state[,] told him he might die at any time & asked if he had been trying to prepare himself for another world he said no, that he thought there was no use, that he had lived in sin so long, that now he need not try to seek forgiveness. Oh! it is so hard to see the men dieing like brutes as if they had no Soul to save[.] I have tryed to talk to them & read to them, but they give me no encouragement, some of them refuse to listen to me. We had presents of Butter, buttermilk, & asparagus, from Mrs. W. P. Farish, this morning also buttermilk & bread, from Mrs. Smith, & butter milk from another lady whose name I forget[,] all of which the men were delighted to get. I went with Dr. Rembert this afternoon in search of some shoes. I suceeded in getting a pair of slippers at a store when there was very little for sale. When I went to pay for them, I handed a Petersburg bill to the boy who waited on me, he refused to take it, when asked why he said because the Town is in the hands of the enemy. Dr. R. asked how he knew, he said he had just heard it. Of course he had heard nothing of the kind & I told him so, I could not get him to take the note, so I paid him with another. Dr. R. rated him soundly though, & I rather think would have whiped him if I had not been present. I found when I got back home, I had plenty of time to make Mrs. Smith a call, I went & found the ladies all at home, I spent a delightful half hour when I was leaving old Mrs. Garret Mrs. S.['s] mother came out & beged me to come in & sit with her a while that she had not heard of my being there until that moment. My time was up though & I could not endulge my inclination to accept her invitation, I heard a mocking bird singing most delightfuly the whole time I was there. Mrs. S. her daughter & two nieces called in at the hospital just before sundown to fetch me a of the most beautiful flowers. She also sent a loaf of the most beautiful bread for the sick men's breakfast. People are getting very kind to the sick, they seem to be awaking to their duty. Dr. Rembert gave us a most amusing account of some of the men. The Virginia Malitia, who have been coming in of late, they are the hardest men to manage the most trifling & complaining, they all pretend to have rhumatism, so Dr. R. has ordered blisters for the most of them, they hate blisters worse than any thing one man he had blistered on both knees because he complained of them, I am perfectly certain there was the nothing the matter with the man. Mr. McMaster asked me if I put any of Dr. Remberts discription in my journal, I only wish I could. Some more sick seventeen in number came in tonight & asked to be accomidated only for the night, they are going in the morning to another hospital they were fortunate enough to get in just before the rain.

Wednesday night. May 21" 62

The morning until ten oclock was misty & damp, the air felt heavy & sultry. Dark looking clouds floated across the sky thretning a rainy day. Before noon it had cleared away quite bright. After I had finished sending up my lunch, I seated me by the front door of the dining [room] where I could get both air & light, I had quite a pile of lables to write & was quite busy with them when Dr. Rembert came in with two other gentlemen, I learned as they passed out of the room, that the two strangers were Dr. Davis the Surgeon of the Delevan[12] & Dr. Williams[13] the medical director, he had come to inspect the hospitals, & Dr. Rembert being the Surgeon in charge of the S. Carolina hospitals was taking him round. No one knew he was coming fortunately every thing was in very nice order, the dining [room] realy looked very nice, the table was nicely laid, with a bunch of fresh flowers in the center. The greater part of the sheets had been changed on yesterday, the beds were nicely made up & the floors were as clean as could be expected. Dr. Rembert says he seemed pleased, as he did not dissapprove of any thing. The men were delighted with their lunch, & dinner today those who were well enough to eat meat up on the wards, had a nice piece of veal. Marie had a letter from home today & I had

12. John Staige Davis, a professor of anatomy at the University of Virginia, held the rank of surgeon and took Dr. Cabell's place as head of the Charlottesville Hospital when he was out of town.

13. Thomas Henry Williams (b. 1822) was the medical director and inspector of Virginia's hospitals at this time. He later became the medical director for the Army of Northern Virginia.

two from two of my friends, laid down to rest a little while before going to the hospital this afternoon & went to sleep, when I awoke I found a strong wind blowing, which did not lul until about an hour ago. It is very warm tonight. There is a very flattering notice of the gallent charge The Hampton Legion[14] made at York town. Newton Fowles was mentioned among the wounded. Dr. Rembert is quite disponding to-night about the way the men at the hospital relaps, he thinks it owing entirely from imprudence in eating. They are not satisfied with the food we take them & go out or send out & buy all sorts of things they fancy. Sevral ladies around are very kind of late in sending us beautiful bread & buttermilk. The latter being a great treat to those who are beginning to recover. Dr. Rembert went down to the depot about noon today & dressed the wounds of 6 or 7 wounded Souldiers, he is a very kind man & grows more & more popular each day.

Charlottesville
Saturday afternoon. May 24" 62

I found Logan very much worse this morning, he asked me to read to him again, which I did, I remained with him as much as I could all the morning, reading & talking to him he told me he was near his end & that he was very happy perfectly resigned to the will of God. I never saw a dieing person so perfectly in their mind, about noon he asked to see a minister, I sent for Mr. Early who lives just across the street, he came instantly, & prayed for the poor sufferer. I was standing by the bed weeping[.] Logan said do not weep for me, I am going to rest, I am perfectly willing to die, I do not suffer as much as you think. When he spoak of his mother, he said she was good & would be rejoiced to hear he had died a christian. He thanked all who had done any thing for him, his eyes rested on me all the time, he told Mr. Early I had done for him as if he were my son[.] I have never witnessed such a death bed in the hospital, I had to leave him for a little while I go back now, I doubt if he still lives, I have not been down to dinner neither has Marie. It has rained hard all the morning, Esse sent for us to go over to

---

14. Wade Hampton (1818–1902), supposedly the largest landowner in the South in 1861, organized the Hampton Legion at the start of the war and equipped it at his own expense to go to Virginia. He had been appointed brigadier general the previous month.

lunch. Mr. Jones presented us with the strawberry's he received last night. Miss Reynolds bought some Goosberrys this morning the first I have seen since I was a child. We have all been shivering over the fire again tonight.

Charlottesville
Tuesday afternoon May 27. 62

I have had a high fever all day, could scarcely get through with my duties at the hospital this morning. As soon as I finished giving the sick men's dinners I came over & went to bed. I slept for two or three hours. The country rings with the news of Jacksons great victory.[15]

Night

I went over & attended to my duties at the hospital this evening. Dr. Rembert & Marie wished me to join them in a walk but I felt too badly. I was glad to dress & seat myself in the large rocking chair by the window in the parlor. Dr. Rembert seems to be in good spirits since he has succeeded in exciting Maries sympathys in his behalf again. I never saw any one so dependant on his friends.

Charlottesville
Tuesday Night. June 3rd" 62

I got over to the hospital just in time to see poor McGee die, he was perfectly in his senses to the last, his was a melancholy case, a match to many others, he came here the fifth of January, was very ill with Typhoid Pneumonia. Dr. Rembert succeeded in getting him up, he tryed to get him a discharge as he would never be fit for duty again. The discharge never came, McGee lingered about, at last he was gilty of some imprudence in changing his clothing, he had a relaps from which he never recovered in the least, today his miserable existence ended, this is the story of many an unfortunate man now in the service of his country. Tis hard to see them die one after another & not be able to help them in any way. Miss Sue Smith & her cousin Miss Winn brought me this morning each a most splendid bunch of magnificent flowers. They also brought some bread for the soldiers. Quantities of Strawberrys are coming in now, they are selling at 25 cts" a quart. Dr. McIntosh lunched with me at the Monticello about noon on Goos-

---

15. Jackson had defeated United States forces at the Battle of Winchester on May 25, 1862, and had captured large amounts of munitions and other supplies.

berry pie & milk. There was several accounts of the fight near Richmond in todays papers.[16] Three S.C. Regiments were engaged, the 4, 5 & Hamptons Legion. Hampton himself reported to be wounded in the foot. No fighting today. The heat still continues. I have been having a very pleasant evening with Doctor Rembert & Marie. It is raining smartly now, Mr. Mills went down to Petersburg this morning to meet his father.

Monticello. Charlottesville Hospital<br>Wednesday Morning June 4" 62

I had literaly to waid over here this morning. The streets were running with water, Nonie was polite enough to escort me over with an umbrella. Dr. Rembert went round this morning. Marie is too unwell to come over, Esse has taken her place for the day. Old Dr. Harris[17] has been passing in & out all the morning. An emense hurd of cattle has just passed, over a thousand in number I should think[,] they were fine looking & much larger than the most which have passed of late. The market affords very fine mutton now[,] we give the soldiers a change ocasionaly, they get very tired of beef. It still pours rain, an immense quanitity has fallen since last night. O! that the enemy may be inconvenienced by it.

Night. My own room

I slept from two oclock until half past four this afternoon, the rain had seased when I awoke & patches of blue sky were visible here & there. We had a small assembly at tea tonight. The two Surgeons having gone to tea at Capt. Taylors I sat with Marie nearly all the evening, she was too unwell to go down stairs. Dr. Rembert has just been in to pay her a visit. Mr. Jones brought me a sweet little boquet of honeysuckle & bleeding heart, when I was at tea, he has exquisit taste in arranging flowers. The Richmond papers have the casulties of the S. C. Regiments engaged on Saturday & Sunday. Louisiana & N. C.

---

16. The Confederate forces lost the Battle of Seven Pines (or Fair Oaks) on May 31 and June 1, 1862.

17. Probably Dr. Clement R. Harris, a contract physician from Augusta County, Virginia.

Regiments seem to have suffered most.[18] I fear much for the results. The enemy seem to have succeeded in perfecting their plans so thurely, & have such confidence of success that I can but feel uneasy. They have every advantage over us. God help us.

Monticello Charlottesville Hospital<br>Thursday morning. June 5." 62

Nothing of much interest has taken place today so far. Again I have no letters from home, I am low spirited & nervous. Not much news of interest this morning. Marie still too unwell to come over, Esse acts in her place.

(Night my own Room)

We were thrown into a great state of excitement & anxiety about six oclock this afternoon, by a report that the Yankees were within ten miles of this place. Capt. Taylor who commands the post, ordered out Scouts, & Dr. Rembert ordered out all the avalable men from all of his hospitals, there was great excitement upon the street. Dr. Rembert did a great deal in a very short time. All of the gentlemen from this house were the first to shoulder their arms & hold themselves in rediness. I was very much worried when I found Dr. McIntosh had gone off with out any thing to eat. Mr. McMaster came in & fixed himself comfortably for the campagne. Dr. Rembert we know could not go as he had to stay behind to see that his sick were taken care of. Mrs. Guinn called & we ladies were entertaining her when I saw Mr. Jones come in. I went out & found that news had just been received while our men were at the depot arming themselves, that the report was false. So in a short time our hero's all came in, & we had a good laugh over the fright. Mr. McMaster has notified us that he will leave us tomorrow for Petersburg. We were very much taken aback, for he is the only representitive of the Association. He is puting us in a very awkward situation, for of course we would not like to stay if the hospital was turned over to the Confederacy. Dr. Rembert & Marie have had their fun about the whole affair. What Mr. McMasters reasons for going are he has not told us. It is now near mid night & I have been suffering with my head all the evening.

---

18. The Battle of Seven Pines had taken place on May 31 and June 1, 1862.

Charlottesville
Sunday Night. June 8" 62

Mrs. Lesesne, Dr. Rembert, Mr. Mills, & myself, stoped on our way
to church to see the body of the noble Ashby[19] which lay in state at
the Farish House. I never saw a more striking looking man. He was
dressed in a full Suit of confederate uniform. His face was perfectly
natural, just as calm & composed as if he only slept. his eyes were naturaly closed his long black heavy eye lashes resting upon his cheek. His
hair beard & moustash are very black & heavy. I saw where the ball
pearced his wrist, the blud was still on the wristband of his shirt, his
coat sleeve was all towrn & {schreded} where the ball went through.
There was a sweet expression about the face, but I never saw greater
determination & courage depicted in any countenance. The body was
covered with reathes of beautiful flowers. A young man dressed in
Confederate uniform staid by the body all day. I did not learn his
name, he seemed much effected & gave the circumstances of his
friends suden death with much fealing. As I understand, General
Ashby was leading on his troops to the charge, his horse was shot dead
from under him, he then led his men on foot, he had not gone far
before a ball passed through his body, killing him almost instantly, he
walked only a few paces after he was struck then fel dead. His old company of Cavelry came down from Staunton this morning about eleven
oclock bringing their flag to attend at his burryal. I heard that one of
them said as he covered the body of his chief with the flag, "he fought
with him under this flag, yes said the young friend, & under it we will
avenge his death." Marie & myself went on to church alone, when we
got by the Baptish church we learned it was the only one open for service, as the funeral of Dr. Leach would take place there with Masonic
honors, we concluded we would go in. The church was much crouded
so we had to go into the gallery, where some gentlemen very politely
gave us some seats, we had to wait some time before the body arrived.
It was brought in by Six of his order, the rest following with the dif-

---

19. Turner Ashby (b. 1828) had taken command of Jackson's cavalry in the spring of
1862 and was a popular and charismatic figure who had been made a brigadier general
two weeks before his death. He was killed while fighting in a rear-guard action south
of Harrisonburg as Jackson's men continued their retreat toward Port Republic on June
6, 1862.

ferent symbles, there was very little worth seeing, & I wished myself away long before I came, Mr. Hogg delivered the adress which was tiresome & uninteresting. We heard that the funeral of General Ashby would take place at the University about four oclock. So as soon as we had had our dinner, Dr. McIntosh told Marie he was going & asked if she would like to go too[.] Marie said she would like to very much if I would go too. We were soon redy, & started off, Dr. McI. with Marie, & Mr. Mills with me, we couldent have had a pleasenter afternoon for the walk. We went into the chapel where we got comfortable seats, there was plenty of time to rest & admire the picture at the back of the Cha{pel}, before the body arrived. It was brought in by his own men, the clergyman who was to perform the service, the chaplin of the Regiment & his friend walking in just before the body. His servant came in & stood near by. There was two adresses, one by the Rev. Mr. Norden the other by the Chaplin of the Reg. —both very interesting. I was glad to hear the Gen. was a man of piety, his private character seems to have been as estimable as his military character. After the services were ended we walked out to the grave which was another half mile off, we had to pass through the college grounds to get there. The campus is a lovely place, just between the two long rows of students rooms stretching for a quarter of a mile on eather side, at the end of which there is a large Gimnasium where the young men have every opportunity of exercising. The grave is in what is known as the university grave yard, which is situated in a very pretty pine thicket & enclosed with a stone wall.

After the services were ended we walked to where the Soldiers are burried, being just out side of the enclosier, a dreadful feeling came over me when I saw how the graves were crouded together. Many of the names have been alredy defaced from the rude slabs of wood put there to identifie each man. A good many graves were alredy prepared and waiting for those who may want them[,] a dreadful sickning feeling comes over me when I think how they are hurryed to their last resting place without one friendly eye to see where they are laid or one loved one to shed a tear over their lonely graves. We had a delightful walk home cool & pleasant, but we were all foot sore & rather faged. Dr. McIntosh & myself puled straws as to which should get the rocking chair after tea, he was fortunate, I had a seat on the soffer though which answered quite as well, Dr. Rembert we found very unwell & in bed upon our return, so Marie went up to sit with him. I have just been up, he says he knew I did not go to see him, but mearly to carry off Marie. I made him laugh a little which I know will do him good.

Charlottesville<br>Monday Afternoon. June 9" 62

Poor Miss Reynolds met me in tears this morning when I went to the hospital. Mr. Mcgill died this morning early & Miss Reynolds is almost heartbroken for the loss of her friend. Some half dozen or more Yankee officers have been parading the town all the morning. I hear they are prisoners on parole, they are alowed to go at large here, with orders to report twice a day at Capt. Taylors office.[20] This I think is very wrong who knows what mischief they may be after, there are many in the Town none too good to give them any information they may wish. I think there are a great many who will welcome the Yankees with open arms when they succeed in getting here. Dr. Rembert is better today able to be out attending to his dutys. Gen. Ashbys Cavalry left about noon today. There has been no mail for two days, owing to a land slide on the road. The weather still continues cool.

(night)

Mrs. Smith paid us a vist at the hospitle this afternoon about half past five she says that several of Gen. Ashbys men staid with [her] last night, the young man whom I had noticed with the body was a cousin of the General, his name is Ashby. The Yankees seem to have attracted a good deal of attention I hear that several of the ladies about the Town have conversed with them. How they could have had the patience to do so is a mistry to me. It is very cool tonight almost cold. The mail came in just at dark. Not much news by the papers. There was a report brought in by some of the men that Jackson had had a battle with Frémont & routed him it was also reported Frémont had

---

20. Forty paroled Federal cavalry officers, captured by Ashby's and Jackson's men, had been allowed temporary freedom of the town. Several got drunk and fought with residents, leading to their rapid re-confinement.

been captured, I fear that fact is not true.[21] I still have no letter from home. Some more sick came in tonight.

Charlottesville
Monticello Hospital
Saturday Morning. June 14" 62

It is oppressively warm, crouds of wounded & sick are coming in every hour, the streets are thronged with Soldiers, hurying to & frow. Officers of every rank below a Col. some sick & some wounded. Dr. Rembert & Mr. Jones have been busy dressing wounds all the morning. Two wounded Yankees were brought in & put on my lower ward[.] I would rather not have them & fear I will not have the patience to do for them, I cant help feeling pity for them, they are human beings. They are our enemys too, wounded & in our power. It will be hard to treat them as I do the other men but I know it is my duty. The heat is almost over powering.

(Night. My room)

I have suffered terably with the heat the whole day. Wished for my box of clothes more than ever, fear I will never see them again. Dr. McI. returned on the morning train. he found the men very well cared for, & did not think it necessary to have them removed. Eight more men came in tonight, they were sent to the Monticello, where they were put is a mistry for the house was crouded to overflow before. There are now 120 men staying there. The Yankee prisoners seem very comfortable since their wounds were dressed. The young men of our army who came in at the same time were very severly wounded, they were taken to the same room when they arrived, but Dr. Rembert thought best to remove them. Dr. Rembert & Dr. McIntosh got into a discussion tonight after tea, which had it not been for Dr. McI.'s coolness might have led to a quarrel, I never saw any one who had better command over himself. Dr. R. is very excitable & says a great many things he is sorry for a minute after. The other is very deliberate &

---

21. Jackson's men had acquitted themselves well against General John C. Frémont and the United States forces in the Battle of Cross Keys on June 8, 1862, and the Battle of Port Republic the next day—the last battles in Jackson's Shenandoah Valley Campaign. Frémont was not captured, but would resign on June 17.

never says any thing but what he means. It is now twelve oclock. The heat is so great I fear I cant sleep.

Charlottesville<br>Sunday afternoon. June 15." 62

Another warm morning, too busy to go to church. Mr. Alexander is still bright, but his wound is very dangerous. Dr. Rembert thinks it very doubtful if he recovers. It is almost impossible to keep him from talking. The men are very kind to the two yankees one of them is polite & grateful for any thing done for him the other is sulkey, says very little & pretends to sleep most of the time[.] I force myself to ask after their health once a day, & see that they get their food regularly. I have never inquired there names nor do I intend to. We did not get over in time for dinner, there were so many to take dinner to on the two wards & such a variety that it took me longer than usual, when I got down to the table the gentlemen had left.

(Night)

I went to sleep this afternoon & when I awoke I found there had been a thunder storm which had cooled the air wonderfuly. I put on my same thin clothing I had worn in the morning & went to the hospital, I almost suffered with the cold, I have been coughing all the evening. We had a funny joak on Dr. Rembert at tea. A man came in & brought some pay rolls which were done up with a half sheet of letterpaper around them, Dr. R. handed them over to Mr. Mills (who was next to him) without opening them, Mr. M. took the paper from around them very carefully he found it had somthing written on it in Dr. Williams hand, a letter had been commenced then thrown aside. Mr. M. saw the meaning of it imediately, Dr. R. took it up & read it, he said what does all this mean, read it again, then said "Williams is the strangest man I ever saw. I will let him know I never asume any thing but what I am intitled to I always signe myself Surgeon in charge of S. C. hospitals Charlottesville because I am, I told him so when he was here." He seemed to think Dr. Williams wanted to take him down in some way. We all began to laugh so he thought there must be something wrong; so he looked to Mr. Mills to explain which he did, Where upon the Doctor indulged in a harty fit of laughter at his own expence. We have a gay time among our Selves.

Charlottesville
Friday afternoon, June 20″ 62

The noise has qui[e]ted down some what so I will now attempt to write. This morning I was over at the hospital by seven oclock as usual to give Alexander & Thomas their breakfast[.] I knew the sentinal so passed in without difficulty. As I was about returning here for my own breakfast, I saw the street almost blocked up by wagons, I had to pick my chance to run between them to get over. As soon as breafast was over I ran up to my room where I could get a good look at what was passing in the street below. Directly Marie came up & said Dr. Rembert said we might go to his office where we would have a better view. Acordingly we were soon there. First came a quantity of Officers & wagons. Then Regt. after Regt. of infantry each with a comanding officer, A Col., Lieut. Col., or Maj. at its head. As one of the Mississippie Regts passed The Col. commanding tutched his hat to us. A great many as they passed looked up at us, & some of the men bowed to us. Young Harvy called out to Marie as he marched along Good morning Mrs. Lesesne. There were a good many we had had in the hospital from time to time, who had joined their Regt. I never saw finer looking men than those in most of the Western Regts. I saw the Selebrated Maj. Wheat of Wheat's Battilion of Tiger Rifles.[22] He is a very large fine looking man but not what I would call handsome[.] The Standard bearer in the 16″ Mississippi is the handsomest man I have seen since I came to Virginia. One of Gen. Jackson's aids is a very handsome man unusualy so. They were passing the whole day. There was some five Divisions that I counted there might have been more. Over 100 pieces of cannon some few very large. I took great pleasure in looking at the beautiful brass pieces captured from the enemy in some of our late ingagements, some of the carriages were marked U. S.[,] a great many of the wagons were marked in the same way. There were many fine horses some belonging to the officers others in the wagons, in fact nearly all the horses were in first rate order the mules were very fat & sleek, as the day began to grow warm the men

22. Major Chatham Roberdeau Wheat commanded Wheat's Battalion of Rifles, a Louisiana battalion attached to Richard Taylor's brigade in General Richard S. Ewell's division of Jackson's army.

began to look a little weary & dusty, all were well clad fine looking men, I only saw one without shoes. I have heard so many speak of the broken down condition of Jacksons Army that I was very much surprised to see so fine a body of men.[23] We see the worse feature of the war. The most of the men we have in our hospital now are from Jacksons army. There are none very sick, only debilitated by continual marching. A few days rest does for them. Nonie Had his little Palmeto flag flying out of the window of his room. One of the Mississippie Regts. cheered it as they passed. There was a fine brass band attached to most of the Western Regts. when they struck up Dixie I became too excited to contain myself, I would have cheered with all my might if I had dared. Capt. Carington's battery[24] looks a little the worse for wear[.] Their uniform is not so fresh & bright looking by a good deal as when they left here. I can now understand how it is an army moves so slowly. Every now & then the men had to stop & let the wagons pass on out of their way. Then the wagons would stop for the men to move on. I was amused to see how quickly the men would get out of ranks when the order to halt was given. I thought it would be impossible to get them into order again, but in a very few minutes after the order was given they would be all right & redy to march off.

(Night)

It is astonishing how very quiet it is. This evening Dr. Rembert & myself took a delightful walk out by Mr. Farishes farm, we could see the tops of the tents belonging to Capt. Caringtons Battery, from one of the hills. We seated ourselves on the stone fence to rest & admire the lovely prospect around, on our way back we stoped at the spring & got a drought of the cool water to wash the dust from our throats. Dr. Rembert was in fine spirits he certainly is a delightful companion. We are all tired & sleepy tonight after the days excitement.

---

23. Stonewall Jackson and his army were leaving the Valley of the Shenandoah to join Robert E. Lee's men near Richmond for a planned offensive on the Peninsula of Virginia against McClellan.

24. Captain James McDowell Carrington had organized this battery in the Charlottesville area; it was attached to the artillery of Jackson's division.

Chapter 6

# July 17–September 3, 1862

*"Tomorrow the association's connection with these Hospitals & the Maupin House ends."*

Charlottesville
Thursday noon. July 17″ 62

An unusualy hot day. I feel my weakness terably.[1] Had a letter from Pa today. There was some mention of Dickie in it. There seems to be much distress in the country, almost every family has lost in these last battles. In the Linchburg paper today there was quite a grand account of the achievments of the Gunboat Arkansass.[2] I hope Dickie is safe I feel anxious to hear. The mail came by Linchburg today the first we have had for some days.

Jeffersons Monticello
Thursday night. July 17″ 62

I had given out the idea of coming up this evening. It has been raining almost all day, & it was so damp & dark this afternoon, that I did not think Mr. Wheeler would come for me. A little after four however he did come to ask if I would venture out, I was so anxious to get away from Charlottesville that I determined to try it acordingly it was arranged for Mr. W. to call for me at five. I was very nearly redy when the carriage drove to the door. Dr. Rembert was going out so he came to the door to say Adieu[.] I realy feel sad to part from him & Marie even for so short a time. I took an affectionate leave of Marie & I was off. I might have enjoyed the ride (my second ride since I came to Charlottesville) had the roads been in any kind of order, but every few yards there was a mud hole then a pile of rocks which kept me roling from one side of the carriage to the other. It took all my little

---

1. Ada had been sick for most of the previous weeks with erysipelas; there are no diary entries between June 28 and July 15, 1862.

2. The C.S.S. *Arkansas* had been involved in action with the United States fleet on the Yazoo River on July 15, 1862, and in the siege of Vicksburg on July 16. Ada's brother Dickie was apparently serving on this vessel.

strength to hold on to the side of the carriage to keep from being pitched out, when we came to the little spring on the side of the road I longed for some of the pure water but there was nothing to drink from. I thought the road dreadful all the way before but when we began to clime the mountain, it surpassed every thing, the recent heavy rains had washed one side of the road into a deep ditch leaving bearly room to get along, in addition to this the road is little more than a bed of rocks, we pulled steadily along however until at last we arrived at the top & then the house came in view. We draw up to the {gate} (a small one) when Mr. W. stoped opened the door & helped me out. Some how I had been under the impression we would drive up to the door, & I was dissapointed when I found I had to walk the distance of more than a hundred yards over the wet grass in my thin slippers[.] I beged to go to my room immediately as I was completely faged out. I found I had not been expected so the room was not redy for me, but I lay down on the bed & rested for about twenty minutes which refreshed me very much[.] I then arranged my hair & went out on the porch, where I found Dr. McIntosh, he had come very soon after we did. About eight the tea bell rang, I went in but could eat nothing, every thing was very good & I actualy envied some of my <illegible> their appetites. Dr. Mac too did justice to what was before him which I was glad to see. The company in the house consists of Dr. & Mrs. Mason & three children. There are also four very genteel looking young men whose names I have not learned, the Masons are of Baltimore, I think most of the young men are from Maryland. I scarcely knew what to do with myself after tea, so I reclined on one of the setees in the hall. A little while after Dr. Mac joined me & we had a nice talk, I proposed to retire & the Doctor got a candle for me, I called him in to show him my room which realy looks comfortable enough, then we went to look at his. I felt his bed & was shocked to find I could feel the slats through the thin bed, I'll answer for it he wont sleep much. I told him he couldent complain of want of room the furniture is sparse, not even a glass in the room. I asked what he would do how would he know if his dress was properly arranged. He thought he might manage, so I left him. The prospects are we will have plenty of rain.

Monticello
Friday Morning. July 18″ 62

Gloomy, gloomy, the rain pours in torents without the least appearance of clearing up. I feel as withered as a plucked flower this morning I scarcely closed my eyes during the night, & when I did I was not refreshed. The bed was as hard as a board, then there was some young man sleeping just above me, who came in late & made a great fuss, then a mouse began to nible in a corner of the room. There was a hundred & one little things to worry me, when I did sleep I was staring & dreaming all the while. I awoke at the first peep of day. I called to Savary to get up, then tryed to take a nap but the flys tormented me so I slept no more, so I got up, not long after Savary came to say breakfast was coming in. I sent her to see if the Doctor was up, he was & nearly redy I hurried to get redy but the bell rang just befor I got my dress on[.] I found Mac waiting for me in the Hall, he looked so white & sleepy I knew my prediction had been fulfilled. He seemed to enjoy his breakfast though & went off a little while after in good spirits. I hated to see him go. I have been lying down all the morning, the want of sleep has almost knocked me up. Mrs. W. has been in to find out what she could do for me & realy seemed concerned to know how she could make me comfortable[.] I beged her to make Mac more comfortable & I would be satisfied. She promised to do so, she very kindly offered to send me lunch or do any thing she could for me. If it would realy clear up & be good weather I think I might bear with most any thing. I must not forget to mention that little Master Tomie Mason has a drum which he delights to beat. It was the first thing I heard this morning. Mrs. M. seems to be a very mild person whom Master Tomie does not stand in much fear of. I hear every now & then you Tomie come out of the damp, still Tomie moves not, it is repeated sevral times in the same toan of voice with the same effect, at last Tomie is taken up bodily & carried in. If this is to go on day after day what is to become of me. no wonder I want good weather.

Three o'clock afternoon

Just up from dinner, never in my life before have I sat down to dinner table without a cloth on the table, I never heard of seting a dinner table in my life before without a white cloth. I dined on a small piece of chicken & a roll, there was no rice on table, for desert there was rice custard. My how I long for the time for Mac to come.

(Night)

I waited patiently until seven oclock, by my little fire, for Mac[.] Mrs. W. came in to ask if she should wait tea for the Doctor. I told her no I had given him up, still I couldent resist looking from the window hoping to see him, when I remembered the river must be very much swolen by the heavy rain during the day. Then I gave up all hope. My how I miss them all, after tea I was sitting here by the fire with no other light in the room, when I saw a little black somthing run out from under the bed, & as quickly run back again, I thought it must be a lizard so I ran out & called Savary & one of the other servants & made them move the bed & look every where they found nothing so I thought it must have escaped through a hole in the window shuter, how I am to sleep I cant tell, I have even a greater horror of a lizard than a snake. Mrs. W. has been in to pay me a visit she says Dr. & Mrs. Mason think Mac & myself must be related for they never saw two people look more alike. Mrs. W. told them she heard me say we were not related, then they came to the conclusion we must be engaged. She says one of the young men not knowing what the Masons had said asked why I did not eat, she told him I had been sick he then wanted to know if Mac was my brother she told him no he was no relation, he said we looked so much alike he thought we must be related, when he found we were not, he too came to the conclusion that we were engaged. I couldent help being amused, but I fear Mac will be provoked. It is no compliment to him to be thought like me now, & certainly no compliment to his taste to think he would choose me for his wife.

Charlottesville
Thursday night. July 31st"

July gone & I still in Virginia[.] Tomorrow the associations connection with these Hospitals & the Maupin House ends. Mr. Mc-Master not satisfied with writing to Dr. Rembert to turn over this house to Mr. Maupin at the end of the month, telegraphed to him again to day that the rent seased & beged he would hand over the house to Mr. M., why some one of the association has not come on to wind up the business. I realy think Mr. Barnwell has treated us with very little consideration, if it were not for our friends in the house who will take care of us we would fair rather badly. However as it is, I dont care. Mrs. Lott[3] after consenting to leave the Harris House, has written to Dr. Rembert a most severe letter accusing him of turning her & her child out of the house which has troubled the Doctor very much. She has acted very badly & given a great deal of trouble. I have attended to my dutys at the hospital all day, feel better only I suffer a great deal with my tooth. Mac looks very very badly I very much fear he will be sick. Tonight after tea [we] were all seated in the parlor when Dr. R. came in & told Marie Miss Reynolds was weeping over at the hospital & asked her if she could not go with him to see what was the matter[.] They had not goten farther than the gate when they met her, she was crying[.] Dr. R. asked what was the matter, she said she would not sleep in the room because there was no key to the door, she was in a grate rage a perfect fury, & all for nothing for she had been told she might sleep in this house tonight, but nothing must do but she must have a fuss. I never have seen any one with a heigher temper. Dr. R. & Marie succeeded at last in quieting her a little. Poor Mac looks too badly tonight.

Charlottesville<br>Monday night. Aug 4" 62

This has been a day of labor & excitement, both Marie & myself were awake until two oclock last night I with tooth ache, took some of McMa—then succeeded in getting to sleep, this morning I got up as usual but had to go to bed again as I come very near fainting. I succeeded in getting up to breakfast was on my feet all the morning, felt too badly to go to the hospital so I was with Mac as much as possible. Mrs. Rembert[4] came today on the one o'clock train. She appears to be a very pleasant nice person but not a bit pretty, the little boy[5] is very handsome, so like the Doctor. It realy is cheering to hear his sweet little voice about the house[.] Mrs. Paten called on Mrs. Rembert this morning thinking she had come a few days ago. Such weather the heat is almost unbearable. I sat with Mac until ten oclock tonight he has

3. An assistant matron at the Soldiers' Home.
4. Esther G. Rembert (b. ca. 1839).
5. Arthur G. Rembert (b. ca. 1859).

been suffering with his head, his room is like an oven. I have no desire to sleep, the moon light is realy very beautiful.

Charlottesville
Tuesday night. August 12" 62

The wounded have been coming in since five oclock this morning. Three or four car loads have arrived some have stoped here others were sent on to Staunton. The Delevan has some two hundred, our hospitals have a few. Dr. Rembert is having about thirty tents pitched at Midway, which will accomidate a great many wounded, the old Methodist church has been pressed for a hospital for wounded, about thirty have been taken there some dreadful wounds among them I hear one has alredy died. The Ladies of the town were down at the depot nearly all day trying to relieve the suffering of those who were left there until places were provided for them. I had a terable fright this morning as I stood at the door waiting to see if I could go into the large ward, my eye fell on a man who had been put there early in the morning with out my knowledge. Such an object I never before beheld, he is shot in the face, his eyes are blood shoten & his face all bandaged up, face very much swolen & the blood trickling from his noze all the time[.] I almost droped on the floor when I saw him my nerves were terably shocked. If I had been only told he was there I should not have minded it. We had a fine rain about noon.

Charlottesville
Wednesday Night. Aug 13" 62

Twas delightfuly cool all night, I found nearly all of my patients better, the good nights rest did them more good than anything else, I forgot to mention last night that Old Burns made his appearance in the Monticello late in the after noon, he is wounded in the leg, he has been talking incessantly ever since he got in he has been put right next to the Yankees. It is too bad for he hates them so much he cant help abusing them. One more wounded man was brought to my lower ward late last evening. Dr. Rembert went over to dress the wound after tea, his leg was taken off just above the knee, he has been very much prostrated all day. I had to have him fed with a spoon. he could take very little nourishment of any kind[.] Edwards fever came on earlier this morning than usual. he complains of feeling badly very weak. Mrs. Tribble & a Mrs. Johnson from the Farish house came round here this morning for Esse to go to the church with them to see the wounded.

Marie & myself were both very much pleased with Mrs. Johnson, she is one of the most patriotic women I have seen in Virginia. She must have been very pretty when young she is handsome now, her figure is very fine & she is remarkably intelligent. Mrs. T. is a remarkably pleasant person. Like most Baltimorians her manners are very fine[.] It has been delightfuly cool all day. Dr. Mac is looking very much better, he went with Dr. Rembert to the Delevan to see some amputations, as he was going out for his ride this after noon he said he felt hungry. I offered him a cracker when I gave it to him I said to him I am afraid you all will never think of me except in conexion with something to eat. he replied, "we will always think of you when we are sick." I have been with Edward ever since tea until now. Another cool night I am impatient to get to bed to sleep.

Charlottesville<br>Friday afternoon. Aug 15″ 62″

It was a dark cloudy morning every one overslept themselves, even I stoal a half hour. It is realy melancholy it is seldom I ever look upon the street that I do not see men with their arms in slings, some with the right arm & some with the left. Ocasionaly may be seen men with crutches limping about trying to see what goes on. Poor Forester looks & is much worse today[.] Tis a sad sight to see his pale hagered face, so young too, If he lives he will have to go through life with one leg, he can never walk again without a crutch. The other young man shot through the face is something better. I believe though Dr. Rembert thinks his case critical too. [In] This warm weather wounds are very offensive I could scarcely stand by young H. long enough to give him some nurishment[.] The flys too are very bad on the lower ward. Old Burns told me this morning his health was very good only his leg hurt him a little, he hoped soon to be in the field again. Dr. Mac is improving very fast[.] I heard him say today he would be able to resume his dutys at Midway tomorrow. Dr. Poellnitz[6] has not yet arrived. Jacksons army has fallen back to Gordonsville[.][7] It is supposed he has between 50 & 60,000 men.

---

6. Dr. J. B. Poellnitz was an assistant surgeon at the Midway Hospital.

7. Jackson's men withdrew from north of the Rapidan River to the Gordonsville area on August 11, 1862.

Charlottesville
Sunday Night. Aug 17" 62

Went to church this morning heard The Rev. Mr. Slaughter, got back in time to give the dinner. This afternoon went over to the reading room to attend service, Mr. Gillmer gave us a very good adress, quite a good attendance of soldiers. They were very attentive & seemed to be pleased. I went to the Monticello from the reading room, in one of the rooms as I walked into the door, I saw four or five men playing cards[.] I was so shocked I could scarcely speak. I went up to them & said Gentlemen sure you forget it is Sunday evening. One of them said, our church does not object to our playing on Sunday if we do not play for gain. I said but you will oblige me very much if you will put your cards up. They did so immediately a little while after one of them came to me & appoligised so politely that I could but accept his appology. When we got home we found that Esse was going home with old Mrs. Carter to spend a few days. After tea, all of the gentlemen went out, so I went to sit with Edward. I am delighted I can have Marie all to myself.

Charlottesville
Thursday Morning. Aug 21st" 62

Esse has come home again. There is an end to all the pleasant talks Marie & myself have been having. She is a most dangerous person we are afraid to say any thing before her, there is no knowing what she will make out of it, I never saw any one who could pervert things as she does. It is distressing to think we should have had such a person among us all this time, one whom we have shown so much kindness to, now to turn against us & abuse us in the {way she} does.

Night

Forester died this morning about twelve oclock. He passed away very quietly, with but little or no pain[.] The wound was so offensive I could not stay in the room. His nurse the young man who came with him was most attentive to him, so kind & gentle with him. I hope he has passed into a better world.

Charlottesville
Monday Morning. Aug. 23d" 62

Esse anounsed to Dr. Rembert at the breakfast table that she intended to leave for Linchburg on Tuesday morning, & asked the Doctor to look out for some one to take charge of her bagage for her. Dr. R. told her the conductor would take charge of it for her. Poor Esse no one asked her to stay any longer, or expressed any regret at her going. Poor girl she has succeeded in making herself very unpopular, God grant I may never place myself in such a position.

Charlottesville<br>Monday Morning. Aug 25" 62

My numerous ocupations for the morning have come to an end at last, I got up this morning & waited for Lavinia to bring the water but she did not come, I then found she too had gone to bed leaving me without any one but Willie & William[.] I sent for Lavinia to attend at breakfast, in the meantime I had gotten every thing in order breakfast was brought in at the usual hour. When I went to the hospital at ten I again received some delightful peaches from Carpenter. Another wounded man has been put on my lower ward, he has his leg taken off just where Foresters was, only his is the right leg & F.'s was the left. He is doing very well.

After dinner

Dr. Rembert must have some body to tease. I generaly am the victim, he got teasing me again as we sat round the table after we had finished dinner, about my diary, he declares he would rather read it than any book destroyed in the Alexandrian libarary, yes says Mrs. Rembert, because it contains so many of *your* sayings, where upon he gave us one of his merry laughs & rushed from the table. Mrs. Webber called about noon, she is here looking after another wounded brother. Poor woman she has trouble.

The weather is charming, just cool enough to be comfortable, very much like our October weather.

Charlottesville<br>Tuesday Afternoon. Aug 26" 62

Esse has actualy gone, she left about two oclock. Marie, Mrs. Rembert, & all of the gentlemen of the house exept Dr. Poellnitz went to the cars to see her off. She will reach Linchburg about six this afternoon. I feel relieved that she is gone now Marie & myself have that room all to ourselves. Dr. Rembert teased Mr. Jones very much about his parting with Esse. He was the last one to come in from the cars[.] The Doctor told him he was glad to see him for he realy thought he had gone to Linchburg & he was just thinking about what arrangements he could make to supply his place until his return. Why said Jones I left the cars before you did, I was in the office at the Monticello before the cars left. Oh! yes said doctor R. you went there to vent your feelings in private, Poellnitz was in your room so you could not be private there, so you went to your shop. Well never mind Jones[,] I will vacate the office for you this evening. Of course every body laughed, Poor Mr. Jones turned crimson. It is quite warm again. The Linchburg <illegible> came out in full dress this morning. I believe it is thought Gen. Pope is trying to get round towards Richmond again.[8] There will be anxious times again.

Night

Spent a very pleasant evening at Mrs. Garrets, with Mrs. Smith & her daughter. It is realy the second time since I came to Virginia that I have taken tea out. Miss Smith played for us first upon the Ban{jo} then upon the piano[.] She executes well & is so obliging. While we were at tea Mrs. Winn another daughter of Mrs. Garrets came in she lives about two miles in the country. Nonie came for us he told us of Maj. Rudd & his wife being here[.] I thought they had called to see us all, so hurryed home, upon getting here I found they had only called to see Doctor & Mrs. Rembert, so Marie & myself sat on the porch enjoying the sweet air & bright starlight. Marie & myself occupie the same bed now[.] Oh! my the releaf not to have Esse.

Charlottesville<br>Thursday afternoon. Aug 28″ 62

Twas a dark gloomy morning the air felt damp & we all hoped we should have the rain we so much need, such large [numbers] of cattle & droves of hogs have passed with in the past few days that the dust is intolerable. A very large drove of hogs passed this morning on the way to Richmond. Edward received me this morning sitting up. He is looking much better & is quite cheerful. A good many of the men from the hospital left for camp this morning, when they got to the Depot they found the cars so much crowded, they had to return. Trains have been passing all day with troops. I had a letter from Mrs.

---

8. This report was inaccurate.

Edward Porcher today, inquiring after a young Hines, his Brother it seams has heard he was with us, I am sorry I can not give any information about him. The most of my men are improving I have very few sick. Today I was very much amused at a little incident which occured on one of my wards, I had been round giving the punch, one of the men who was not taking it asked me if he might not have some, I laughed & said it was for the sick & left the room[.] I went on the other ward & gave it to those who were to have it & as I came down thought I would go in & give the man who had asked me for some a little, as he has been quite complaining for a day or so, just as I got to the door I saw through the crack two water mellons lying on the bed[.] I walked in the room & found they had thrown the bed quilt over them as they saw me, so I said, well Mr. Abel if you will not eat any mellon I will give you the punch you asked for. He declared they were not his, I said to the men you need not have troubled yourselves to cover them I have eyes all round. I dont know whose they were. Mr. Carpenter gave me some more beautiful peaches today[.] I ate part & gave the rest to Dr. R. & Mac. We had a silent party at dinner today, Mr. Jones & Mr. Arthur have gone in search of wild medicens again today.[9]

Charlottesville
Friday afternoon. August 29″ 62

I have just heard that Mr. Barnwell & Dr. Lafar have arrived, we are all too glad they are come at last, now I hope the business will be settled. Edward has a return of fever again today. The weather still dry & quite warm again. Had a letter to write to Pa this afternoon but felt too dull. I still suffer from absent mindedness, some times I find it impossible to collect my thoughts.

Charlottesville
Saturday morning. Aug 30″ 62

I got Nonie to go with me to try & get a pair of shoes. I could not find a single pair redy made to fit me. I ordered a pair of gaiters which the man said he would let me have by today week, he charged me eight dollars for them. Mr. Barnwell called in to see us, he is

9. The Confederate medical service encouraged the use of natural medicines as a way to circumvent shortages of traditional drugs.

looking remarkably well & is in fine spirits. He told us Mrs. Madroy had been sent home from Petersburg & Mrs. Lott has gone North, only four of the nurses he brought on from Carolina still remain, they are Mrs. Rion,[10] Marie, Miss Clarke[11] & myself. Dr. Lafar spent last evening with us, he is very careful not to say any thing about Petersburg. I think him very much altered he comes to dine with us today. Mrs. Rembert is charmed with Mr. Barnwell, she thinks (as we all do) that he is very handsome & most elequent. The war news is most exciting & incouraging. Mr. B. says the Administration is in fine spirits, I am afraid though we are inclined to depreciate our enemies rather too much.

### Night

Dr. Lafar dined with us, & was much more talkative than last night. Edward is better again. Though not out of danger yet, he gave me a kind message from his mother this afternoon. I am afraid he is inclined to over rate my little attentions. The clouds are begining to over cast the sky. Oh! that we may have rain. One of my ward masters was taken very Sudenly ill with Pneumonia. Dr. Rembert was sent for a few minutes ago to go over to the hospital to see him.

### Charlottesville
### Sunday Morning. Aug 31st" 62

I almost overslept myself this morning it was so dark & cloudy, when I arose I found it had rained in the night, I thought I had heard it but was not sure. The mist rising from the mountains is perfectly beautiful. It looks like colum after colum of light smoke curling on heigh. I am too unwell to go to church the damp air affects me very much[.] I am sorry I could not go Dr. Mac asked me to go with him, I hope to hear Mr. Barnwell at the reading room this afternoon. I have just looked from the window & two men are passing in the street one with his right & the other with his left leg off, they get on much better with crutches than could be expected. It is sad to think of the hun-

---

10. Eliza Rion (ca. 1822–1863) of Chesterfield County, South Carolina, was the head matron of the Midway Hospital.

11. Frances Jane Clarke (1826–1896) was the sister of Ada's two future husbands and would marry Thomas J. McCutcheon, a physician in Mannville, South Carolina, in 1868.

dreds of disabled men this war is producing, many will be of no possible use to them selves or any one else. I heard of one poor creature who had both eyes shot out at one of the Richmond battles, he will be nothing more than a burden all his life. My men are all better today, Eugene was sleeping so quietly when I went in to see him that I did not wake him. It is so cloudy it must rain again before dark. Edward seems to be doing very well this morning he is a most kind hearted affectionate person. God grant his sickness may be sanctified to him, he thinks I trouble myself a great deal about his diet, but if he only knew how much more I am troubled about his Soul. I fear he is very careless now.

Night

Mr. Barnwell dined with us today it seemed like old times to have him back again. He gave us a beautiful adress at the reading room this after-noon from the text "And he said Tomorrow" Taken from Exodus. His prayer was most beautiful and appropriate, nearly all of us from this house were present[.]

Marie, Mr. Mills, Nonie & myself walked up to Midway after the soldiers tea this evening, we went in to see Mrs. Rion until Dr. Mac was redy to come down, Mrs. R. was very glad to see us & insisted we should stay until Miss Clarke came in. I never saw a more patriotic old lady, I asked after her son[12] & she told me he said something about coming on to this State, she does not wish him to do so, but said she "I would sooner put a tomb stone over him, than he should be a coward." Dr. Rembert Marie & myself had a long talk tonight after tea, first about Dr. Poellnitz then about our going home, Dr. R. insists upon our staying here this Winter he declares if we go the hospital will go to the dogs, he realy seems anxious to keep us. I am willing to stay if I realy can be of use, I am very much troubled about it some times, I realy want to go home very much but if duty requires me here I will sacrifice any private feeling & stay.

Charlottesville
Tuesday Night. Sept 2d" 62

It has realy been a charming day Marie & myself went out about eleven oclock to call on Mrs. Carter & Mrs. Paten, we found both too

---

12. This could be any one of the four of her sons who were old enough for military service.

sick to receive us. We then continued our walk & I called at Mrs. Mallory's to pay the milk bill. The Sun was just pleasantly warm, & I only wished we had little more than an hour to stay. We had a present to the Hospital of vegetables from Mrs. Frank Minor[13] this afternoon. Yesterday we had a can of Buttermilk from Mrs. Tom Farish.[14] We have had another talk with Dr. Rembert tonight about I going home. He still begs we will remain, I am glad to stay & do what I can for the relief of our suffering soldiers, but the Servants are so bad & give so much trouble, I am much inclined to go. I should hate too to go at this time, I know it would put Dr. Rembert to much inconvenience. Still I would not for worlds stay a moment longer if there was the least reason why I should go. I do not wish to be indebted to any one for even a morsel of food, I know that both Dr. R. & McIntosh are my firm friends, still I do not wish to be dependent on them for any thing more than the kindness they have always shown me.

We are receiving accounts of our briliant victory constantly Mr. Barnwell went to Gordonsville today, & returned in the mid day train he said the news was confirmed that we received on yesterday.[15]

Charlottesville<br>Wednesday Night. Sept 3d" 62

There was nothing but worry, worry, all the morning[.] Lavinia tryed herself to see how much trouble she could give me. Mr. Maupin came in to see Mr. Barnwell & Dr. Rembert told him about her, he had her well whiped. Of course all that troubled me, then too Mr. Barnwell & Dr. R. were having a pretty warm discussion & I was uneasy for fear they might come to some misunderstanding. I was worried too because I couldent make up my mind whether it were best to go home or not, at last I determined to ask Dr. McIntosh what he thought about it, we went for a walk after I had finished at the Hospital. After I had put the facts of my case before him, I asked for his

---

13. Frank Minor ran the Ridgeway Academy in Charlottesville.

14. Wife of Captain Thomas L. Farish; their East Jefferson Street house was commandeered by George A. Custer in 1864, and Farish was captured in civilian clothing when he returned to protect his family. Condemned to death as a spy, he was saved by Custer, who convinced General Philip H. Sheridan to parole him.

15. Confederate forces were victorious at the Second Battle of Manassas or Bull Run, August 29–31, 1862.

advice, he said he could see no reason why I should not stay that I could do just as much good as ever & could just as well do what I came to do now, as at first. he said also, that if we left he thought seriously of going himself. That our being here kept him. It was nearly dark when we got back home, Mr. Barnwell, Mrs. Smith & Miss Sue were here. Mr. B. took tea with us, Mrs. S. & her daughter had been to tea & could not join us, they insisted upon our leaving them in the parlor until we had finished. They told us they had just heard that our army was within ten miles of Alexandria, & would be in today.[16] God grant it may be so.

---

16. Confederate forces did not take Alexandria.

Chapter 7

# September 5–November 4, 1862

*"Oh! I am getting to long for home, for peace, that we might once more enjoy the comforts & conveniences of our beloved homes."*

Charlottesville
Friday night. Sept. 5″ 62

A few wounded came in today all S. Carolinians, mostly from the upper districts. They are miserably dirty & rag[g]ed, some are shoeless. They were delighted to see a lady from S. C. one said Madam we are glad to see you & would be glad to see more from our state there is a old lady there I call my own I would like mighty well to see. Poor fellows tis a sad sight to see them so mamed, none of them are severely wounded.

Charlottesville
Sunday Night. Sept 7″ 62

I begin the week with a new book the second since I left home. Four months have elapsed since I sat in the same room with the one I finished but yesterday, new upon my lap, thinking how I should begin. Many many things both pleasant & unpleasant have transpired during the time. It is gratif[y]ing to me to be able to state that I have received nothing but kindness from those around me. I did not think of being here until now, circumstances have decided me to stay at least for a while longer, Though my inclinations tend homeward. Virginia could never be a pleasant home to me. I often find myself longing for home. When I go among those poor men now in our hospital & tel[l] them I am from Carolina, they cant resist shaking my hand & saying I am mighty glad to see you. There is a devotion for the State among her people which belong's to no other.

Charlottesville
Monday afternoon. Sept 8″. 62

Not feeling very well I came up here to my room from the dinner table & left William to wash up & put the dishes away. I went down again a few minutes ago, & found that the dishes had bearly been washed, & that was all, the Silver was on the dinner table, the cloth not removed or the knives cleaned. when I called William & told him about his neglect, he was so impertenent that I slaped him in the mouth before I knew what I did. He ran off yelling as if I had hit him with a cudgel, he never rested until he made his noze bleed then ran to his mother saying I had done it. Old Willie was like a lioness in a moment[.] I never in my life saw any thing with such a temper she was perfectly frantic she went on at such a rate that I told her if she did not take care I would have her whiped too that I was determined William should be whiped tonight she said no one should tutch either her or William. I went to the Hospital & went about my duty's as usual expecting to find Old W. over her passion when I got back I never was more mistaken. She & Lavinia were both raving when I got back, I said nothing but determined to tell Dr. Mac as soon as he came in, accordingly I did, he took William off, as soon as I had finished telling him. I never heard such a row as ensued, William yelling as if he was being murdered, & old Willie abusing & thretning Dr. Mac with all her might. The Doctor locked him up as he had to go to Midway & had not time to whip him then. After tea Dr. Rembert was informed of the matter & they went out to give W. the whiping[.] I beged Dr. MacIntosh not to whip old Willie as she was generaly such a good negro. It seems that while they were whiping W. she went up to the door of the room where they were & burst in telling them to stop whiping her child that they should not whip him. The Gentlemen determined at once that she must be whiped too so they caught hold of her & puled her in the room. From their discription of it they must have had a dreadful time of it. They finaly had her taken to gaol where she is to remain until Mr. Maupin comes down. I am worried almost sick about it all.

Charlottesville
Tuesday Night. Sep 9″ 62

I arose this morning after an almost sleepless night, with a dreadful headache. Savary has been doing the cooking, I suppose I will be compeled to give her up to it now, as Dr. Rembert has decided to give up old Willie. It will inconvenience me very much but I feel in some way bound to do what I can to lessen the expence of getting another cook, I realy begin to feel that I am one of the most unfortunate of human beaings. I am always doing something or offending some one without intending it. Now tonight Dr. Poellnitz became offended with me for a mere trifle when I never dreamed of hurting any body's feelings. Dr. Rembert took it up & spoak the first cross word to me he ever did. Dr. R. becomes more & more sensitive about Dr. P. every day.

Charlottesville<br>Wednesday Night. Sept 10″ 62

Splendid news today from the West, Cincinnati is ours, so says a telegram received here today our brave men are rejoicing greatly. Two of my men had a hand taken off, one on yesterday & one today. Sturgess had his taken off on yesterday the Doctor tells me he stood it bravely he seems to be suffering a good deal today, so is Moser, who had his off today. Both Dr. Davis & Dr. Allen[1] have been down today, they assisted with the opperations. Three of the men who were shot in the head had to have pieces of bone taken out, they were very much exhausted by the opperation. They have been put on Maries ward, it being the most quiet. I am feeling very sick & badly. Today when I went to give the dinner at the hospital I forgot that Dr. Davis & Dr. Allen were to be there, several of the men were standing in the passage on my lower ward waiting for the bel to ring[.] I spoak to them & passed on, I was intent upon geting to where the table was & geting through with my dinner that I did not perceive some gentlemen who were standing there, when I got to the table I saw a very pleasant looking man seated by it[.] I took a good look at him & he at me, I thought I had seen him some where & bowed[.] I then heard Dr. McIntosh say Dr. Davis Mrs. Bacot, astonished I looked up & found Dr. Mac looking very much amused[.] I bowed to Dr. D. then Dr. Rembert introduced me to Dr. A. it was an amusing scene altogether, I got away as soon as I could, without seeming to run[.] Dr. R. amused himself all dinner time joaking me about Dr. Davis he says Dr. D. made so many inquiry's about me, that he even had to spell my name for him. Marie with her mischief has proposed to Dr. R. to invite him down to tea that he may become acquainted with me. I am suffering very much from sickness at my stomach, I can sit up no longer.

---

1. B. W. Allen was a faculty member at the University of Virginia and a surgeon at the Charlottesville Hospital.

Charlottesville
Thursday Night. Sept 11″ 62.

I was very sick all night, & found myself too sick & exhausted to get up for breakfast this morning. Marie for the first time since she came had to sit at the head of the table, I wish I could have seen her[.] Dr. R. has pronounced my disiese jaundice without seeing me, he may have thought on yesterday I was going to have it. I went down about half past ten & found Edward just going up to my room with the morning paper for me. I went to the Monticello but could not stay long, the smell of the wounds made me very sick. I am laughed at where ever I go, but I am by no means as much coloured as either Dr. McIntosh or Mr. Jones.

Charlottesville
Satuday Night. Sept. 13″ 62.

Most of the wounds are doing finely[.] I could not go to the hospital until after ten this morning as I was again unable to get down to breakfast. Poor Sturgess got me to write to his wife for him, he has lost his right hand & yet he bears it with so much fortitude & manliness[.] I can scarcely bear to go into the hospital now the wounds are begining to smell terably, we try to keep it as clean & nice as possible, but seems to me a dreadful poisonous smell hangs about the whole house. some times when the wind is in this direction we can even smell it over here. Little Arthur has been quite sick all day, both the Doctor & Mrs. R. are very uneasy about him, I think it one of the most miserable climates I ever knew of for children. Old Willie left today, very quietly, she did not say goodbye to any of us. Mr. Mills got home just before we went to tea he found his brother, but could not move him, he is comfortably cared for in a private house & has a friend staying with him. We have no idea of the suffering many a poor man lyes down by the roadside & dies with out [a] friend to close his eyes even. I am too sick to write any more, this is certainly a most disgusting desiese.

Charlottesville
Sunday afternoon. Sept. 14″ 62

last night after Marie came up to bed, I beged her to go down & get me a glass of cider[.] She did so, I drank it & was greatly relieved, I had been tossing about for two hours or more unable to sleep or rest in any position five minutes at a time[.] I had no sooner drunk the cider than I felt pleasantly & soon fell into a delightful sleep from which I did not awake until six this morning. I found the men all doing as well as I could possibly expect at the hospital this morning. There is one on Maries ward a Mr. Stone who is not doing well he has unfortunately taken Erysipilis in his wound which I fear will kill him. He has been moved into one of the tents to prevent its spreading among the others on the ward. I went to Willfords tent to see him this morning he has fallen off dreadfuly, but looks better than he did sometime ago. Dr. Rembert & Marie still joak me about Dr. Davis. It is amusing Mr. Mills did not perceive until after breakfast, that I was jaundessed he took a good look at me then roared, asked if I too was in love. Dr. R. says that is the case, of course it is only a piece of his fun. I was lying on the bed this morning reading a paper & noticed that cotton at the north had goten up to 58 cts" per pound. Yes said Marie next year you will be quite a speck I will send Tedd to see you, I had more than half suspected for some time that Marie would like to make a match between her brother & myself. The Sun has scarcely been out today, the weather is delightful.

Charlottesville<br>Monday Night. Sept 15" 62

Nine months have passed since we pressed Virginia soil, a nine months of both pleasure & pain to me. I often think I would be too delighted to see home again but I know I would not be contented to stay away. I would be delighted to go into Maryland now with our army to attend the sick & weary who have no one to speak a kind word to them or give them a cup of water. what is to become of our sick is a matter of great consideration to me. With the army still advancing & no hospitals nearer or easier of access then Culpeper there must necessarly be great suffering. A few goods are being brought in by Jews, but they are so heigh it will be impossible to get any thing. Miss Sampson came up into our room to pay us a visit this afternoon. She is full of life & is good company. I imployed myself the most of the afternoon picking lint. I am feeling a good deal better today the cider has certainly been of considerable benefit so far. It is a lovely night, I longed for a buggy ride this evening, I havent even had a walk for more than a fortnight.

Charlottesville
Sunday Night. Sept 21st" 62

It was such a lovely morning that I determined to try & get to church. If I had had on a pair of good thick shoes I would have enjoyed the walk. Mr. Mead read the service & Dr. Harold preached, I was too far from the pulpit to hear well & Dr. H.'s voice is very weak. I dont all together like his manner he is too affected. I met an old gentleman a Capt. Hall from Newberry S. Carolina at the hospital this evening he came on to try & get a furlough for some young men, living near him. Mr. Mills & Mr. Jones asked Marie & myself to go & walk with them, we accepted the invitation & went as far as Mr. Farishes grounds. I enjoyed the walk very much it being the first of any length I have had for some time. Tea was redy when we got back & we hurried through with it that we might get off to church. Dr. Rembert & his wife went together, Marie & Mr. Mills & Dr. Mac & myself we got in while the congregation were singing. The church is very plane & un-assuming no carpet on the floor & the benches uncushioned, the whole church looked bare & comfortless. The services were conducted in the Presbyterian stile. Mr. Early conducted them, his subject was the Prodigal Son. I have often heard Mr. Early read the buryal service but never heard him preach before. His remarks were very good but he let himself be carryed off beyond his depth, his voice is very weak & you felt all the time that he was over straining himself. I liked the dis-course thought it calculated to do a great deal of good. Edward was the only one left in the house except little Arthur[.] on our way to church Dr. Mac told me Edward was going to Richmond tomorrow. He is go-ing to try to get a furlough home. Oh! I am getting to long for home, for peace, that we might once more enjoy the comforts & conve-niences of our beloved homes. It is roumered today that Gen. Lee had sent a statement to the war department that he had entered Maryland with eighty thousand troops, & he now recrossed the Potomac with just half that number.[2] I cant believe the report still I feel uneasy. I fear

2. While Lee had taken far less than 80,000 men across the Potomac, he had lost a large number of them by the time he returned during the night of September 18, 1862. After the Battle of Antietam on September 17, over 13,000 Confederate casualties—out of a force numbering perhaps 40,000—were reported.

Maryland is not going to come to our relief a few of her sons may be loyal but not so many that we might risk our army with in her borders. God help us, we can do nothing of ourselves.

Charlottesville
. Thursday Morning. Sept. 25" 62

It is one of the loveliest of fall mornings, the air so cool & blue, more than half of the house hold have gone to Monticello to spend part of the day. I put them up a nice lunch as they would not be back to dinner. I have just returned from the hospital, several of the men beged me to intercede for them with Dr. Rembert for a recomendation upon which they can get a furlough, they have a friend going to Richmond who has promised to try & get them for the poor fellows. I felt as if I could have gone & beged the Surgeon General[3] for them myself. One of the men called to me just as I was running through the gate, Mind lady I depend on you to get it for me, you are a S. Carolinian & we trust to you. I promised to do what I could another came up & said I thank you Mrs. Bacot for what you have done for me I can never forget you for it. All this is very gratif[y]ing to me, & I thank God I am able to do something for my country for I feel that I am serving my country when I can do anything for the men who are fighting for my country.

Charlottesville
Thursday Night. Oct 2d" 62

My dutys at the hospital have been pretty much the same as usual today. At dinner Dr. Rembert offered me his horse to take a ride. I accepted & Dr. Mac proposed we should go about half past five. I sent to the Godwins to borrow a saddle & skirt as I had none of my own. I received a very polite note from Miss Mary Godwin regretting she had neither, so I sent to Miss Sampson, there I got the saddle but could get no skirt. I was determined to go whether I had a skirt or not, so I put on my old black silk, it being pretty long & without the hoop I found it answered very well. Dr. Mac helped me up by taking my foot in his hand, I failed the first trial but succeeded a little better the next, I could have goten up very well if I hadent goten into a laugh. I created

---

3. Samuel Preston Moore had been the surgeon general of the Confederate Army since the summer of 1861.

quite a sensation, as many of the soldiers as could get on the little porch came out to see me mount & the gate was filled with darkees. We went out by the Marylanders camp & beyond the mill. Oh! I enjoyed every moment of the time the air was so fresh & pure, & I enjoyed being on horse back once more, before we returned the moon had been up some time & Jupiter made his appearance in time for us to admire his splendor. Marie & Dr. Rembert went up to see if Mrs. McKennies[4] house was for rent, they found the old lady at home & learned she entended remaining here during the winter. What we are to do about a house is something more than I can conjecture, unless we can buy furniture or rent enough for this one. Mr. Charlton Wilson[5] took tea with us this evening.

Charlottesville
Saturday Night. Oct 4″ 62

It has been an entencely hot day. Dr. Mac came home with a sick headache about one oclock. I took him a cup of tea which revived him, but he was too sick to go to dinner. Mrs. Maupin spent the day with us, Mr. M. & herself came down to make out the list of broken glass & china & to find out what was missing generaly from the house, preparatory to the sail which will take place in little more than a week from now. I very much fear there will be some misunderstanding & some heard feeling against Mr. Barnwell. Mrs. M. was very friendly to Marie & myself. Mr. M. is a very sharp cunning man, thinks much of making money, but is just & upright. Mac came down to tea but his head pained him so much he lay on the sofa the rest of the evening. It is beautiful moon light but very warm.

Charlottesville
Monday Night. Oct 6″ 62

As soon after breakfast as we could get off, Mr. Jones, Marie & myself got into the old waggon & went up to Mrs. Daniel's[6] to look at her things which are to be sold tomorrow. Such a time as we had going

4. Possibly the mother of local entrepreneur, militia colonel, and surgeon Marcellus McKennie.

5. Dr. Rembert's secretary at the hospital.

6. Probably the owner of the Daniels boarding house, which was currently serving as part of the Soldiers' Home.

from house to house, looking over old rubish & standing about at last we succeeded pretty well in picking out what we wanted. We first went to Mrs. McKennie to try & rent furniture for our room, she could not rent us any but said she would gladly lend us what we required, dear old lady she was so sweet & kind, said she was very fond of all the Carolinians she had ever known, & would gladly do what she could for them. We had quite an amusing time with old Mrs. Fitch the old lady is the greatest sharper I have met with, she is only a little ahead of the rest of the people here, who are nothing more or less than a set of sharpers, with a few exceptions, Mrs. McKennie for instance, she has been very liberal. We went over to the Harris House to see the ladies there, Mrs. Guinn has grown so fat that she no longer requires her curls to fill her face. It took us until twelve oclock before we could get through[,] at last we were redy to jump into the waggon & start home[.] I could never have made up my mind to ride through our village in such a waggon. If every body here did not do the same I could never think of doing it here. Dr. Rembert has been in since eight oclock this morning he took breakfast with us. We had a magnificent sunset the air is cool & pleasant but the dust suffocating.

Charlottesville<br>Sunday Night. Oct. 12" 62

It was so wet & disagreable a morning that I did not go to church. Nonie is still in bed & Dr. Rembert says he is threatened with Typhoid fever. Marie of course is very much distressed about him, I wrote to Mrs. Smith this evening to know if I could get a room at her fathers for this week, she came over to see me & said they would let me have a very nice room & furnish lights at 50 cts" per day. I of course will take my meals at the hospital & furnish my own wood if I require a fire which I certainly will if the weather continues as cool as it now is, we have had a fire all day. Dr. Rembert has remained in town tonight, both he & Dr. McIntosh have been as kind as possible to Marie & Nonie. Dr. R. has advised Marie to night to move Nonie out of the house tomorrow, so I will go to Mrs. Smith in the morning to see if I can get a room for him. God help us in our trouble. Marie has been weeping all the evening. What will become of her if she looses Nonie, God only knows.

Barracs Charlottesville
Wednesday Afternoon. Oct 15″ 62

Marie says we should call our rooms the Barracks.[7] They certainly deserve the title, soldiers are coming & going all the time. The sale commenced this morning about ten oclock, we had a good view of everything they put in the yard for sale, from Dr. Macs window. Dr. Mac made sevral very good bargans for us. The things were going for a mear song. Mr. Maupin stood by in an agony, he looked the picture of dispare, as the things were put up, he would say how much they were worth & give their history. It was very amusing the people seemed much more disposed to laugh & talk than to bid, so the auctioneer called out ladys & gentlemen less talking & more biding. We had Doctors Harrold[8] & Hamner[9] to dine at the hospital with us. Dr. Harrold is very pleasant & full of fun. He remarked to me that his wife was delighted she was coming where she would have no trouble with house keeping. Dr. Hamner has very little the appearance of a refined gentleman, he is tall & rawboned, a man over fifty I should judge. He seems pleasant & affable in his manner.

After dinner Mr. Wilson went for the mail, on his way he was arrested by Peolie the Sargent of the guard[10] as he was dressed in soldiers cloths & had no pass with him. Mr. W. told him he was now acting as Dr. R.'s secretery but Peolie was not satisfied so Mr. W. refered him to the Doctor they both came up together into the office where they found the Doctor. Peolie said "do you know this gentleman Sir" yes said the Doctor he is my sectery[.] I hope you are satisfied now Sir, said Mr. Wilson & walked off in the most dignified manner, much to the amusement of all. I saw a flock of fourteen wild geese this afternoon flying south ward. Miss Sampson has just come up to see us.

---

7. Until the final decision was made to stay on at the Maupin House, Marie and Ada stayed at the Monticello.

8. Probably Dr. J. A. Harrold, an assistant surgeon at the Charlottesville Hospital.

9. Probably W. W. Hamner, a contract physician at the Charlottesville General Hospital.

10. Unidentified; probably a member of the Provost Guard, a militia unit formed in Charlottesville in August 1862 to guard the General Hospital and commissary stores.

The Barracs. Charlottesville
Thursday Night. Oct. 16" 62

Not one of [us] attended the sale to day, last night about two oclock Capt. Mallory[11] came up to Dr. Macs room to ask him to go out to a place about six miles in the country where the cars had met with an accident. It seems two cows were on the track causing the engine to be thrown from the track pulling five of the first cars after it. they were thrown down a very steep embankment crushing them all to pieces & killing & wounded many of the soldiers in them. Dr. McIntosh discribed it as a most horrable scene, he heard the wounded crying & groaning with their wounds long before he reached the place. Many of the unfortunate victims were lying around large fires made on the side of the road while the dead were scattered here & there among the men. Dr. Rembert went out about ten oclock, where they all remained until near three when they came up with the wounded which were taken off at the Delevan. I am told the chamber furniture sold well, the bedsted we used went for over $50, the parlor furniture also sold well, a Jew merchant gave ten dollars apiece for the chairs & the sofa brought $50. So Mr. Maupin's face wore a smile instead of a frown today. Nonie is very much better. Dr. Poellnitz has been in a very bad humor today he would scarcely speak to me. Mrs. Rembert was in all the morning she gave us the key to Dr. P.'s ill nature it seems some one told Dr. Rembert that he had been drinking again where upon the Doctor told him if such was the case he must make up his mind to leave here immediately. Poellnitz denied most biterly that he had taken any thing, he suspected Marie & myself of telling on him, how he would deny having taken any thing I dont see for I know positively that he did, & that he was affected by [it], though neither Marie or myself had told on him.

The Barracs. Charlottesville
Friday Noon Oct 17" 62

I had a good nights sleep last night the first I have had since I came over here. My walk in the evening did me a great deal of good, I went to see Mrs. Old Mrs. Rion & Miss Clarke & was much pleased with

---

11. William Barton Mallory was currently the captain of the Provost Guard and was also a member of the 19th Virginia Infantry.

the latter, she like ourselves is a volunteer from S. Carolina, & a very nice lady like person. This morning before I was out of my room Miss Carington was up here in search of Dr. R. she was here yesterday after noon to see him about the filling of the place Mrs. Guinn has just vacated. Mrs. Chockran it seems wishes the place given to a Miss Gay a maiden lady a Virginian & a very nice person, & Miss Carington came down to see about it so much afraid was she that he would give the place to some one else, about ten oclock Miss Gay came down to the Monticello to see Marie & myself, she wished to be taken over the hospital as she had heard we had every thing conducted in the best way especialy the dietry department. I took her round upon my two wards & explained as well as I could how we managed the diet. Dr. Rembert has gone up to see Mrs. Chockran about Miss Gay, as he had given the place to Mrs. Pool.[12] Old Mrs. Carington the mother of Mrs. Chockran came down & objected so strongly to Mrs. Pools going up to the Harris House as a companion for her daughter that the Doctor thought it best to go & see them all together. The weather is most delightful[.] Mrs. Maupin told me this morning I might go to cleaning up the house now. Accordingly I put two or three hands to washing the windows.

### Afternoon

The Doctor got back while we were at dinner, he says old Mrs. Carington went up with him to see Mrs. Chockran & they were very much opposed to Mrs. Pools taking the place the old lady said if Mrs. P. was put there her daughter should leave, that she should not stay to associate with such a person[,] that she had no acquaintance with Mrs. P.[,] that they had never heard of her before & the like[.] Capt. Chockran said he would take his wife away if her wishes in the matter were not consulted, Mrs. C. herself was perfectly willing to stay & do every thing in her power to sute the Doctors convenience, that she had no objection to being with Mrs. Pool, but her husband & mother said positivly she should not if Mrs. P. was put there, what could the Doctor do, but say he would try & make some other arrangement for Mrs. Pool & give Miss Gay the vacant place at the Harris House. why is it that people cant agree & make every thing as pleasant as possible,

---

12. The wife of Mr. Pool, the steward of the Monticello Hospital.

I for one will try & be different from every one else in that respect & be contented with what ever place the Doctor chooses to assign me.

Night

I went over to the Hospital rather earlier than usual this evening as I had a bed to prepare for Mr. Cooper who has taken a room with Mr. Wilson, he is wounded in the foot. I also went to the kitchen to see Miss Sampson, I found her very busy getting something redy for the men's tea. I saw the men get their tea & was at the door speaking to Mr. Tarrer (who looks remarkably well & seemed very glad to see me.) when Dr. Mac came in & asked me if I would take a walk with him before our tea. I was too glad of a run in the fresh air to refuse, so we walked to Mr. Farishes gate & back, I fear very much that there is some very serious misunderstanding between Dr. R. & Dr. Mac, from being the best of friends they have become almost enemies. I fear too that Dr. Poellnitz is the cause of it. I am very much distressed about it. There was two young men S. Ca's & their sister came in to the hospital from the country today where the eldest of the young men has been staying. The woman came up to me & asked if she could stay with me tonight, I told her no that I had but the one room, she then asked where the women staid that came to the Hospital I told her none ever came to stay, but that I could give her a room for the night which had nothing in it. That I would have a bed moved in there for her & would try & make her as comfortable as possible. I saw two very large potatoes in one of the wards as I went round, one of the men had bought them for thirty cents a piece. Often have I known them to sell for less than that a bushell. I am too sorry I did not get the little clock that has directed my movements ever since I first came here, it sold for 9 or 10 dollars, I dont know who bought it. I know I shall miss it when I go back to my room.

The Barracs. Charlottesville
Monday Night. Oct 20″ 62

I tryed hard to effect our move today but did not succeed quite, I moved over Dr. Mac, & a part of our things but not enough for us to go. Marie Nonie & myself are the only ones over here tonight. Dr. Mac insisted that we should let him stay in Nonies room & Marie stay with me but Marie was afraid to leave Nonie even for a night, so we had to stay by ourselves. I am too much fatigued even to sleep[.] I have been first at one house then the other the whole day besides having the whole Hospital in my charge for Miss Reynolds has now gone regularly to bed. I have so much to think of that I cant think of anything. Miss Lewis came into the hospital to see why I would not send them the rashons as they have been getting them, because said I, I did not know you had been getting rashons, I know nothing about it. But said she if I were in your place I would have known, I told her I had my own dutys to attend to & did not meddle in any one elses. That if Mr. Pool[13] said she could have what she wanted I would have no objection. She then said she heard from Miss Carington that Dr. Rembert had said the kitchen was nothing more than extra expense[.] I told her I had nothing to do with that, she must see Dr. R. if she wished to know about it, That I knew nothing about it that I had purposely kept out of it. She was very vexed, & said if that was his opinion as she had been formost in getting up the kitchen she would be in putting it down & they would all go where their efforts to do for the soldiers were better appreciated. Dr. Mac has staid with us until bed time, said at parting he could not bear to leave us all alone.

Maupin House. Charlottesville<br>Tuesday Night. Oct 21st" 62

I have not had a half hour to rest this day, I was up at half past six having slept very little during the night. There was some soldiers belonging to a Maryland Reg. encamped just out of town, who were on a regular spree, before their departure, they left this morning. The whole town was disturbed with them until a late hour last night. I hear there was a large frost this morning I am sure it was cold enough. The wind has been very heigh & cool today, I could scarcely keep my feet in crossing the street. At last we are fixed enough to sleep in the house, but we still take our meals at the Hospital as we have not the servants we most need yet.

Mrs. Poellnitz & Col. Bratton[14] come today. Dr. Poellnitz has asked the Col. to stay here, although we are in such confusion, I think it the

---

13. Mr. Pool was the steward of the Monticello.

14. Probably John Bratton (1831–1898) of the Winnsboro District in South Carolina, a physician who had quickly risen to the rank of colonel in the South Carolina regiments serving with General John B. Hood's division of Longstreet's Corps of the Army of Northern Virginia and who had been captured at the Battle of Seven Pines. Bratton was promoted to brigadier general in 1864 and served as a state senator and member of Congress after the war.

most inconsiderate thing I ever heard of[.] This afternoon Dr. Mac walked into his room & saw a man lying asleep on his bed, he could not tell what it ment. He had never see Col. B. nor did he know he was in the house. Dr. P. had deliberately taken him into Dr. Mac's room without saying a word to the Doctor about it. Just before tea he told the Doctor he had taken him there to take a nap, that the Col. was going to stay with us tonight. Of course there was nothing else to do but let him stay. What I saw of him at supper impressed me very favorably. He is a tall well made man, with a fine head & rather a handsome face, upon the whole a striking man, very quiet & dignified in his manners. about a half hour ago Dr. P. sent to ask me for a candle for Col. B., I asked the girl what he was going to do with it, thinking he was in Mac's room & I could not imagine what he wanted with a candle as Mac had candles in his room, the girl said he was to sleep in a room on this floor, so Marie said no he could not, & told the girl to ask Dr. P. to come to our room that she wanted to see him, he came & she asked him what room the Col. was to occupie, he said Dr. R.'s that he had given him permission to put him there. We of course could say nothing more. I am now ocupieng Nonies room as it has no fire place, & he has mine with his mother until he is well enough to go about. My bed is a lounge made something on the order of a stretcher only much narrower with a straw bed on it such as the soldiers use. Dr.'s R. & Mac are very much conserned for fear I am not comfortable. I am suffering with my head & back so much that I cannot write any more though there is much I would like to say.

Charlottesville
Friday morning. Oct 31st" 62

I am too homesick this morning, I told Dr. Rembert I could not make up my mind to stay any longer. Savary has been giving me trouble, I fear I will have to sell her she could not stand the test, I declare it has made me feel dreadfuly. I found Miss Nelson at the hospital distributing flowers & potatoes. She had taken poor Elder a little sago jelly which he was enjoying. Johnson came out of his room today. The weather is charming only a little too warm for my comfort. A Telegram came here this morning to the effect that England France & Spain had demanded a suspension of hostilitys from the North, & if it is not granted they will reconize us.

Charlottesville
Tuesday Night. Nov 4" 62

I have been very busy today packing, I find things have accumulated very much, since I first came on. Dr. Rembert & the ladys have been telling me all day how much they will miss me. I was thinking so much about going home that I forgot the beef was short at the Hospital & I could not get any for dinner. I had to go out & try to get chickens, but they were not to be had, so I had to get Eggs at 75 cts" a doz, I succeeded much better than I had any idea I could in getting up a dinner. David left this morning for Richmond he is to engage rooms for us tomorow. Mr. Barnwell came today, he is only here until tomorrow, he will go part of the way to Richmond with us, he paid Marie & myself a great compliment by saying he would be delighted to have us with him in Richmond, that we had done our duty so faithfuly that he would give us any post we might desire, from his account of the living in Richmond I dont see how we can go there. He says he was charged two thousand dollars for a house, he now pays 600 dollars for three rooms, I realy was sorry to leave so pleasant a household even for so short a time. Mac made me a present of a beautiful book tonight, I am just beginning to realize how I will miss him when we get back for then he will have his wife to pet him, but I must not be selfish. I feel too sorry for Marie she of course cant bear the idea of being left behind.

Chapter 8

# November 5, 1862–January 18, 1863

*"I . . . feel that my duty is in Va. now."*

Gordonsville<br>Wednesday noon. Nov 5" 62

After considerable fixing this morning trying to leave every thing in as good order as possible, we started for the depot. Marie, Mrs. Rembert & Miss Jessie Herald walked down with me Mrs. H. bid me quite an affectionate adieu & hoped it would not be long before I would return. Dr. Rembert & Nonie also were at the depot to see us off. Mr. Barnwell came with us this far. he was very kind telling me to call on my way back & he would take me round to see the Hospitals & show me what ever I wished to see. He also instead of giving me transportation which would have kept me a day longer in Richmond, lent me 100 dollars, telling me I need not be in a hurry to return it. Dr. Mac has had to stand up all the way to this place, the cars are so much crowded, my what a throng there is here officers & men hurrying here & there all runing up against each other. The old lady who sat next to me when she had finished her lunch gave the rest to a poor soldier passing. I never saw any one more grateful he ate what there was & when the last was gone he came to the window & bowed to the old lady again. There goes the whistle, we are off.

Richmond Night

Such a jam as there was in the cars the gentlemen had to take turns to sit. Dr. Mac had to stand most of the way, Gen. & Dr. Jenkins[1] of S. Carolina were on hand, they stood very near me most of the time & I could hear their conversation, the Gen. is very affable Dr. Mac knew them & they passed the time very pleasantly. A Bridal party got on bord at Gordonsville they were married this morning at church,

---

1. Micah Jenkins (1835–1864) — a graduate of the South Carolina Military Academy and founder of the King's Mountain Military School at Yorkville, South Carolina — had been serving with South Carolina regiments in Virginia since the start of the war and had been made brigadier general in July 1862. He was killed by gunfire from his own men in the Battle of the Wilderness in 1864. Dr. Jenkins was presumably his brother.

the groom was a very young looking Surgeon. The crowd at the depot was imense it was some time before the Doctor could get a hack, we succeeded at last & came to the Spotswood, where David has procured me a nice little room, the only objection to it, being so high up. I thought I would never reach it when the boy was showing me to it. Dr. Mac soon came for me to go to tea. David met us at the parlor door as we went down, & we went into tea together. They gave us some very nice rolls & a passable cup of tea. Dr. Mac has gone for our passports, we leave here in the morning between three & four.

Petersburg<br>Thursday morning. Nov 6" 62

We started this morning about four oclock from Richmond. It had been raining all day & it still rained a little, we ran down here in about two hours, I got my feet very wet getting out. I prefered to dry my feet by the fire to going to the breakfast table, Dr. Mac & the Captain went, They say I did not miss any thing by stoping. I see from the window crowds of soldiers, some of them poorly clad & shivering in this cold morning air. The gentlemen say it is time to start.

Waldon, one oclock

The rain comes down fast & every thing is driping wet. The guard was very strict at Petersburg, stoping us at two entrances one where we showed our passports the other our railroad tickets. at last we got off. We have determined to go the central rout as we find we will have to stay here until 6 oclock this afternoon if we go by Wilmington. Not many ladys going South. We are traveling very slowly. A great many soldiers & officers going South on furlough.

Raleigh 6 oclock afternoon

We change cars here again, & miserable work again getting from one car to the other. just one puddle after another, fortunately though it did not rain, I got my feet soaking wet this time, I have been sitting by the stove trying to dry them but have only partly succeeded.

Charlotte N.C.<br>Friday Morning. Nov 7" 62

We travled all night we have only goten this far. we had another bride & groom on bord last night, nothing could have been more out of taste than the brides dress. It was amusing to see them they imagined they were not seen as there was only one light in the car & that down at the farther end, so they endulged in a few kisses. I slept more than usual, having a whole seat to myself. Dr. Mac was very kind & attentive, we had no supper, but I did not feel the want of any. we arrived here at six[.] The morning air is very cold real icie, we have come to the same hotel Pa & myself stoped at about four years ago. I made the acquaintance of a very pleasant young lady a Miss Woodson of Charlottesville, she has travled with us all the way, her face was very familiar but I had never heard her naim, we stoped at the same hotel & she told me her name & that of her escort. I happened to know his sisters Lizzie & Lydier Wood. The breakfast was very good, except that instead of Coffee we had Rye. The morning air is delightful, so much pleasanter than yesterday.

### Chester N.C.

Twelve oclock the cars stop here half an hour for dinner. I did not get out. Miss Woodson bought some ground nuts & invited me to partake. Capt. Wood[2] has just come in he says he was invited to partake of some of the soldiers free dinner, I noticed that last night when we stoped at a place called the shops for supper a boy brought in a basket filled with provision for the sick & wounded. I have noticed that since we got into N. Carolina provision seems to be much more abundant & decidedly cheaper.

### Winnsborough

The old town as far as I can see looks just the same as when I passed here about four years ago. An old lady with her servant has just passed through the cars with a basket of food things & a bottle of wine for the sick soldiers, one can not help noticing the difference of feeling towards soldiers in N.C. & S. Carolina to Virginia, there they try to make all they can out of them, in the two states mentioned they are given almost every thing. Oh! there is no place like Carolina.

### Columbia S. Ca.
### Friday Night. Nov 7″ 62

We found after getting to the depot that if we went on tonight we would have a dreadful time at Ringsville so we determined to stop here for the night, the Doctor too seemed to wish us to do so, after some difficulty the Capt. got our bagage off, it had been marked for Florence

---

2. Possibly Captain Thomas Wood, quartermaster for Albemarle County, Virginia.

& at first they told us we could not get it — by a little purceverance we did get it & came to Nickersons Hotel my room is comfortable but nothing extra[.] our tea was not inviting Rye for Coffee & the milk more than half water. however I was not very hungry so it did not matter, there was plenty of nice hominy & Butter which was a treat to all of us as we have not seen any for so long.

Mrs. Maxwell & her husband are here tonight[.] I saw her before her marriage but as she did not reconize me I did not speak to her. I could have almost fancyed myself in Charleston so many Charlestonians are here, Maries friend Mrs. Ford is also here she is leaving in the morning for the up country. My two the Doctor & Captain sat with me a while then went out to make some purchases. I enjoyed myself listning to the conversation of the ladys, I have not heard so much kind feeling & sympathy expressed for the soldiers in Virginia the whole time I was there as I have heard here tonight. The gentlemen came back about half past eight[.] I never have seen the Doctor is such fine spirits. He invited me to go to a consert with him, but I feel a little fatigued from my three day's travle, then too we make a very early start in the morning.

Kingsville  
Saturday morning. Nov 8″ 62

We had to get up at five this morning to take the cars for this place. They gave us breakfast before we left. Oh! my how I miss my coffee. When we got to the depot we found that a part of my bagage had been left behind of course we could not wait for it, I very much fear it is lost. This is the coldest morning we have had yet. The ground is white with frost. There were so many around the fire when I came in that I could not get to it for a while. We have to stay here until three oclock this afternoon. I have met a very nice old gentleman here the Rev. Mr. Erlish the father in law of Mr. LaCost whom I nursed at Charlottsville. Dr. Player is also here so the time has not hung so heavily on my hands as I anticipated, I dont think I have ever seen a more desolate place.

Gen. Harlee's. Mars Bluff. Night

The Captain left me at Florence as he had to take the other train for Society Hill. I found after he had gone that we would be detained some time at Florence owing to a dreadful accident which took place with in a quarter of a mile of the depot. The engine of the midday train blew up killing three men & wounding the engineer so severely he is not expected to live. Soon after leaving the depot on the other side of Timonsville some one threw a brick at the cars which hit the window by which Savary was sitting, broke the glass & hit S. on the face. The conductor Mr. Brock was very polite when I got to this depot he handed me off & took me to the fire in the warehouse. Mr. Pearce then came up & spoke to me, & I requested him to write a note to the General & ask if he would be kind enough to send me up home. The carriage was more than an hour getting to the depot, the servant said the Gen. & Mrs. Harllee asked if I would not spend the night & they would take me up in the morning, I concluded to do so as it was a long ride & Saturday night too & I thought it would be fatiguing the horses too much. Mrs. H. was very kind & seemed very glad to see me. She has given me her best room & I have a very nice fire, It is very cold.

Roseville
Sunday Night. Nov 9" 62

I had a night of tolerable comfort at the Generals, not that every thing was not as nice & comfortable as possible but I was in such a state of excitement & it was so cold I could not sleep, as soon as Savary made the fire I got up & dressed. We breakfasted about nine, Miss Henning Miss Ford & Miss Butler were staying with Mrs. H., I had thousands of questions to answer, at last we got off to church. I did not stop, I met cousin John on the way, a little way from here I met Pa going for me, Sister is still in bed & looking very badly, the little baby is a nice little thing her name is Ada Graham partly in compliment to me. The other children are all the picture of health & were delighted to see me. Pa is looking remarkably well & Peronneau is as fat as possible[.] I met with a most harty welcom, the Servants too flocked around me. Flora has grown very much & I think her quite improved. Her curls have been cut but I dont know that she looks any the worse for it. Pet is here having come up last night, he looks well & has turned out quite a beard. He brought Louise to see me this evening she is very thin, Irene Jane & George also came over. Some of my flowers are looking pretty well but I have lost a great many, I succeeded in gathering a very pretty bunch this afternoon just in time to save them from the frost.

Roseville
Friday Night. Nov 14" 62

Pa was up at five oclock this morning & off to Florence by six he went to see our negroes off but there had been a colission on the North Eastern road about half way, injuring both engines, but no life was lost. So the negroes have to remain at Florence until tomorrow morning. I walked over to see Mrs. McCall this afternoon, I had a very pleasant time[.] Mrs. McC. & Nett both seemed so glad to see me. Nett was knitting an undershirt for Gregg, she showed me one she had finished it is realy very nice, our people are up & doing the Yankees will never subjecate us, for we are willing to endure every privation. Every one about this part of the country that I have seen, seems patient & hopeful of course there is necessarly much distress, for there is no family that has not some portion of it in the army. Every woman is exerting herself to do somthing to make the poor soldier more comfortable. I was also at Mrs. McLendons this evening I find Flora has outgrown & worn out all of her cloaths, how I am to get her fixed up for the winter I can not now tell, I could do better if my time were not so limited.

Roseville

Saturday Night. Nov 15" 62

Pa was going to the village this morning so I concluded to go as far as Arnmore with him notwithstanding it was so showery. I found Mr. Gray[3] at Old Hannahs house cutting up the beef. It was so nice I sent Mrs. Shackelford some of it. Although I was not in calling trim I went in to see Mrs. S. as I heard she was about moving away, I found her sister Miss Eliza Ford & a Miss L. were with her. I was much pleased with Miss F. she is a very stilish looking girl with most pleasing manners. Mrs. S. too seems to be a nice person she met me very corduly though I had never seen her before. she expressed herself much pleased with Arnmore & regreted being obliged to leave. Old Hannah gave me a glass of milk & a potatoe at dinner time which I enjoyed. My negroes seem to dislike the idea of my leaving home again. They beg me to stay with them, poor things what would they do with out some one to take care of them. The inclination to stay at home is very strong some times, but when I think of what I can do for the suffering Soldier, I am willing to forgo every pleasure & return to my dutys. I went in to see Mrs. Gray who was preparing the thread for my dresses. I pity the poor woman with so many small children. My faithful old Hannah has kept every thing very nicely for me. Mr. Gray wanted me to ride over the crop but I had not time. God has blessed me abun-

---

3. Mr. Gray was acting as Ada's overseer at Arnmore.

dantly, may I be sufficiently greatful. My negroes have all been well & I have made a fine crop[.] It was nearly night when we returned. Sister was sitting up still having remained up all day.

Roseville<br>Tuesday Night. Nov 18" 62

It has been a beautiful bright day almost as warm as Spring. Leah almost bled to death at the noze. She bled nearly all night, it was stoped about seven oclock but commenced again about ten, the Doctor was sent for & arrived in time to save her life. There was great excitement among the negroes, they thought "aunt Leah was going for dead." Mrs. McCall Nett & Mary spent the day with us[.] Nett is still my sweet friend. Sister gave me one of her dresses today which I can make fit me with very little alteration. It rains hard & is very warm. Mr. Moore & Miss Martin called this afternoon. I weighed this evening more than I ever did in my life, (139 lbs") I have never been in better health[.] I have Oh! so much to be thankful for.

Roseville<br>Thursday Night. Nov 20" 62

The rain has poured in torants all day, & is now. The old House leeks all over, there is not a dry spot on the piazza. Pet came up last night, he has ten days furlough then returns to camp. Cousin Fannie called this morning between the showers. she was in the blues decidedly. I feel sorry for an[y] one who has so misserable an oppinion of the Government & its heads. Pa went to muster this morning in all the rain, when he returned he found he had left his gun behind leaning by a tree on the field[.] Nice order it will be in when he gets it if he ever does.

Roseville<br>Saturday Noon. Nov 22d" 62

The sun shone bright & clear into my room this morning rousing me from a delightful nap which I indulged in after the children left my room. Mr. Gray came in to see me on some business about an hour ago, while I was talking with him, Peter walked into the room[.] I did not moove to speak to him, but he came up to me & shook me by the hand & kissed me, he inquired after my health & I after his, nothing more, Oh! how my heart thrilled with pain[.] I had hoped never again to see him, but perhaps it is best. He has an appointment in the Confederate Hospital at Florence. I have seldom seen him look worse.

Night

Sister very nervous. I hate the thought of leaving her in such delicate health, but feel that my duty is in Va. now. I am more anxious to get back than I care to confess[.] Miss Julia Lesesne came up with Mrs. T. Pa has gone to call on her. Pet dined with us, he went out & killed two birds for Sister this afternoon[.] Sister received a trunk from her husband today with some thing Mrs. Saunders[4] had sent to the children, when they were opened I never saw such smiles of delight as brightened the faces of Louie & Sissy. Wm" sent Louie an overcoat which delighted him beyond discription he put it on & struted around to show it. Gump must see it so off he ran to find him. It is clear and quite cold tonight. I wish very much I could be of the happy party going to Newberry tonight.

Roseville
Saturday Night. Nov 29" 62

I feel wearyed out tonight. Cousin Tom[5] came down this morning he pulled out one tooth & put in three plugs for me, I hope now my teeth will go through the Winter. Pa went to Darlington today, I sold some fodder to the Government at $2 a hundred, the agent represents the need of it very great. Wm. told us of one of the dreadful sights he saw in Virginia. The Yankees had been in posession of the place, & we had driven them back, in one end of the garden a man had been buried but so shallow was the grave, his hand was sticking up, lying on the ground in another part of the garden was a sute of Yankee cloths with human bones in them, some poor wretch had died there & the birds had eaten him, in the house stretched on his blanket on the floor lay another corps blackened & dry in the position he died, with one leg drawn up. He had been left to die alone, left to die horable idea. Oh! how many tales simelar to this could be told, yes & of our own men. Oh! war the horrors of war.

On the Cars
Wednesday morning. Dec 3d" 62

I got to Florence just in time last night to take the cars. My friends were on board. David came to the carriage to meet me, the Dr. seemed

---

4. Jacqueline Bacot Saunders's mother-in-law.

5. Thomas Westfield Bacot (b. ca. 1822) was a surgeon-dentist.

delighted to see me, & Fannie met me as if I had been an old friend I think her rather pretty than other wise. She is spritely looking with very pretty eyes a sweet expression about the mouth & beautiful teeth. Walter Gregg was at Florence he realy seemed glad to see me. Although we were on a sleeping car to Wilminton it was any thing but comfortable to me. Others seemed to enjoy them as I heard many snoring around me[.] we arrived at W. about one oclock only remained there long enough to get the baggage taken from one car to the other. There is a great crowd going on, the cars were as much crowded last night as I have seen them in Va. refugees are returning to W. now, all danger from the fever is past. We got to Goldsborough about seven oclock, did not get out to breakfast as we had lunch with us. It rained nearly all night after we left W., & is still pouring. Mac is as kind as ever to me, David too is very courtious, he occupies a seat by me. So far we have escaped accident.

Charlottesville<br>Monday Night. Dec 8″ 62.

Marie very kindly said she would keep the key's & let me rest for a day or so. I have not been out today. Fannie has been in my room most of the day. Mrs. Rembert is quite sick so Marie is with her most of the time. Dr. Rembert & Dr. Mac received orders to Richmond to stand their examination, the Doctor leaves tomorrow & Mac goes next week. The snow has not melted in the least, I dread the idea of going out into the cold. I am so much pleased with Dr. Harrold, I sit next to him at table while Marie continues at the head of the table, I am delighted we have so nice a family[.] Mr. Mills & Mr. Jones take their meals at the Hospital, which gives us much more room at table. Dr. R. seems very nervous about his eximiniation. Arthur has improved wonderfuly. He calls me Aunt Coats so sweetly.

Charlottesville<br>Monday Night. Dec 15″ 62

Marie turned the keys over to me today she did it in form, I have had a very busy day. Fannie finds it hard to stay behind while Mac goes to R. As Mac took his seat at the dinner table he gave me a bright smile & said he was very glad to see me in my old place again. Dr. H. too said he was very glad to have me at the head of affairs once more.

I am trying hard to get things in order. I have Mr. Coats[6] now as Marie has Mr. Haden[7] though Mr. H. is general ward master & supervises the whole. I have one poor man in a dieing state tonight. Most of the others are improving. The wounded from the battle fields of Fredericksburg most of them have gone to the Delevan. Some persons in town say they heard canonading very distinctly today. The weather could not be more favorable for a battle may God be with us.[8]

Charlottesville
Tuesday Night. Dec 16" 62

I never remember a more boistrou[s] night in the midst of March than last night was. every window in the house rattled & the shutters stormed at a most furious rate. Fannie & I went to see Mac off this morning, we got down to the Depot about twenty minutes before the train started, Mac stood talking to us until the conductor called out all aboard he shook hands huradly with me & gave Fannie one long, long embrace & was off. we stood on the piazza of the ware house watching the cars move off, but they only moved a little way to give room for another train which came up filled with Soldiers which got onto the Richmond train[.] we stood watching the crowd & trying to see Mac from the cars, but we could see nothing of him. The crowd began to disperse & we found we were the only ladys left, so I told Fannie I did not think it propper to remain any longer especialy as we could not see Mac by remaining as he was locked in the ladys car & could not get out. I was busy all the morning at the Hospital. although Mr. Pool is stuard & his wife pretends to look after things generaly there are many things Marie & myself find we must direct. The Servants seem to have a much higher respect for us, there fore we can manage them more easily. When Dr. Poellnitz came in to dinner I noticed he had been taking something. He talked a great deal to Dr. Harrold which is not usual & talked about his own private affairs which I did not suppose he would do if he had been in his right mind[.] I was sitting with Fannie just before the tea bell rang talking & laughing, when I heard some

---

6. A wardmaster at the Monticello.

7. Another wardmaster at the Monticello.

8. There was no battle in the vicinity of Charlottesville after the Confederate victory at the Battle of Fredericksburg on December 13, 1862.

one come to the front door & try to get in. The door was locked & he kicked & banged away until Jane went to open it. It was Dr. P. he was so drunk he could he could scarcely stand, when Jane opened the door she invited him in but he stood there bowing with his hands in his pockets & said he would not come in until he knew why the door was locked, so Jane left the door open & came in to the room she had bearly shut the door when he began to call Jane at the top of his voice, finding she did not go to him he stagered in & went to his room. Poor Mrs. P. she has the sympathy of the household. She could not come to her tea, Dr. Paten called after tea to see Dr. P. but he was not fit to receive him[.] I had two sweet letters today one from Pa & the other from Dick containing his photograph, I am sleeping with Fannie to-night I promised Mac to take the best of care of her[.] I am very very much pleased with Fannie she is a dear warm hearted girlish person full of life but not thoughtless[.] Mac is all devotion to her. It is very, very late Fannie & I have been talking regardless of how time was passing.

Charlottesville<br>Saturday Morning. Dec 20" 62

Oh! how I wish I could be in Dear old Carolina today where the people are celebrating the second anniversary of their independence or rather their withdrawal from a hateful Government. Here no one thinks of it except the few Carolinians who are here. Old Mrs. Rion & ourselves celebrate the day with a Sumtious dinner. When I went to the hospital a little while ago, I found the men all drawn up over the fires it is so entencely [cold] no one seems to be enclined to move. The dead house has just been finished. I hope we shall very seldom need it. I found the men very much better, none ill except one poor man who has been lingering for several days, yesterday a priest came all the way from Staunton in an open buggy to see him, I could but admire his zeal, for it was a terable night to be out. He received Mr. H.'s tele-gram, asking him to come, just in time to take the stage, but there was no room for him, so he hired a buggy & road all night, that he might add one to his church.

Night

Mac came looking very happy but much thiner than when he left. He met with a very warm reception from us all. Fannie went to the depot to meet him. We sat down to dinner directly after he got in. All of the gentlemen complimented me on the dinner & all did full justice to it. Marie wanted to know if it was in compliment to the day or to Mac. I told her it was both. Both Fannie & Mac sent for me this afternoon to go & sit in their room, but I did not go because I thought they would rather be left alone as they had been separated for several day's. I begin to feel the effect of the hospital upon my spirits alredy. Marie is delighted that Mac has returned so she can have me with her this bitter cold weather.

Charlottesville<br>Thursday Night. Dec 25" 62

   This is now the second christmas I have spent in this place. We were disturbed by the noise in the street long before daylight I had just gotten out of bed this morning when Charlie & Mary both burst into the room crying Christmas gift. Child like they had been all around at every door. It was rather hard to collect our family[.] at breakfast I gave Marie her present & sent one to Fannie & Mac, before they were out of their room. I received a beautiful Prayer book from Mac & Wordsworths Pastoral Poems from Fannie. Fannie wrote in hers (Sister Ada from Fannie)[.] Marie saw it & declared she would tell Dr. Rembert, I beged until she partly promised she would not. The children were as happy as possible with their presents. I was busy here until eleven, then went to the hospital the men were in fine spirits, we took the dinner to the wards first then went down to the dining room & prepared the dinner for the rest. They had plenty of Turkey ham Mutton, Rice, potatoes, bread Pies & apples. It was two oclock before we got home, We had our dinner at half past three. a sumptuous one it was too. Mrs. Rion sent us down a present of pies & rusks this morning. The dinner was going off very pleasantly until Dr. Poellnitz chose to get in a passion about something Dr. Harrold said I felt too sorry for little Mrs. P. she looked as if she would have sunk out of her chair. Every one of the ladys in the house have been teasing me to let them see the book Fannie gave me, I would not because of what was written in it. Had a nice long letter from Sister. Have just returned from the Hospital wher I have been giving the men their Eggnog. We are to have an oyster supper here tonight. I must dress for it is time I was down seeing about it.

After Supper

   I soon succeeded with Savary & Janes help, in getting every thing. The oysters were pronounced very good, all except myself ate very hartely of them. Dr. P. was on the stool of repentance, so the supper passed off beautifuly. I was much complimented on the days entertainment. A little while after we had finished supper, Dr. Mac Fannie & I made the eggnog for the rest of the party & a plenty of fun we had over it. I was the last to come up stairs, found Dr. Rembert in our room talking to Marie. As soon as I came in both of them began to beg me to show the book Fannie gave me[.] before I could make an objection Marie gave it to the Doctor, he then got hold of my Journal & was reading away, I caught him & tryed in every way to get it from him, but could not for I became so weak from laughing I could do nothing. I succeeded at last in getting it away. Dr. Harrold came to the door a few minutes ago & asked Dr. R. to go up again & see Martha,[9] she has had another convu[l]sion. I am too unwell & tired to think of offering to sit up. Dr. H. has just sent for Marie.

Charlottesville<br>Friday Morning. Dec 26" 62

Marie sat up until near six this morning, then I went up & staid until breakfast. The poor girl had one convu[l]sion after another until I thought she must die, once I thought her quite gone & ran in for Jessie & the other children, she revived a little & I made fresh mustard plasters & put them on. The whole family are in the greatest distress, poor Dr. H. wept bitterly he said she had been his pride, to me it is an awful thing to see a man weep. Our family at breakfas[t] was very small.

Afternoon

Martha still alive, they tryed hard to get a daguerrotype of her just before dinner, but she was too restless, she had a convu[l]sion every few minutes, she is almost gone now. Miss Tenel an acquaintance of the H.'s dined with us today, I never saw a greater odity. There seems to be a gloom spred over the whole house. Dr. Rembert insists upon my going with him to the party tonight. I have not the least inclination to do so. Savary's trunk has come at last every thing safe.

Night

It is a sad, sad sight to see a young girl die. Tis sad to quit this beautiful world while all is bright but "Gods will be done." Martha I have no doubt is taken from much evil. God grant she may enjoy that rest which is only

---

9. Dr. Harrold's daughter.

to be found above. Mac & Fannie went up to see her tonight, the room was so warm & close that F. came very near fainting. There is a profound stillness through the house, & gloom on every countenance. Of course none of us went to the party tonight. I sit up not that there is any thing to be done but mearly to be with Mrs. Harrold.

Charlottesville<br>Saturday Morning. Dec 27″ 62

I sat up until seven this morning Martha still breaths, but is considerable weaker than the first part of last night. She is uncon[s]cious & has not spoken since yesterday morning. It is agonizing to her poor parents to see her life spun out so as they can do nothing for her. The weather is gloomy & disagreeable.

Night

I had just laid me down to rest a few moments about four oclock this afternoon, when Jane opened the door & told me Martha was dead, I went up & found the family all around her weeping bitterly. Dr. Harrold was on the bed by her, in an agony of grief, he covered her hand with kisses & bathed it in tears. Yet he was resigned. Miss H. Jane & myself dressed the body. Never befor did I ever do such a thing except to dress Peters little baby when it died but then that was so different[.] I have always had the greatest horror of tutching a dead person. I got through remarkably well much better than I had an idea I could. Fannie Mac & myself offered to sit up with the body tonight, but Dr. H. said it was not necessary that he would shut up the room, & keep a light burning & that he would go in ocasionaly during the night. Jessie is staying with us tonight.

Charlottesville<br>Tuesday Night. Dec 30″ 62

Hated dreadfuly to get up this morning. It was dark & misty nothing to invite one up, being housekeeper I dare not endulge, perhaps it is best. Just before dinner I came in from the Hospital it was raining a little, met Mac & Fannie at the door just going out for a walk beged F. to pay me a visit instead which she did. Mrs. Rembert & the Doctor came in soon after & we had a pleasant little party. I was very sorry to be obliged to brake it up to go down to dinner. Fannie said Miss Carington had called & invited all the ladys of the house to attend a party at her mothers on New Years night. I am sorry, I think I know why it

was given though I may be mistaken. There seems to be considerable
feeling against us here, we heard here the other day that it was understood that we did not wish to associate with the people of the place.
Why I cant tell, Miss Carington has been staying at the Harris House
& making herself rather too officious. Dr. Rembert told her of it a few
days since & she appoligesed. I think now she is very anxious to make
amends for all by inviting us to spend the evening with her. This is my
opinion. I may be mistaken. I hope I am.

   Dr. Poellnitz's time at the Monticello will be up on Thursday, then
Dr. Harrold takes charge. A very pleasant change for us. I have been
with Fannie most of the time I have been at home today. Mac reports
Mrs. Rion no better both Dr. R. & himself think her in a very critical
state. I was to have sat up with her again tonight but Miss Carington
was there so I thought I would wait until I was more needed. No mail
today. wonder what can be the matter.

Charlottesville<br>
Thursday morning. Jan 1st" 63.

   I went up to Midway about nine oclock with Mac last night found
Miss Clarke & Miss Hewit alone with the old lady, Mac felt her pulse
& pronounced her sinking very fast, as soon as the blisters were dresed
the two ladys went to their room to lye down for a few hours, while
Mac & myself watched. About twelve Miss H. returned, & I persuaded
Mac to go home as he could do no good by staying & he was feeling
very unwell himself. We could do nothing more than sit there & wait
for the end which we saw must be very soon. we gave her drink as long
as she could swallow to ease her last moments[.] about two oclock her
breathing became very very short & painful at twenty minutes past the
spirit had fled, she entered upon the New Year in another world. We
called Miss Clarke & she had help called for us, Miss H. & myself
dressed her, I could scarcely divest myself of the idea as I looked upon
her hard masculine face that it was not a soldier. She was a very peculiar looking woman. Her head was large & covered with short coars
gray hair, her features large & bony which all together gave her very
much the appearance of a man. We did not get through laying her out
& the room fixed before four. It was nearly five before I lay down to try
& take a little rest. I got up at nearly seven & walked home with Ma-

tilda, I could not endulge in a long nap as it is New Years & I must make some preparation for a nice dinner.

Night

Our dinner passed off very quietly. Dr. & Mrs. Poellnitz left just as we were about to be seated at table. Poor little woman I feel very much for her, to have to travle with an intoxicated husband is anything but pleasant. They had to wait several hours at the Depot as the cars were very much behind time, Frank McQueen & Boyd Brunson arrived here late this afternoon on their way to Fredericksburg. They have taken board at Mrs. Smiths. They dine with us tomorrow. Dr. Rembert & Marie, Mac & Fannie went round to Mrs. Caringtons to the party when they got to the house they found it closed & no lights, they knocked at the door & the gentleman who is boarding there came down & told them, that Mrs. Carington & her daughter were both absent at the Harris house that they had not been at home for more than a week. We had a fine joak on them when they arrived at home, Dr. R. & M. would not take their tea before they left they were so sure they would get a nice supper of Oysters. Mac & Fannie were wiser. They all came up & spent the evening with me & a gay time we have had, Mac went round to call on Frank & Boyd. He found them in good health but very tired from their long ride. We dont know what to make of being invited out to spend the evening, & finding the doors closed. It looks very much like an insult. These Virginians are strange people, so, so unlike our Carolinians. It is a lovely night I would not have objected to a walk myself.

Charlottesville
Friday noon. Jan 2d" 63

We have just returned from Mrs. Rions funeral. It was a sad, sad sight to see the Hurse moving slowly along followed by all the men from our Carolina hospitals who were able to be out. She had nursed many of them through severe illness, & now they were paying her their last respects[.] we followed the body to the church first where Dr. Harrold read the service for the dead most beautifuly. Not more than half a dozen of the Town people were present. The body was then taken to the Town Cemetery (all following in the same order as we did to the church,) when the Services were concluded. The friends of the old lady & some of the soldiers filled in the grave. As I turn my steps homeward I could but think who of us would next be taken, & I felt deeply sory that so useful & energetic a person should be cut off so sudenly. Mac feels his loss deeply, he knows he will never get any one to fill Mrs. Rions place. Mrs. Pool is like no body, she cant begin to half way fill the place. I believe Miss Hewit & Miss Clarke are to remain Miss C. as Matron & Miss H. as nurse. Mrs. P. will attend to the dining room.

Night

Frank & Boyd dined with us, they are both the picture of health. They gave us very amusing accounts of their stay in the Valley & their escape from the enemy. The weather still lovely, we have had several applications for the vacant room here. Mrs. Mason called on Fannie & myself this afternoon.

Charlottesville
Saturday Night. Jan 3d" 63

We had a bitter cold night, the frost & ice remained upon the ground until near noon today. I found Abbot had died in the night he asked for me before he died. He was from Georgia & a very nice man. Dr. Harrold is making a good many changes. I have now a very nice Servant on my wards. The hospital will I know compare with any other in the town.

Frank McQueen & Boyd Brunson took tea & spent the evening with us. B. has improved very much he has made the most of his opportunities. They stayed until after nine[.] Mac had no one to talk to & almost went to sleep. I found Dr. Rembert in here when I came up, he remained with us about an hour. He could not resist teasing me about David, told me he heard the Captain was coming on here[.] I said I was very glad, would like to see him. I was telling the Doctor that Mr. Haden had fixed a screen on my ward for a servant to sleep behind, on my ward & I was very much put out about it. I have no idea of having my ward turned into a negro house. Haden is a perfect Yankee & cant see our objection to the negroes sleeping on the wards. I do not object to their sleeping on the wards but I do object to their beds being left there in the day.

The weather has moderated.

Charlottesville
Thursday Night. Jan 8" 63

The day has passed off quietly. Nothing new from the army. Mr. Jones invited me to take a horseback ride with him, I could not go on account of the cold. Fannie has been with me down stairs since tea Mac & herself are the only ones who seem to feel for me. Marie still confined to her room. Dr. R. staid to take an EggNogg. He asked me how I would like to be Matron of an Hospital, I said I would not object, he then asked me if I would go to Midway, I said I would like to, he was delighted, I think if Mac approves of my going I would like it very much.

Charlottesville
Friday morning. Jan 9" 63

Fannie quite sick this morning. Mac of course very much worried, I mentioned to Fannie that Dr. Rembert had asked me to go to Midway, she is very much opposed to my going says if I do she will go too. I am full of work today, Jane has not time to help me.

Afternoon

Went out with Dr. Rembert to purchase cloth for Sheets & Draws for the Hospital. Succeeded in getting 600 yds" at 75 cts of unbleached shirting for sheets, & 300 yds" at $1.00 of twilled for Draws. It is a splendid afternoon, wish I could take my ride, went to see Fann found her head still aching very much, beged me to put my cold hands to her head. Mac is very much opposed to my going to Midway, begs me to stay here, says he would like very much to have me there but wants me here more. Fannie is down on Dr. R. for wanting me to go; how am I to get out of the scrape? I have told Dr. R. that I would go, if I tell him Mac objects to my doing so, I know he will be very angry, wish I had not said any thing about it until I had consulted Mac. I feel highly complimented that I am held in such estimation[.] I have promised Mac & Fannie not to go if they are opposed to it. I feel almost as if it were my duty though as I would have a larger field for doing good. But Mac is my friend & I will be guided by what he says. There goes the hospital bell I must go.

Night

What am I to do what is my duty Oh! God show me what I aught to do. Mac asked me to go up & sit with them after tea, I came in first to see Marie, found Dr. Harrold paying her a visit, when he went out I said Mac objected to my going to Midway. Marie then said you had better tell Dr. R. so then, for he is now writing to his sister to come on & take your place[.] I sent & asked him to come in that I wished to see him, I told him what I wished with him, he was very angry at first for he thought he had the matter all settled without further trouble, then for me to say Mac had advised me not to go was too much. He thought it would be more patriotic for me to go than stay here. We talked about it for some time[.] at last I went up to see Mac & Fannie again & told them all Dr. R. said. Mac seemed a good deal put out, for he said Dr. R. had rather taken advantage of me by puting it in the light he had, he knew how to work on me. I beged Mac to advise me that I would act on his decision Oh! he was so very very kind to me, just like a dear brother & beged me not to be troubled, that he wished me to remain here, that I had my hands full & did as much as I could, that if I did more it would be at the expence of health. Fannie was very much excited & said every thing in her power to keep me. Finaly I told Mac to think it over & tell me what he thought best in the morning. Marie is in bed & wants the candle put out, no sleep for my weary limbs this night. Oh! how I wish I like Fannie had some dear one to decide for me & tell me what to do, to love & care for me.

Charlottesville<br>Saturday Noon. Jan 10″ 63

Mac was true to his promise, he told me that after much thought & consideration, he still was of the opinion I had better stay where I am. that I was not born in the same station of life that Mrs. Rion was[,] that I had never been acustomed to labour, there fore I could not undergo what she did except at the expence of comfort, pleasure, & health[,] that it was my duty to take care of myself. That he & Fannie could not think of giving me up. I promised I would not go so the matter is decided. The weather is shocking. The snow fell thick & fast for two or three hours until every thing was well covered. It then begin to rain. I had a time getting home from the hospital where I spent the morning.

Night

The weather has been so dissagreeable all the afternoon that I did not venture out. Marie is much better. Fannie was out of her room, feeling quite well again. I had a nice letter from my dear boy today, so good in him to write to me two to my one. Dr. R. has been in, teasing me about my extravegant notions, thinks the war has given me much higher notions than I had before[,] says he thinks I have lost a great deal of my piety. he will go any length to tease me.

Friday Night. January 16." 63
Charlottesville

There seems to be quite a panic in Town on account of the sickniss here. I never heard of so many deaths in a place of the size in my life. Smallpox is spreading in private familys as well as in the hospital. The Town Council have inflicted a fine of $5 on all who neglect to be vaxinated. Rained last night, wind still high & quite cold again. We had a pleasant time at dinner today. Miss Nelson's box arrived about noon she sent us a fine lot of eggs, a duck & two fine chickens. we gave the men a very nice lunch today they enjoyed it. Boyd came in after tea we played whist until ten oclock Mac & Fannie beat Boyd & myself every game. It realy did me good to see Mac enjoy it as he did. He is looking very badly again but seems quite cheerful. I was vaxinated again tonight. It is bitter cold.

Sunday Night. Jan 18." 63
Charlottesville

I actualy suffered with the cold going to church this morning. The ground has been frozen hard all day. Dr. Harrold had to ride ten miles out in the country to preach for Mr. Nelson. Mac went out to walk with Boyd & I spent the afternoon with Fann, we amused ourselves boiling candy. quite a treet these war times. I could scarcely make up my mind to move from the fire long enough to attend to my duties, but I am blessed not to suffer with the cold more than I do. Oh! I have so much to be grateful to all might[y] God for. These are times when I am perfectly happy. I have all that is good for me & much, much more than I deserve. My only distress is I can not be as good as I ought. No news of importance from the army in this State, in the South west we are looking for an attack very soon[.] I hear too the enemy are making great preparations to attack Wilmington. May God protect us, if they should succeed the country for many miles round will suffer. The whole line of railroad will be in danger.[10]

10. This attack on Wilmington did not materialize.

# Epilogue

The friendships Ada Bacot made in Virginia had a major impact on her life. One of her new friends, Frances Jane Clarke of Charleston, was a nurse at the Midway Hospital in Charlottesville. Internal evidence from a diary Clarke kept during her time in Charlottesville reveals that her brother Thomas, then a first lieutenant in Company H of the Infantry Regiment of Hampton's Legion, was wounded at Second Manassas and came to the Midway for treatment on September 7, 1862.[1] Bacot probably met Thomas Clarke for the first time in Charlottesville and then renewed her acquaintance with him on a visit to Kingstree, South Carolina, in 1863. Ada married Thomas Clarke on November 10, 1863, at her home church in Mars Bluff, South Carolina. Her regular pastor, Augustus Moore, officiated. Clarke had been too ill to serve with his regiment for much of the past six months and did not return to active duty until mid-January 1864.

Bacot was still a wealthy woman at the time of her second marriage, and she and her family were sufficiently concerned about her property for her to execute a premarital agreement. This agreement conveyed Ada's property to her father in a trust for Clarke's and her use during their joint and separate lives. After their deaths, the property would go to their children. If Ada and Thomas Clarke had no children, the estate would go to her brother Dickie and her niece Ada Graham Saunders. The contract and attached schedule of property revealed that Ada Bacot owned the 700-acre estate of Arnmore, twenty-eight slaves, thirty bales of cotton, miscellaneous crops, a share of her mother's property in Mississippi, some slaves from Mary Hart Brockington's estate, and shares in the Wilmington and Manchester Railroad.[2]

Bacot's friend James McIntosh was delighted by the news of her marriage. He wrote, "it has been my lot in life to form but few friendships

---

1. United States Census of 1860, South Carolina, City of Charleston, Fourth Ward, 364. Chalmers L. Gemmill, ed., "Midway Hospital: 1861–1863: The Diary of Miss Clarke of South Carolina," *The Magazine of Albemarle County History* 22 (1963–1964): 185–86.

2. Marriage settlement of Ada W. Bacot and T. A. G. Clarke, November 10, 1863, Ada W. Bacot File, Darlington County Historical Commission.

& from none of them does memory call up such pleasant reminiscences, as that one which gives to me the privilege of expressing for you, the warmest the best wishes of a friend. . . . you [are] married, which accords exactly with the advice I've been giving my friends for the past twelve months."[3] Ada was apparently planning to live in Atlanta, and McIntosh asked her to write him about the condition of military hospitals there, as he wished to transfer away from Virginia. Her brother Dickie also wrote, asking if she was still thinking of settling in Texas.[4] Eventually, Ada Bacot Clarke decided to stay in South Carolina.

Ada's new happiness did not last long. Thomas Clarke was killed in action by a shot to the head in Dandridge, Tennessee, on January 17, 1864, just two days after his return to active duty. Seeking to console Clarke's widow, one of his fellow officers and friends wrote to Ada that "frequently would he turn to me and say 'Welch, I am the happiest man alive, & I have one of the best wives man was ever blessed with.' "[5] Ada was pregnant; she bore a son, Thomas Alfred Chives Clarke, on September 1, 1864. Her father, Peter Samuel Bacot, died of yellow fever only a month later. Just seven months before, he had invested $4,300 of his remaining cash in Confederate bonds. After Clarke's death, Ada remained in South Carolina at her plantation, Arnmore; her sister-in-law Frances Jane "Janie" Clarke, who had also left the medical service, kept her company for a while.[6] Apparently they nursed together at a Confederate hospital in Kingstree, but there are no details available about this service.[7] When the war ended, Ada

---

3. James McIntosh to Ada Bacot Clarke, December 6, 1863, private collection of Lillian Clarke James.

4. Richard H. Bacot to Ada Bacot Clarke, December 17, 1863, South Caroliniana Library.

5. S. Elliott Welch to Ada Bacot Clarke, April 18, 1864, private collection of Lillian Clarke James.

6. James McIntosh to Ada Bacot Clarke, March 2, 1864, private collection of Lillian Clarke James; Richard H. Bacot to Ada Bacot Clarke, February 24, 1864, South Caroliniana Library.

7. Henry H. Riggs to Ada Bacot Clarke, October 30, 1866, private collection of Lillian Clarke James.

Bacot Clarke signed an oath of allegiance to the United States in order to protect her still-substantial property.[8]

After the war, Ada remained close to her in-laws and her brother Dickie. Dickie ran a steamboat on the Cooper River, and he and her brother-in-law, James Clarke, speculated on barrel staves before they went out of business in the late spring of 1866. Dickie then joined forces with his brother Tours Loire Bacot and his brother Peter Brockington Bacot's brothers-in-law, George and Thomas Trenholm.[9] During this time, Ada's sister Jacqueline and her paternal uncle Richard Bacot lived with her.[10] Ada was not always well in mind or body at this time; she worried about raising her son alone and did not take care of herself. Dickie chided her gently: "I'm afraid we'll have to charge it all to 'Arnmore' for you *allways* get fat when you go away for awhile."[11]

Thomas Clarke's brother James was around Ada and Arnmore a great deal during these first years after the war. He had left Charleston in 1862 to live in Kingstree. He and Ada grew closer, and a little over three years after Thomas's death, on February 21, 1867, Ada married James at Christ Church in Mars Bluff. As before, there was a marriage settlement, but this time her property was put in trust to Dickie for herself and her heirs. The new appended property schedule, witnessed by J. A. Clarke, included Arnmore, all its appurtenances, and her one-sixth share of the 960-acre Roseville estate which was shared equally among Ada and her brothers and sister after her father's death.[12] Ada's marriage to James Clarke would last longer than her other two; James Clarke died in 1894. Their wedding cake had been a fruitcake, and for the first twenty-five years of their marriage, the Clarkes had a slice of it each year on their anniversary.

---

8. Ada Bacot Clarke Loyalty Oath, June 20, 1865, private collection of Lillian Clarke James.

9. Richard H. Bacot to Ada Bacot Clarke, December 24, 1865, and May 8 and September 15, 1866, South Caroliniana Library.

10. Richard H. Bacot to Ada Bacot Clarke, February 1, 1866, South Caroliniana Library.

11. Richard H. Bacot to Ada Bacot Clarke, February 1 and December 4, 1866, South Caroliniana Library.

12. Marriage settlement of Ada B. Clarke and James E. H. Clarke, February 21, 1867, Ada W. Bacot File, Darlington County Historical Commission.

Ada and her new family lived in Charleston until 1877, and all four of their surviving children—Mary Jacqueline (1869–1882), Edna Anne (1870–1944), William (1872–1874), and James Henry, Jr. (1874–1953)—were born there. One child, John Bacot Clarke, died at birth in September 1867. James had been trained as an accountant and was involved in various business ventures. Ada lost her plantation Arnmore in 1871; 575 acres of the property were foreclosed on by creditors and sold at a sheriff's sale.[13] Family tradition holds that she had mortgaged Arnmore to save Roseville. In 1877, the Clarkes returned to Roseville and took over the running of the plantation. They began a joint farming venture with a neighboring family, the Mc-Cowns, and called it the McCown-Clarke Company. A number of businesses operated on the Roseville's premises, including the Mc-Cown-Clarke Mercantile Store, a cotton gin, a lumber mill, a machine shop, and a grist mill. The company was one of the first to introduce tobacco cultivation to the Darlington area in the 1890s. After James's death, Ada Bacot Clarke supervised her family's share of the business with the help of her unmarried daughter, Edna, and her eldest son, Thomas Clarke. When Thomas married in 1889, he and his bride moved into a tenant house, the "Sans Souci," about a mile from Roseville. The McCown-Clarke Company was a large and prosperous enterprise, servicing an entire community; the store even issued its own money. Thomas Clarke was successful in business and Democratic politics and was a member of the South Carolina State House of Representatives at the time of his death in 1909. Ironically, he died of erysipelas, the same disease Ada had contracted while nursing in Virginia. The family's personal and financial fortunes declined after Thomas's death. Ada Bacot Clarke died two years later. Thomas's eldest son, Howard Sanborn Clarke, was arrested in 1914 for the alleged murder of his wife. He was imprisoned until 1927. The cotton gin blew up in the early 1920s and was never rebuilt; the store burned down in the 1930s; all the plantations except for the house at Roseville and the Sans Souci and its land were sold or foreclosed on during the Depression era. In 1948, the McCown-Clarke Company was dis-

---

13. Horace F. Rudisill, personal communication and enclosures, September 26, 1992.

solved and the remainder of Roseville sold out of the family.[14] The most recent word on Roseville, which is located one mile off I-95 in Florence, is that it is being renovated as a bed-and-breakfast inn.

Most of Ada's siblings stayed in South Carolina after the war. Her sister Jacqueline, who had married a North Carolinian, remained in close touch with her family back home. Dickie kept moving west after the war. He settled for a while in Missouri, where he married a widow in the 1890s, and reached the west coast and San Diego by 1911.[15] Tours Loire stayed in South Carolina, and A'Jane spent the rest of his life near Roseville, helping to run the McCown-Clarke Company. Ada and her brother Peter and his wife had reconciled after the war. Peter practiced medicine in Florence, South Carolina, but he fell on hard times; in 1881, his wife and children lived with the Clarkes when Peter lost his job with the state health department. His wife died the following year, but Peter lived until 1924.

Ada Bacot Clarke's long life came to an end on April 11, 1911; she was seventy-eight. After her early bereavements and disappointments, she had come to enjoy a satisfying life. Although her wealth decreased after the war, she and her family were able to make a living from her lands under the new economic order. One of her sons, Thomas Clarke, represented the district and his family in the state legislature under the new political order. Her Civil War experiences as a Confederate nurse, recalled by her descendants with pride, marked a turning point in her life. For it was the positive lessons she had learned about herself and her abilities during the war and the friendships she made in Charlottesville that brought her the personal satisfaction and independence of her later years. The Civil War may have been the tragic undoing of the South, but it was the making of Ada Bacot Clarke.

14. This information was provided by Anita Clarke Curl, a great-great granddaughter of Ada Bacot Clarke through Thomas Clarke.

15. Richard H. Bacot to Peter B. Bacot, December 1911, Peter Samuel Bacot Papers, South Caroliniana Library.

# For Further Reading

Bleser, Carol K., ed. *In Joy and In Sorrow: Women, Family, and Marriage in the Victorian South, 1830–1900*. New York: Oxford University Press, 1991.

Brockett, L. P., and Merry C. Vaughan. *Woman's Work in the Civil War*. Philadelphia: Ziegler, McCurdy and Co., 1867.

Brooks, Stewart. *Civil War Medicine*. Springfield, IL: Charles C. Thomas, 1966.

Clinton, Catherine. *The Plantation Mistress: Woman's World in the Old South*. New York: Pantheon, 1982.

Cumming, Kate. *Kate: The Journal of a Confederate Nurse*. Edited by Richard Barksdale Harwell. Baton Rouge: Louisiana State University Press, 1959.

Cunningham, H. H. *Doctors in Gray: The Confederate Medical Service*. Baton Rouge: Louisiana State University Press, 1958.

Dawson, Francis W., ed. *Our Women in the War: The Lives They Lived, the Deaths They Died*. Charleston, SC: News and Courier Co., 1885.

Faust, Drew Gilpin. "Altars of Sacrifice: Confederate Women and the Narratives of War." *Journal of American History* 76 (March 1990): 1200–1228.

_____. *The Creation of Confederate Nationalism: Ideology and Identity in the Civil War South*. Baton Rouge: Louisiana State University Press, 1988.

Fox-Genovese, Elizabeth. *Within the Plantation Household: Black and White Women of the Old South*. Chapel Hill: University of North Carolina Press, 1988.

Jordan, Ervin L., Jr. *Charlottesville and the University of Virginia in the Civil War*. Lynchburg, VA: H. E. Howard, 1988.

Maher, Sister Mary Denis. *"To Bind Up the Wounds": Catholic Sister Nurses in the U.S. Civil War*. Westport, CT: Greenwood Press, 1989.

Massey, Mary Elizabeth. *Bonnet Brigades*. New York: Alfred A. Knopf, 1966.

Moore, Frank. *Women of the War: Their Heroism and Self-Sacrifice*. Hartford: S. S. Scranton, 1868.

Pember, Phoebe Yates. *A Southern Woman's Story: Life in Confederate Richmond*. St. Simons Island, GA: Mockingbird Books, 1974.

Rable, George C. *Civil Wars: Women and the Crisis of Southern Nationalism*. Urbana: University of Illinois Press, 1989.

Simkins, Francis Butler, and James Welch Patton. *Women of the Confederacy*. Richmond: Garrett and Massie, 1936.

Sterkx, H. E. *Partners in Rebellion: Alabama Women During the Civil War*. Rutherford, NJ: Fairleigh Dickinson University Press, 1970.

Taylor, Mrs. Thomas, et al., eds. *South Carolina Women in the Confederacy*. 2 vols. Columbia, SC: The State Company, 1907.

# Index